A SILENT PATRIOT
OF BANGLADESH

A SILENT PATRIOT
OF BANGLADESH

H. P. Roychoudhury

PARTRIDGE

To order additional copies of this book, contact
Partridge India
000 800 10062 62
orders.india@partridgepublishing.com

www.partridgepublishing.com/india

Contents

To those souls of the district of Sylhet who sacrificed their lives for the cause of independence of India and for the cause of liberation of Bangladesh.

[Nikunja Behari Goswami]

An Outline at the Outset

- **Are the Teachings of Gandhi to Demoralise the World?**
- **Why Non-Violence and Not Violence?**

It was because non-violence works in a sleeping voice, while violence works in a roaring voice. Gandhi was a soldier of independence of India, but he prefers to fight under the cover of a saint and without arms. Gandhi's mystic befooled the Hindus by carrying out the movement against the British using religion in a twisted way. The ethics of Hinduism is to sacrifice as nothing would be left in this world after sometime, and tolerance should be the virtue of human beings. He transformed the virtue of tolerance into 'non-violence' and befooled the common Hindus. The ethics of Hindu religion dictates the mind-set that if anything is to be offered to the 'Almighty', that must be offered with pure and purified mind-set. Thus it had brought a system of purifying self by remaining in fasting and then offering something to the 'Almighty'. Gandhi had used the

'FASTING' in the movement to befool the people to accomplish his hidden desire.

What he did only to befool the Hindus, he knows Muslim religion never believe in the virtue of tolerance or non-violence or fasting? As such Gandhi kept the movement confined to Hindus only. He was an Inner Temple Law graduate; he was a lone genius to see the future of India and the future of Bengal. His movement of non-violence was in the way of 'non-cooperation' or 'civil disobedience movement' although he had tested the gravity of the movement earlier in other places, where it could not brought effective results, but it got fruitful result with huge participation of Bengali Hindus only in Bengal. Why did he avoid the Muslims in the movement? He designed the movement 'non-violence' based on the ethics of Hindu religion that is 'tolerance' very carefully to bring segregation between Hindus and Muslims. Thus his success of movement in Calcutta and in other places of Bengal had encouraged him to proceed with his vision of destruction of Bengal, destruction of Bengali leaders by communal hatred, and shifting of power centre from Calcutta to Delhi. The vision of Gandhi was the destruction of Bengal through communal violence using the ethics of Hinduism in the form of non-violence.

Violence is the source of life, construction, expansion, and also destruction, while non-violence is nothing but destruction. God has given the human beings the strength for the protection of life and energy for better thinking for the exploration of life. Violence is the source of life, but again violence finishes a life. God has given human being the energy, the thinking energy apart from the strength to utilise it for the betterment of life. On the other hand, the meaning of non-violence is not to utilise your strength and energy and only to bring natural destruction to self. Are the teachings of Gandhi to demoralise the world? Violence brought the atom bomb, but behind the atom bomb, people explored the nuclear energy to build the space rocket; violence brought the civil war in the USA, but behind violence, USA built its nation, a nation of superpower; violence brought the French revolution in France, but behind violence, France brought 'democracy';while Gandhi utilised non-violence in British India and brought destruction to India by dividing India and killing Indians.

1 Who Is the Silent Patriot?

[1]

He was **Nikunja Bihari Goswami**, a silent patriotic worker, who had sacrificed his life starting from his boyhood to the end of his life to the service of the people under the influence of our national leader Gandhi, and keeping his ideals in mind, he spent the last day of his life. His dedication to service was so much that he could not get time to think for himself and passed all throughout a lonely bachelor life. He was the third son of a respected school teacher Sri Nadia Chand Goswami born on 5 April 1913 in a village Kalapur, of Thana Srimangal, under Sylhet district of undivided India at present under Bangladesh, and the end of his life came on 29 August 1993. He left the house at the age of 17 and had taken shelter in an Ashram called Kulawra Ragalkur Ashram now in Bangladesh and dedicated himself to the service of the nation as directed by Gandhi from the heart of undivided India. After his death, many people were writing about his leadership, how he could successfully cross over a stretch of forty miles starting from Fultala to Malawvi Bazar of the district of Sylhet along with twenty thousand tea labourers to place their right of demand of casting votes in the referendum of Sylhet to decide the fate of Sylhet to be included in the partition part of India or Pakistan. More than five lakhs of tea-garden labourers were deprived of casting their votes by the then government of Assam, while only by fifty-five thousands votes, Sylhet was tilted towards East Pakistan at the time of partition of British India. After the partition of India and subsequently after the separation of Sylhet from Assam, he could have been shifted to Assam as Sylhet was a part of Assam just before partition and also as he was very much acquainted with many places of Assam during the activity of independence movement under different stages of fight against British, but he did not; he remained in East Pakistan along with the left-out people. During independence movement, he was all the time in the forefront of the movement had it been 'the Mass Civil Disobedience Movement' of 1930 or 'Quit India Movement' of 1942, and he was imprisoned several times and kept in jails of Sylhet, Moluvibazar, Jorhat, Silchar, and other places.

As an ardent devotee of Gandhi and a faithful volunteer of Gandhi who had passed the different moment of his life in different situation that had arisen at the moment of independent movement without hesitation. He had no definite place to rest at the time of continuing with the movement, but otherwise, he was resting in Ashram and rarely at home making the best part of his life in Rangalkur Ashram. He had remembered the spectacular moment of his life in that Ashram once in one occasion he could touch the feet of Netaji Subhas Chandra Bose in the year of 1938 and felt the excitement of giving every drop of blood of his body as he had wanted once the blood of Indians for freedom. In another occasion, he remembered he could touch the feet of M. K. Gandhi and felt the emotion to give up the British cloth, felt the temptation to learn the techniques of making clothes by Charka, making his own useable things such as soap, and growing of necessary vegetables by his own effort. Throughout his life in Ashram, he was the most enthusiastic person to implement Gandhi's principle of Saach Bharat, cleaning of toilets, growing of food, and making of own clothes.

Indian people have the good luck to know a lot of the early life of the present president of India from his speech addressed to his beloved students. The teachers' day of 1915 was a memorable day of India, as the president of present India Shri Pranab Mukherjee has himself described his early life by giving a spectacular speech in front of the student just before the Teacher's Day (5 September 2015), describing how he could travel long a distance of five miles every day and how naughty he was as very often he was forgetting of going school with some false pretext, but he was under the care of his mother, and under compulsion, he got ready to go to school.

Here we find in the life of an unknown **Patriot** (Nikunja Bihari Goswami) an inborn desire to sacrifice his life for others and never had any sort of desire of pleasure for himself that had been either for power, wealth, or love for a woman, an instinct human nature present in each and almost all human beings. Here we find a man who had lost his mother at his early age, as such there was nobody to look after him other than himself even at his tender age. There was nobody to guide him, but he was lucky with an attachment with a library that had given him the opportunity to read books, books of all stream, and that was the golden opportunity for him to know the world, the people, the place, and what-not.

[2]

Suruj Kumar Das was writing about Goswami, who was one year junior to him by age, and said that he had lost one of his younger dear brothers at his sudden death. He was writing Swami Vivekananda who said, 'As you have been born as a human being, keep a mark in the society before death.' Thousands and thousands of people have been born or will be born and thousands would die, but how many of them could have got successful to keep their marks in society? The late Nikunja Bihari Goswami was one who had kept a mark in society. His life was full of action and activity. Keeping himself active in the service of the human being and in the service of society for more than sixty years, he had taken leave forever on 29 August 1993 at the age of 80.

He remembered the year 1947, the country was divided, he left for India and his dear younger Goswami remained in Pakistan, but their communication never got detached although they were living in a different country henceforth. Rather in the last five years, their relation had improved a step further. He was remembering the past incidents of Goswami, a thrust of fear had arisen in his mind once. It was the year 1930; anybody dares to violate the circular of Cunningham, he would be kept in jail. The young Goswami under the call of Satyagraha violated the law and went to jail without fearing the act of torture, and he had preserved such kind of sentiment for the cause of the nation throughout his life. At that time he was a child of a school, later he was taken up to SriMangal lock-up along with many others. Even at his young age, his mind was ready to go to Satyagraha by passing fondness of family bondage and likewise he dedicated his whole life remaining as a man of Ashram and never became a family man.

Of course, behind his dedicated life in Kulawara Rangarkul Vidya Ashram remained as a lifelong bachelor, a servant of society, rightly or wrongly a follower of Gandhi, however memorable the guidance of few personalities like Dhren Das Gupta, Prunendu Kishore Sen Gupta, and Abaladas was unforgettable. After getting arrested and living life in jail, at his young age of class VIII student, he never got any chance to take education in any institute, but he continued his study in the Ashram under the instruction and guidance of the guardians of the Ashram, which made him a good writer and a good editor of a paper in his later life and also in no way less than anybody to make name as an outspoken speaker.

15 August 1947, India was divided and Pakistan was formed. Most of the Hindu people of the country were leaving the country, but he remained there under all difficulties and remains dedicated to the service of the people. During the military rule of Pakistan under

the cloud of the liberation movement of East Pakistan, a plan was chocked out to kill him, which compelled him to leave the country and take shelter in India for a few days. But as soon as Bangladesh was liberated, he came back to his place and engaged himself in the service of the people, in the supply of food and shelter to thousands and thousands of people who had returned to the country from India just after the liberation of the country, the country being devastated by breaking and burning of every house and every office by the military rulers of West Pakistan. Even after the formation of Bangladesh, he had to face many problems in order to do the service to the society, but he himself remained cool and remained dedicated to work as a silent servant of the society.

During the turmoil period, he was also entrusted to continue to work as editor of *Jana-Sakti* paper to enlighten the people in their desire to the service to society. At that time he came across with Dr Mahanambrata Brahamchari, who uses to travel to different parts of the country imparting the hope of serving as human beings in the midst of the hopeless state of condition of human life. He advised the present generation to pick up the ideals of his life, which would give them the best peace of life as a human being.

[3]

Binoy Krishna Das was writing Umesh Chandra –Nirmalabala-ChatraBas is situated in the area of Chai-Bandar of Sylhet. The ChatraBas is related with the memory of late advocate Umesh Chandra Das and his life partner Nirmalabala Das. Due to the request of their sons and daughters, Veteran Nikunja Bihari Goswami accepted the responsibility of ChrtraBas to look into the interest of students and since that time he continued with the multiple works to help the students in their study. It was at the beginning consists only of land and two to three most ordinary rooms without any brickwork.

Krishna Das was continuing with his writing that he was almost of his age. Goswami was born in April 1913 and he was born in August 1914. Goswami hails from Kolhapur of SriMangal Thana and he hails from Gurabhui of Kalawara Thana. Goswami started his learning in SriMangal and he started his learning in Karimganj, now a part of India. In the period of school life, he used to meet him sometimes in the village, but after 1930, he used to meet him in jail and also sometimes in meeting, or in procession of nation's liberation movement. By the time Goswami joined

Kulawara Ashram, the Ashram is situated three miles away in the east of Kulawara Railway junction, which was created by late Prunendu Kishore Sen Guta and Dhrendra DasGupta, leaving their education in the university in order to create a learning centre, a self-organising volunteer centre to do all kinds of service for the benefit of mankind.

However, at last Britain have left the country, India and Pakistan formed, all those were in jail went to their home, many of those left the country to get silver medal, again many of those who could not complete their study went back to complete their study, but again many of those left nowhere. Those who were left in Sylhet were Pruendendu Kishore Sen Gupta, Aminur Rashid Chowdhury, Durgesh Deb, Sunil Das, Nikunja Bihari Goswami, SriRama Kanta Das, SriSuresh Chandra Das, and Smt Suhasini Das. Among all the three Prunendu Sen, Nikunja Goswami, and Suhasini Das did not return home. Staying in Rangarkul Ashram, they started their work with a new spirit of service. They set up a primary school, a haemo-medical centre, a centre for oil production from oil seeds, a centre of making of thread with Charka and making of clothes, a centre of production of homemade vegetables, fruits, mango, jackfruits, and pineapples.

East Pakistan Congress committee was formed. The well-known Jaminder of Sylhet Brojendra Narayan Chowdhury, advocate and commissioner of minority, Bsanta Kumar Das, Central Labour Minister Prundendu Kr SenGupta MP, and people representative Nikunja Bihari Goswami, all together were allowed to form the Maulivi-Bazar Minority Board. He himself also became a member of the tea garden of the board and thereby got the opportunity to do a little service to society.

Mr Das is expressing with a pain in his mind that in the matter of personal life he was completely opposite to him. He was a lovely son of his family grown up under the care of parents, brothers, and sisters, but Goswami was neither under the care of his father nor much of his mother as he has lost his father at his tender age and mother a little later. He was under the care of his parents, but Goswami was completely free and carefree. Goswami was concerned with politics and common people, but he was concerned with family. Goswami was the secretary of tea labour union, looking for the interest of both the tea-garden owner as well as the tea-garden labours, but he was looking for the interest of the family only.

It was the year 1958, a meeting was going on in the assembly hall of East Pakistan at Dacca under the guidance of commerce minister and labour commissioner Mr Ali Hassan with regard to export of tea, where Prundendu Keshor SenGupta MP, joint Secretary Durgesh Deb and Nikunja Bihari Goswamu were present. In the second day at seven o'clock, all of a sudden morning news announced that the country is now under military rule. Commerce minister was arrested immediately. Goswami went to his hotel where he was staying in the city of Dacca, and he was told that everybody must return today in the night train that those were seating at different places to avoid arrest. But today Goswami is no more, nobody would go to Dacca for the cause of common people, and nobody could arrest him.

It was 8 October 1993, Friday, Nikunja Bihari Goswami left for heaven leaving this world. All volunteers of the Ashram including a large gathering of Hindus and Muslims together prayed for the departed soul under all religious customs. Accumulation of a few thousand people including Hindus and Muslims in the prayer meeting signifies his popularity and love for the people. At last all activity was completed under the guidance of Smt Suhashini Das, the sole guardian as well as the protector of the Ashram with a mournful mind.

[4]

Dr Jatindra Saha is saying that it was the year 1962; he was living in Dacca in Rup-Chand lane of Bangla Bazar. It was summertime; he was relaxing in the summer vacation period, where the pressure of teaching was almost absent. One day one of his close friends Netai Paul came to meet him with a gentleman, who was no other than Nikunja Bihari Goswami. He was dressed in Khaddar cloth. His very appearance strikes him as such that he was not only a pious religious man, but also he was a man of heart full of love and lustre. He was very much pleased by talking with him.

By the end of August of 1962, he went to Sylhet for a few days just before he went to America. At that time he got the opportunity to meet with Goswami, talked with him, and exchanged ideas and views with him. That closeness of a few days had made Goswami very dear to him as if he is one of his relatives, and since then he used to call him Gosai-Mama (Uncle Goswai). In 1982, Goswami went to England because of his invitation. He has fought for country, fought for society throughout the whole life in exchange of nothing but of hard life facing jail and torture time to time. People think to do something for the family because of his love for the family, Goswami thinks to do something for society because of his love for society. He thinks the whole society is his family. Every person of society is his near and dear one. But society also has not forgotten him; society is also indebted to him that was the reason why Goswami had been requested to go to England in his later life. Complying with the request, Goswami went to England, that was the matter of great pleasure to him.

The writing of Dr Saha about Nikunja Bihari Goswami is expressed by the name 'birth and death' that carries a deep meaning of understanding. In any human life, there occurred many incidents, but the incident of birth and death is two of the most important incidents of anybody's life. The time in between birth and death is called life. According to Hindu religion, life passes through different stages. The first stage is called the stage of childhood. Goswami even at his childhood stage entered into the field of serving society that is found to be seen rare in human life. Besides this, after attaining the independence of India, there were many congress workers who attained high posts in official works, in administrative works, and many by indulging in political activity became minister. But Goswami without looking to any 'gain-full' activity turned to 'gain-less' activity by the mental desire of sacrificing his energy of activity for the cause of society. According to Hinduism, the man who can pass a life free from the bondage of love and the temptation of desire should be proud of getting the highest degree of peace in life. To know the existence of 'self', one requires knowing the art of meditation to see beyond.

There is no end of thought and discussion of life and soul. As soon as a soul begins to grow at mother's bailey, the life begins to grow. It is difficult to believe how a soul takes the shape of a body. Apparently, although it is unbelievable, in a scientific world, there are many instances that justifies the fact. The word *energy* indicates the strength of power. Though the energy could not be seen, it is the source of electric power and the source of all work. It is not possible to see what the energy present inside petrol is. But it is the burning of petrol that drives a motor car or flies an airplane. As such the existence of human soul as well as human life cannot be nullified outright although human soul is not visible. The world-famous scientist Einstein and his famous equation $E = mc^2$ is very much known to the scientific world. Scientifically E stands for *Energy*, which is not visible like soul and m stands for *matter* as good as human body. Thus energy with body of matter is identical with that of soul with matter-like body. The fact of the matter is that any matter can be transformed into energy as such energy can be transformed into matter. It is to be remembered that matter can exist in different forms, as such if energy can be transformed into different types of matter, then the unseen soul can also take up different forms and different body matter. Electricity, light, and heat are the different forms of energy. Light is visible energy, but electricity and heat are the forms of unseen energy. The movement of unseen electricity through electric wire produces light and heat. Similarly the movement of unseen souls with that of a visible matter of human body can produce life. According to Dr Saha, Goswami was freed from the bondage of mother's love at his early stage, because of the death of his mother at an early age; he could devote himself for the service to society at the expense of a mother's love. In 1929 there was a devastating flood in the district of Cachar. The SDO of Maulivibazar at that time Muhammad Ali Chowdhury gave him the opportunity to work for flood victims. Goswami actively participated in the flood works. During that time he got the opportunity to meet with Sri Prunendu Kishore SenGupta, who was a devoted social worker and a congress worker. That was the turning point of his life. On seeing the kind of service of the congress volunteers for the country and society, he was charmed so much that he determined to devote himself for such works and remained faithful to that kind of activity throughout of his life till death.

Further Dr Saha was writing about Goswami's student life. He was brilliant and he was never satisfied with the limited teachings of the school. Thus along with school teaching, he used to study other books of geography, literature, and life history of great scholars such as Bankim Chandra, Rabindranath, Nabin Chandra, Sarat Chandra, and many others. He also studied religious book such as Ramayana, Mahabharata, and book like Gitanjali. All those academic activity indicated that had he been in education instead of going in the path of service to society, he would have brought more floral for him apart from earning plenty of money.

Having being a meritorious student, he left the school for his inner call to serve the society discarding the love and sympathy of his father and other family members. Overcoming all obstacles of near and dear ones of all respected persons of the family, one day he fled away from the house with one cloth and without ticket and reached to the volunteer centre of Kulwara to work for the independence movement. It was difficult to understand what kind of secret force tempted him at his tender age to leave the house.

Every birth is ascertained by death. But soul has no death. There are many people in the universe of different colours, such as white, black, or brown. There is no selectivity on the part of a soul to acquire a body in the mother's belle. But after birth, the human's nature, the character, or efficiency in work differ, as such someone becomes a scientist or a poet and remain immortal by dint of their performance of works. But again there are many who remain illiterate in spite of all effort because of blindness or any other body deformation. If it is believed that God is the creator of all human beings, then the question arises why someone is enjoying a happy life life-long but again someone other is unhappy life-long because God has differentiated the two souls. Why? There must be something else. That justices the fact that a new birth depends upon the performance of one's earlier birth. A human being changes his rotten old dress and takes up a new dress, similarly in Hindu religion, it is believed that a soul gives off a sick body and takes up a new body. Again just as wind takes up the sweet ingredients of flower along with it, a soul takes up the good or bad ingredients of the earlier body to the new body. This was the reason why people are found with different mentality. It might be said that the veteran Goswami had taken up the power of servicing desire from his earlier birth.

[5]

Let us begin to write the Linking Unit of the Patriot with the different aspects of his life.

The life of the **Patriot** (Nikunja Bihari Goswami) is related with the ideals of Gandhi, no matter good or bad, but the fact of the matter is that he has passed his life keeping those ideals in the secrets of his mind. The news of rioting at Naokhali had brought Gandhi to Noakhali, he was there with a group of people to bring a semblance of brotherhood and an attempt to restore peace and as such a description of Gandhi's Naokhali visit is described herewith.

Let us write the facts highlighting Gandhi's Noakhali visit.

The British government became weak due to continued death of British soldiers in the war front of Second World War that started since 1939. Under those circumstances after the end of war in 1945, the new prime minister of Britain Mr Clemens Attlee was thinking to relinquish its administrative power in India to Indians. The devaluation of British power had encouraged the Indian politicians how to occupy the power of chair. Every power-monger politicians had contemplated his or her political strategy. Indian people are religious minded from ancient time onwards. People are suffering in tension and uncertainty. The country would be divided, where to go, where to live. This sort of question had made the people restless. People were passing sleepless night. Noakhali was a Hindu majority place. Many of the Muslim people thinking the place Noakhali might not be a place for Muslims as the majority people are Hindus. Let us start the burning of Hindu houses; the Hindus would be compelled to leave the places. This was the beginning of the Noakhali rioting. The huge Hindu population began to shift to safer places, making it a place of human slaughter.

On getting the information, Gandhi had decided to go to the actual places to console the people to resist from inhuman barbaric onslaught. Many senior people gave importance to Gandhi, but many young did not hear him. Their demand was they wanted their land; they did not want Hindu people as the country was going to divide on the basis of religion. This was logical, but at the same time very painful. The common people understand little, they could not see future. But they obey their leaders, the leaders of their community, and leaders of their religion as mostly the people are religious right from their birth, what they have learnt from their parents as well as from the community in which environment they have grown up. These young people were engaged in burning and killing as they were the devoted soldiers of the community. The fault lies with the thinking of the leaders. Gandhi had started the religious movement, the movement based on **non-violence** as good as tolerance of Hinduism. Gandhi's idea was to bring more people in the protest against the British.

(There is a picture here, not shown because of the restriction of copyright that shows how Gandhi and Nehru were in discussion in 1942. Without Nehru in the Delhi chair, how could Gandhi accomplish his inner desire in disguise?)

Thus religion directly or indirectly became the issue of target. Few political leaders thought of himself on his own way how to capture power, how to occupy the powerful 'Delhi chair'. Henceforth religion became the easy target to divide the people in their process of occupying the power of chair. Both neither Gandhi nor Jinnah nor anybody else thought for the people of India, the survival state of poor Indians, not the question of their status of life. The goal of Jinnah and Nehru was the 'Delhi chair', while the aim of Gandhi was the 'name and fame' under the banner of non-violence, if not they could come to an amicable solution, a solution where all Indians could live in tranquillity of peace. But their desire for power and fame did not allow them to look for peace but instead indulge them to go for religious violence and hatred to fulfil their desire. The illiterate ordinary common people were instigated to kill one another and create a situation of no return other than the division of the country. Thus the burning fire of religious hatred was started at Noakhali of Bengal at an opportune moment after the beginning of Gandhi's non-violence movement at Calcutta. It was pity to see that the act of 'non-violence' has turned into violence.

To carry out the duty of leadership, Gandhi thought it right to visit Noakhali in view of hearing rioting where Muslims were threatening the Hindus by burning their houses and by the fear of killing. In view of controlling Noakhali Rioting, Gandhi had undertaken a Peace Mission to Noakhali. After the end of all happenings of killing, kidnapping, large-scale conversion, looting, burning of Hindus alive, and burning of houses, Gandhi had appeared with his *saint*-like face in the name of peace mission, hoping his presence might bring back peace. But peace cannot be one sided. There was no

Muslim leader in the peace mission, which might be a mistake on his part.

It was his belief that his presence would stop burning and killing. But later he had realised that Muslims had lost faith over him. The public speeches of the leaders of ML had created a communal atmosphere that would take long time to reduce. As such he decided to return to Calcutta, otherwise his presence might be misunderstood by the Muslims. Of course it had reasons because everybody knows that he had a magnetic power to mesmerise the Indians like a magician. It was also true that he mesmerised the powerful Bengali rulers of British India except the Muslims with his *saintly covered image*.

He was in South Africa; he was humiliated there in the streets, in the moving bus. But he had noticed that when he was thrown out of the bus, the African people gathered around him to know the facts. Thus he had grown up with a concept that humiliation attracts public sympathy. This concept of public sympathy had made him a power-greedy saint to mislead the majority of Hindus. He had kept his idea in his inner mind to apply it at an appropriate time at an appropriate place. His aim was to be a political leader, a leader at the top but in disguise. On his return to India, he had made his place in Congress Party, but he had found that the greatest hurdles were coming from the Hindus of Bengal and Hindu Bengalis. A powerful man of Bengal of that time was C.R.Das, the giant figure of law in Bengal, who was even being magnetised by Gandhi at the outset, who had at the outset devoted whole heartedly to Gandhi's movement. He gave up the British dresses, the dress that he had used generally to get clean in French, but finally he had to differ with him on political ground and had formed a new party, called 'Saraj Party', which had compelled him to keep a distance with congress.

The young Netaji Subash Bose of Bengal, who had dared to threaten him with the election of congress president, was another irritant to him (Gandhi) to reach to the goal of his mission. Not only that, he even humiliated him by defeating his candidate Sitramayya Pottabhi. Although Gandhi had to burn himself with humiliation, he had compelled him (Netaji) to leave the post of presidency. That everything he had done very nicely without any suspicion and that too was done in disguise. Although Netaji was successful to be the president second time by passing him, he had formed a yes-man group with Northern Congress leaders as well as with the groups of defeated candidate Pottabji of the South. The yes-men group of congress did not permit the congress president,

Netaji Subhash, to form the working committee on his own without taking the opinion of Gandhi. This humiliation had compelled Netaji to leave the office. This was how Gandhi did work under the cover of **saint-face**.

He was very much conscious in his activity towards the contribution of the Hindu elite of Bengali people. The Bengal as well as the whole of India was proud of the contribution of Swami Vivekananda, Rabindranath Thakur, Bipin Paul, the Rishi Arabindu, C.R.Das, and Subash Bose. To fulfil his inner desire, he had to do something that would graven the contribution of all these Bengali elites. On seeing the rising of Muslim power under the instigation of Jinnah, he had thought it the right moment to utilise the Muslim force to downgrade the Hindu force of Bengal. It was the reason why he remained aloof in the moment of crisis and stood firm with his weapon of 'non-violence'. Everything was done in disguise. The situation turned bad to worse, a position of no return. The only solution was the partition. Gandhi was disheartened and remained aloof. The proposal of partition was undertaken by Patel and Nehru, and his consent was taken afterwards so as to get it approved by a majority vote. Thus although he was a neutral man of *saint*, his activity turned him a man of religion. However he had maintained his saintly image sometimes in open public, sometimes in disguise in every act of his life.

He not only had disagreed with the Bengali Hindus, but he had also disagreed with his trusted Muslim colleague Khan Abdul Gaffer Khan, who was called 'Frontier Gandhi', who was not even been consulted before giving consent to the creation of Pakistan. This was shocking and painful no doubt. But Gandhi might have thought otherwise. As Pakistan is going to form, it must survive with sufficient land and people. As the Land of North-West Frontier Province is very near to Punjab of Pakistan, as such he might have thought it must be sided with Pakistan. Gandhi might have in desire of expectation that let both India and Pakistan be formed with sufficient land and manpower and let both the country get the opportunity to flourish and live happily side by side as a friendly brother country. He could not think that both the nations would involve in inner fighting in future.

Who was Khan Abdul Gaffer Khan? He was a politician as well as a spiritual leader. He believes in non-violence like Gandhi, although he was twenty years younger than Gandhi. He was born on 1890, while Gandhi's year of birth was 1869. He was a much disciplined man. In 1929, he founded Khudai Khidmatgar (Servants of God), for the movement against the British. This Khudai Khidmatgar Force is like that of an army unit well dressed, well trained, but they never fought with the British with weapon as they are the followers of Gandhi. Gaffer Khan was also called Badshah Khan. He never believed in the policy of the Muslim League and their demand for the separation of Pakistan. He travelled with Gandhi, Nehru, and many other congress leaders to organise volunteers for the non-violence against the British in different places of India. He had been offered with the post of congress presidency, but he refused. He said,'I am a solider of Khudai Khidmatgar; I have to fight along with them.' He added,'I would give Weapon of Prophet, no power on Earth can stand against it.' But the sad part is that he had not been consulted before giving consent to the creation of Pakistan. He was utterly shocked and sad. He decided to form 'Autonomous Pashtunistan', but Pakistan arrested him and kept him in jail for the period 1948–1954. He was arrested again in 1956. His health was deteriorating with ill-treatment and without care. He was kept by Pakistan under house arrest and finally he died in 1988 remaining under arrest.

It was the belief of many people that he (Gandhi) was in complete belief that unless these Hindu elites of Bengal, who were in the helm of British rule, were removed or their power being destroyed, the centre of power could not be shift to Delhi. The united Bengal was powerful and all activity was carried out in Calcutta and not at Delhi. He was in belief that unless a man of his choice was seated at the chair of Delhi, his inner desire could not be completed. The facts of his life had revealed that his every act of achievement was accomplished at the shadow of disguise. The act of reducing the activity of Hindus of Bengal in disguise was also a plan of his life to achieve the highest post 'Father of the Nation' in the emotion of the dark of saintly cover. Why it said so? The following matter of facts would clear the facts of doubts:

(Gandhi with a dress of a 'half-necked fakir'[according to Winston Churchill] with well-dressed Jinnah in picture, which could not be displaced because of the copyright restriction, that explains the secret of understanding.)

He was considered a saint person, a person after getting a law degree of barrister at the highest court of the law of Inner Temple, London, who had sacrificed his bar-at-law dress and had taken a dress of a 'half-necked fakir' (according to Winston Churchill), so to say, the dress of a villager, just to cover his inner mind and expose his outer face, as a face of saint just to win the majority mind-set of Indians who were mostly illiterate, poverty-sicken, and lashing a downtrodden life and get the recognition of the leader of downtrodden people.

He was considered a leader above Hindus and Muslims. The independence movement was once thought to be fought united, but finally there had occurred a loss of faith towards Muslims leading to loss of right and loss of unity. But there were a good number of Muslim leaders who never had wanted the division of the country. But Gandhi did not apply his mind-set to convince both the parties for the unity of the country. It was probably in his inner mind that after initial violence and revolt, good sense would prevail when love of unity would restore to bring back the feeling of brotherhood and a never-ending peace of destiny.

Even after the declaration of 'Direct Action' on 16 August 1946, Gandhi was indifferent. Neither had he made any attempt to stop the declaration nor had he taken any step to counter it. Why? It was because his intention was to get up with the volatile situation to the extreme point as it is useless to talk with anybody when the person was in an emotion of violence. Thus the emotion of violence initially had taken a few lives. Everything was going on in disguise, although apparently it appeared that he was not in the picture. But again he was the supreme head of independence movement in disguise. It might have been in his mind that after an outburst of emotional spark of violence, the good sense would return to bring back the peace with the love of brotherhood.

Lastly, independence declaration was going to be accomplished on 15 August at Capital Delhi. India was divided into two parts, India and Pakistan, on the basis of religion and Punjab, as well as Bengal was also divided and the land had been demarcated for Hindus on one part and for Muslims on the other part as per Radcliff declaration and people had already begun to shift to their respective places, under the volatile atmosphere, but Gandhi instead of honouring independence at Capital Delhi, he had chosen a place in Calcutta to stop any more rioting and prevent the Muslims to cross over from West Bengal to East Pakistan. The place that had been decided by Radcliff for the respective religious people was prevented by Gandhi, not by force but by the soft weapon of Hindus 'fasting'. This was how he had designed his plan along with his like minded men such as Nehru and Patel. Thus Hindus perished in East Bengal by *rioting* and in West Bengal by the weapon of non-violence and the weapon of 'fasting'. On 12 February 1947, A.K. Fazlul Huq had stated that 'Gandhi's presence in Noakhali had harmed Islam enormously'. Finally he was compelled to return.

(A picture of Gandhi along with Hindu volunteers in the mission of March in the streets of Noakhali could not be shown because of the restrictions of copyright.) (Gandhi in Noakhali, 1946)

The visit of Gandhi to Noakhali did not help in controlling the situation of rioting as the peace mission did not involve any Muslim leaders. Muslim could not recognise that Gandhi was a leader who would speak for the interest of Muslims. They had considered him a Hindu leader, who had been looking for the interest of Hindus only since the demand for separate homeland for the Muslim. Thus his visit had agitated the Muslim more and the depth of violence and spray of killing increased. On 7 April, more than a month after leaving Noakhali, Gandhi had received telegrams from congress party workers in Noakhali, describing attempts to burn Hindus alive. Party workers even had stated that the situation in Noakhali is going bad to worse and that the Hindus should have been better to quit before going to perish.

The unknown Patriot Goswami, the Rangalkur Ashram mate Smti Suhashini Das, along with twelve other volunteers accompanied Gandhi to visit Noakhali but volatile situation went bad to worse. Even Gandhi's life was in danger. It was because of these volunteer's careful approach, the mission was kept away from attack. Gandhi had taken a goat from India. He had kept that goat with him in Noakhali. Local Muslims had stolen that goat and ate it. Mohandas Gandhi had to discontinue his mission halfway. Why did he have undertaken the Noakhali visit? According to many, it was to cover up his miss-doing to get him free from suspicion. Neither had he talked with Suhrawardy, Fazlul Huq, or Jinnah to stop mass killing nor ask the congress volunteers of 80% people to strike back. It was because he did not want to stop it. His philosophy was not to speak with a man who is in emotion of violence and never to strike violence with violence. Let the Bengal burn and let the Bengalis destroy no matter. Let the natural things to happen, good sense would return. Independence came, but Bengal was divided, Punjab was also divided. Millions killed and millions displaced. The destiny of the people was decided by the best wishes of the leaders.

[6]

Let us continue to write the Linking Unit: The greatness of a great leader gets reflected in his actions which exposes the thoughts of his inner mind. Why Gandhi had created a Sabarmati Ashram and trained many volunteers only of one community? What was its activity? Why did it not become a non-religious servicing centre? Is it not degrading his image? Is it the image of Gandhi, a leader of the people of India above religion? Let us talk of 'the greatness of a great leader'.

Let us highlight where was the greatness of a great leader? The greatness of courage was seen in the action of performance. What Gandhi had shown in the mass civil disobedience movement, on 12 March 1930? Gandhi had set out from Sabarmati with 78 followers on a 241 mile march to the coastal town of Dandy on the Arabian Sea to collect salt in protest of the British monopoly on salt, Indians being deprived of salts, essential materials of Indians required to taste food, without taxes. Encouraged by the courage of Gandhi, on the Eastern sector, the unknown Patriot, Nikunja Bihari Goswami, at his beginning of youth, jumped into the streets of Assam to protest in the spirit of Gandhi's mass civil disobedience movement. It was against the circular of Lord Cunningham, the then DPI of Assam, who had asked the students not to disobey government in any affairs. In 1932 Nikunja Bihari Goswami went to jail; in 1933 he again went to jail in Bhanu Bill Peasants strike.

After passing the days in jail, Goswami had returned to his Ashram and had remained busy with the usual duty of Ashram. In the midst of political unrest, he had thought of a big gathering and amusement. He had a discussion with all the volunteers and finally they had arrived to the decision that as the annual function of the Rangalkur Vidyalay was coming nearer, they must have arranged it in a befitting manner inviting the young favourite leader Netaji. In the year of 1938, he was kept as in charge by the volunteer groups of Ashram to look after the national leader Netaji Subash Chandra Bose when arrangements had been made to invite him to grace the occasion of the annual function of Rangalkur Vidyalay. It was a great joy and a learning lesion for volunteers and youngsters. Even in 1939, during war time again, he had been inducted with the responsibility of looking after Netaji including the arrangements of security when he had been visiting Silchar.

Goswami was not at rest any time particularly at that time, the wartime when the atmosphere in India was very much volatile. Although war was not on India or on Indian soil, Indians solider were involved, the dying of Indians soldiers had brought a crying outburst throughout the country against the British rulers. The young Indian volunteers were waiting impatiently for the orders of their national leaders to jump into action for the sake of the nation. Goswami became restless in action as soon as Gandhi had declared Quit India Movement in 1942. Although everybody knows Gandhi's movement was non-violence, it was that moment the sign of undeclared violence became visible everywhere. There was complete cut-off of communication link by the disruption of communication wire; the movement of railway became standstill due to disruption of railway track here and there. The government machinery had failed to discharge their duty due to non-cooperation of the employees. Practically there was no government at that time.

Goswami, by his well-organised set of working system of volunteers, had spread the message of Gandhi in every corner of towns and villages of Sylhet. He was a devoted worker of Gandhi. He along with his volunteer groups had spread the message of peace in every street and in every corner of the streets. But the government did not like the activity. According to the government, he was spreading hatred as such his activity was considered anti-government activity and he was kept in jail custody. After staying a long period of eighteen months, he was released in 1944. By the time he was sufficiently grown up to realise the good or bad. He was first shocked to see the growing trend of hatred of Hindus and Muslims on the basis of religion. Everybody will perform everybody's religion, without any objection. There was no harm or interference in the performance of individuals' religion. He was thinking religion was not the issue of hatred. There must be some other cause due to which one hates the other. At last he was successful to discover the reason of hatred. It was nothing but food, short of food, scarcity of food. It was the period of wartime, scarcity of food was prevailing everywhere and in every corner of doorstep. People had lost the civility in procuring food in the presence of food scarcity, humanity suffered. Finding opportunity few political leaders had turned the situation in their favour to divide the nation on the basis of religion when the scarcity of food for a particular community of religion no longer would exist. Gandhi wanted equal opportunity to both Hindus and Muslims. Gandhi was never in favour to strike back to quell the rioting with strong hand rather wanted them to be satisfied at their wish, so he preferred to succumb to their demand.

Probably he had understood that Muslims had not considered him as their leader. Muslims had restored their belief on Jinnah and Jinnah's two-nation theory. Realising the mission of non-violence was a complete failure to stand against the mission of violence of Jinnah, he had preferred to surrender, otherwise the chair of Delhi might have been occupied by the militants of Jinnah and the rule like that of Babur would have been prevailed. The underwater thinking was going on to save him from the curse of a defeated leader; a leader even with the support of 80% of the people had failed to get independence of United India. His surrender had turned the attention from violence to non-violence. Thus his failure to liberate a united India had been turned into the glory of nonviolence and he had sat the seeds to become the father of the nation in due course of time even though the division had lost the lives of millions and the future insecurity with the feelings of religious hatred of Hindus and Muslims. There was no record in the history that a person becomes the father of the nation by dint of an act that would bring millions of lives in danger. The greatness of a great leader had culminated in the joy of personal glory, but the unknown patriot could not find any joy in the prevailing atmosphere of religious hatred and finally in the division of the country, so he had preferred not to be the party of Hindu leaders of the North anymore, who had divided India, divided Bengal, and even divided Assam, a part of it called Sylhet, what was a part of Assam for more than seventy years(1874–1947) during the British period, the people who had learnt to live with the people of this region, who had acquired the pleasure of living with simplicity bestowed with belief and faith unlike the people of Bengal, had now snatched away from Assam.

The unknown spirit of **Patriot** had preferred to die along with the downtrodden Hindu people, and also along with the company of poor tea-garden labourers, who were compelled to stay in East Pakistan for survival till death, forgetting the attraction of power, pleasure of wealth, or the luxury of life. It was not India or Indian people, who had discarded him and his followers, but it was the Indian leaders—Gandhi, Nehru, and Petal, in particular—who had betrayed him and many more like him.

[7]

The Linking Unit: The independence movement although started in 1885 after the formation of the Indian congress and came to an end in 1947 to bring happiness and improve the status of life of the respective units of India, and in particular the two units of Bengal is discussed here as it is the vital state that was the pioneer in the sphere of growth to India and also to the downfall and hence now it is the time to assess the present status of the people of the two regions, a record for the poster generation, to do good to the people of the next generation, because the record of the past is the source of guide line for the activity of the present keeping the vision of progress for the future. Let us see the two Bengals.

The lives of Hindu Bengalis in both the Bengals was disturbed very much after Partition. The **Patriot** had chosen his life in East Pakistan, the Hindus who were living there knows very well that they had to face hurdles in every step of their life as they were living in a part where the law of Islam was the basic ideals of ruling the nation, although sometimes on political ground, it was said that the country is democratic in its function.

But in the mind of **Patriot**, many questions had arisen looking to the plight of Hindu Bengalis in India. Hindu Bengalis in West Bengal (WB) thought to be the happiest people as they got their desired land after the partition, the Land of WB, that had been developed very fondly and dearly by the British, the series of industries had been erupted by the British to make it economically the most sound region, and above all, the

British had evaluated the most spectacular capital of the British empire by the nursing of three villages to the city of Calcutta. The British had started the teaching of English first in Calcutta in Presidency College, Calcutta. Many Bengali, particularly Hindu Bengali, came out with outstanding knowledge in English, and many had explored their knowledge of thought in different sectors, in the field of invention of new culture, in the expansion of arts and literature, in exploring trade, and very much in power politics. His curiosity was to know what had happened to those talented individuals, who had been counted as ideal thinkers of the nation; the proverb was, 'What Bengals thinks today, India thinks tomorrow'. It was a pity to see the conditions of Bengalis in the city of Calcutta since partition, the partition victims are occupying the footpaths with small business stall to survive, spreading across the major streets making the city a tent House of Hawker and not to speak of the conditions in the rural areas. Was it the rightful thought of foresightedness of S.N.Banerjee, the outstanding orator, who could excite thousands of youngsters to sacrifice their lives for the cause of any adverse activity, in the killing of British in disguise, who was the creator of Indian National Congress?

The **Patriot** had seen the right of Muslims in East Pakistan and later in liberated Bangladesh where the Muslims men and women, boys and girls, and old or youths are cherishing with a feeling of ownership of '**my country**', however small, however poor that might be. But coming to Calcutta, the **Patriot** had realised that he was missing the charm of ownership of '**my country**'. It might have for missing of something in WB, where the Muslims have gotten in EB, but the Hindus have not gotten the same in WB. It was because WB unlike EB is a part of secular democratic India, where Hindus and Muslims enjoy equal democratic right. But the **Patriot** had failed to understand the logic of great Indian leaders in dividing Bengal. Bengal was divided on the basis of religion because according to Jinnah Bengali people having with different religion cannot live together as they were Hindus and Muslims. On that basis East Bengal was created for Muslims and West Bengal was created for Hindus. But in secular India in WB, Hindus and Muslims are living together with equal rights. If it was the belief of Indian leaders, a belief that Hindus and Muslims could live together, how they could agree with the theory of Jinnah, **two religion–two nation** for Bengal. If Bengali Hindus and Muslims could live together, the Indian leaders had understood the facts earlier, how they could divide Bengal? Therefore the logic to divide Bengal because of two religions did not hold good. Something else was hidden in between this logic. That was nothing but the destruction of Bengal. How?

[8]

Bengal and Bengalis at the point of destruction is noted here in a nutshell. It was nothing but to destroy the source of power centre of Bengal. Unless Bengal was divided, the power centre could not be shifted either to Delhi or to Karachi. It was a recognised fact that Bengali people are fighters, genuine fighters, and get very much emotional easily to fight to the last; the nature of fighting is present in their inherent character. It was the reason the battle of Plassey was started in Bengal to defeat Sirajud-Daulah by Robert Clive of British, it was also the reason why Jinnah had started the 'Direct Action Day' at Calcutta instead of Punjab to create a part of India as Pakistan what was created mainly centring Punjab from geographical point of view, and likewise Gandhi had started the non-violence movement at the city of Calcutta with the intention of spreading the emotion of non-violence across the whole of undivided Bengal instead of Hindi-Heartland, to get the British to realise that without compromise, it would be difficult to **Rule** India anymore. Gandhi knows very well, without the cooperation of Bengali youths, and Bengal, his movement could not have brought success.

Let us discuss why Gandhi had chosen Bengal 'the starting and ending centre' of independent movement. Gandhi had returned to India with a political mission to secure the highest throne of India. His principle of movement was based on two ideals, 'non-violence in front of public' and 'political action in disguise behind the public'. The strategy of the movement was based on the following outlines:

- All non-violence action must be in front of public
- Political action to remove Netaji should be behind the public
- Political decision to divide the country should not be in front of public, but it must be in disguise, and at the back of the public
- Political decision to form Pakistan without taking the consent of all Muslims of India should be kept in secret till the final announcement
- Political decision to keep the Land of Frontier Gandhi in the dark till the declaration of Pakistan

He had started his experiment in Champaran district of Bihar in 1917, Kheda district in Gujarat in 1918, against

British for compelling the peasants to grow indigo against food crops, but the movement came to an end without any impact.

Coming to the political scene of India, he had noticed that Muslims were not very much involved in any kind of movement along with the Indian National Congress, rather they were with Muslim League since its formation in 1905. In order to befool Muslims, he had decided to support the Khilaphat Movement of Muslims in India in 1920. It was a pan-Islamic, political protest campaign against British India to get the support of the Muslim rights in India. But the Muslims of India had realised his inner mind and discarded his support. In this respect, the mind-set of Gandhi can be understood through a series of question and answer as written as such in the net as well as in different papers.

[9]

Let us find the reason why did Gandhi support the Khilafat movement in spite of the fact that the Turks had killed 2 million Armenian Christians in the Armenian genocide. Turkish military officials, soldiers, and ordinary men sacked Armenian villages and cities and massacred their citizens. Hundreds of thousands of Armenians were murdered. With the change of government, Armenians hoped for the best. But young Turks wanted most of the people to be converted to 'Turki' by heart in the Turkempire. Accordingly their way of thinking brought a danger signal for others, non-Turks, and especially Christian non-Turks, who were faced a grave threat to the new state. Armenians organised volunteer battalions to help the Russian army to fight against the Turks in the Caucasus region. These events, and general Turkish suspicion of the Armenian people, led the Turkish government to push for the 'removal' of the Armenians from the warzones along the eastern front. Thus the young Turks created a 'Special Organisation', which in turn organised 'killing squads' or 'butcher battalions' to carry out the worst genocide of the history. The young Turks did it because they were dedicated to their religion.

[A picture is here where Turks are taking Friday prayer all together, which could not be shown here because of photocopy restriction. Indian Muslims supported the Turks because they are also dedicated to Islam.]

During World War I, Turkey was a party to Central Powers (Germany, Austria-Hungary, and Bulgaria) and very soon it was going to lose against the mighty stronger British force of the British empire. The Britishers won the cooperation of Indian Muslims in the condition of the exchange to help or treat the Turks generously after the war. But the war promise was not honoured as such the Indian Muslims started the Khilafat movement in India in support of the Turkish government. Gandhi supported the movement with a secret mischievous intention to win the Muslims' heart. Many people questioned, is it not treacherous and mischievous and against the ethics of humanity? Gandhi is writing a letter to Hitler to stop the war on the ground of peace for humanity. But here in the movement he is supporting the genocide indirectly. Thus the ethics of Gandhi was in a dilemma of humanity and genocide.

In Khilafat movement, Gandhi was supporting the Muslims of India who were in favour of genocide to Armenians. Where is your ethics of non-violence? When Gandhi is talking of humanity, he should be above of any religion of mankind or community of mankind. He was applying here the religious force against the ethical force. But in Indian independence, he applied the ethical force against the religious force. It was started in 1930 at Calcutta in the civil disobedient movement, as a non-violence movement. Non-violence is the opposite side of tolerance, which is the ethics of Hindu religion. Muslims did not join the movement as such the movement brought communal violence and disunity opposite to Khilafat movement. So he was acting as saint, but he applied the rule of politics in opportune time to fulfil his inner ambition. But again he never forgot to talk of humanity and mankind. Who can forget that he created Pakistan at the cost of millions of death of Punjabis and Bengalis, if not a genocide like Armenians? Why? All goes in one direction to make Nehru, the PM of India, but apparently Gandhi was not for any post, but he knows Nehru will not keep him down.

Again he had started on an experimental basis a non-cooperation movement in a small village of Gorakhpur district in UP on 5 February 1922, against the Rowlett Act (1919), by dint of which anybody can be kept under detention without trial indefinitely. But a large number of protesters participating in the non-cooperation had turned violent, leading to police firing. In the incident, twenty-two policemen had died at the hands of an angry mob. The movement was called off immediately. Thus Gandhi's experiment had turned into an event of complete disaster.

After carrying out movement in the Hindi-hard-belt, he had turned his attention towards Bengal. Gandhi in a very clever way involved himself in the social works in villages and earned a reputation a man of poor or downtrodden. By the time he had changed his dress a dress of a Fakir and made himself a *saint*. But he never left politics. He became a man of God to the public. He knows his political limitation, so he was under the shadow of Nehru family as he worked under Motilal Nehru and came into public prominence. It has infused one vision in his mind to make Nehru the PM of India after getting independence. To achieve it, he required to shift the power centre from Calcutta to Delhi, because in the centre of Calcutta, the leaders of Bengal were very much prominent and popular. It was only the leaders of Bengal who could challenge Nehru to occupy the chair of power at Delhi. He designed a plan in his inner mind to start a non-violence movement in Calcutta. To start up with the mission, he faced opposition from the Muslims, but the movement takes its own turn depending upon the situation, the mind-set of people, and the future of the residents. It turned to communal violence, a set back of the movement. Everybody wants to get something but not at the cost of bloodshed. However the movement brought an atmosphere of communal hatred under the shadow of non-violence at Bengal. **How?**

As a man, Gandhi was calm and quiet, pious and religious. Violence was never in his character. He knows Bengalis were never afraid to take arms and fight for their right, but at the same time, Bengalis are religious, very much religious. Keeping the religious sentiment of the Bengalis in mind, he was thinking how to start a movement and utilise the Bengali Hindu force in the process of movement to achieve the goal of independence. He designed the outline of the movement, a religious movement, what he called non-violence. The Hindu religion is based on two ethics, sacrifice and tolerance. He converted the virtue of tolerance into non-violence. He passed a resolution at the session of Nagpur to start with the independence movement under the shadow of non-violence, such as civil disobedience movement. Objection came from Jinnah.

He did not give importance to the objection of Jinnah. He thought that letting the movement start, Jinnah would be talked to and to some extent he was confident to bring Jinnah with him; when both united, Hindu and Muslims would fought with British. With this belief in mind, he came to Calcutta to start the movement only with Hindus. The natural question arises why did he start the movement only with the Hindus? Of course it was the character of Gandhi, whatever he thought in his mind, he never discloses it to anybody and he dares to implement it by his own endeavour. It was the reason why he disagreed with Motilal, C.R.Das, Lala Rajpat, and Tilak; it was because he thought in his mind a religious non-violence movement. He proceeded alone to implement it. At the outset, he changed the dress and transformed into a *saint* to win the heart of common people. It was in his mind that if the Hindus join the movement in large number, the Muslims will follow for the unity of brotherhood as the brothers of the Hindus and Muslims of Bengal for the greater cause of independence of India.

It was a volatile situation at that time in Calcutta. Under the guidance of Bengal leaders, many young boys were engaged to kill the British in secret. As a result, many young Bengali youths were hanged and many more were sent to cellular jail in Andaman for life imprisonment. The suffering of pain was prevailing in the hearts of all young and old, male and female, rich or poor Bengalis. As soon as Gandhi came with the weapon of 'non-violence', every Hindu individual jumped into the movement with a belief that a Messiah of God has come to the land of Bengal to save the youths of Bengal. But who knows that few stray fellows who were neither with the opinion of Jinnah or Gandhi would arrive here to vitiate the atmosphere with a threat of violence nor dare to destroy Bengal by the violence of blood.

The ethics of Hinduism is the virtue of tolerance and sacrifice. Gandhi utilised the virtue of tolerance to non-violence and had made all the Bengali Hindus of Bengal a strong supporter of the movement. However, the giant lawful personality man like C. R. Das, or personality like literary giant Rabindranath Thakur, and few like others did not join the movement. Jinnah could not be convinced and the Muslim mass in general except few did not join the movement as a result the movement being turned into a Hindu movement of civil disobedient movement in 1930. Of course it was a setback for Gandhi as the Muslims did not participate in the movement. As Gandhi failed to convince Jinnah by repeated discussion, he did not enquire or was interested to talk with any other Muslim leader as it would be useless in view of the negative support of Jinnah. It was because Gandhi wanted Hindu-Muslim unity through the process of movement, although he knows that in the Nagpur session, Jinnah objected to it. His strong belief to win over Jinnah did not succeed.

Gandhi was doubtful with his movement of non-violence at the outset. He wanted to start it only with the Hindus as the Muslims right from the beginning did not want to join the movement. His idea was experimental. But he was astonished on seeing the mass upsurge to join the movement. He was in Fakir dress as he was dealing with the common poor people as he thought that he should be at par with them in *dress*. It made him a man of God as if he became a messenger of God to all Hindus. As such he was behaving like a magician as a mystic, using a Fakir dress. Thus all Hindus were mesmerised by his saint-like behaviour although he was not doing any activity of saint rather he kept himself busy with politics of its own way without taking into account the other's view to think for a better future. Of course he had something in mind never disclosed to second man or discussed. It was he who had his own secret plan. Unless vigorous movement is in Bengal, there cannot be excitement on behalf of British India to talk to hand over the administration to Indians. Every movement has two effects, good or bad. However the non-violence movement gave the birth of communal violence under the instigation of few short-sighted people. This could be brought under control, but if the people become power-hungry, the emotion of violence could be utilised to bring the greatest disaster. Jinnah utilised the emotions of violence for the formation of Pakistan actually for Punjabis, but a bonus point for Bengalis was the East

Pakistan. Today East Pakistan is no longer a Pakistan but Bangladesh.

Muslim did not join the movement. Gandhi did not care for that because his intention was to carry out the movement on experimental basis. This was Gandhi's first success to shaken British India to give the signal to British government that the quicker the British left India, the better is for the British otherwise the bigger movement in the British India might have led to total disaster. Gandhi was worried with the birth of violence, but still he was hopeful to finish hatred and violence. At last the Declaration of Direct Action on 16 August 1946 disheartened Gandhi. He tried his best to talk with any Muslim leader but without success. He never prepared any force to counter the act of violence by violence, which is against his personal ethics of law. It was the inner voice of Gandhi to surrender to humanity and never take arms to stop the rioting; his belief was that God will fulfil your dream. If the people are happy by the division of India, let the people enjoy the happiness. If Jinnah wishes to go away with Pakistan, let him go and enjoy the happiness. If the division of Bengal makes the Bengal leaders happy, let them enjoy the happiness. Destiny will make a man the leader of the nation.

He came to Calcutta, 30 April 1930, and had decided finally to start the civil disobedience movement after consultation with Indian National Congress, Calcutta. It was a movement of non-cooperation with floods of people. More than one lakh people had been imprisoned. The movement had not remained limited in Calcutta, but it had spread to districts, districts to sub-divisions, and sub-division to villages. The Muslim league did not support the movement. It continued only with the Hindus because a section of the Muslims were in support of the demand of Muslim League (ML). The people all over Bengal starting from city to town, village to remote village had spread the sky with the slogan of Mahatma Gandhi, Gandhi-Ki-Joy, as if a messenger of God has come down to Earth to change their fate of destiny. But they did not know that at the back of Gandhi's non-violence, few people contemplated violence to bring bad days for Bengal. He had come here to use the mighty Bengal to carry out the mighty movement of non-violence. If the Bengal and the Bengalis were not in the forefront of the movement of non-violence how he could succeeded to compel British to leave India and how he could reach to the throne of India. The fortune was in favour of India, today India is a free nation, and he was fortunate to become an international messiah of an unknown international weapon, the weapon of

'**NON-VIOLENCE**' known all over by dint of which India had achieved her independence as it had been declared by Nehru, the first prime minister of India although violence had erupted in the acts of non-cooperation, and also violence showed its ugly face in fighting of Netaji's Azad Hind Force. Apart from all pain and pleasure, the happiness lies in seeing India is an independent sovereign democracy.

Similarly, the British after getting exhausted with the movement of Bengalis in their open protest in the streets and in secret killing of British in dark of night, they had thought unless the powerful Bengalis were destroyed, the ruling of British was difficult. It was the reason for which in one stroke, they had divided Bengal (1905), and by another stroke, they had shifted the capital from Calcutta to Delhi (1911).

The same theory was applied by the northern leaders of India to deprive Bengal during independent movement so as to shift the power centre from Bengal to Delhi and Karachi. There was no difference in the logic of depriving Bengal and the Bengalis. In the final stages of independent movement (1946–1947), the Hindu leaders of Bengal had been totally eliminated as there was no leaders of either active or alive at that time. The real freedom fighter Netaji Subhash Chandra Bose was out of the picture. The prominent leaders, who had been in the command of the scene of holocaust of the independence movement, were Gandhi, Jinnah, Petal, and Nehru. The people of India were looking towards them and they had a belief that their leaders would bring independence to them, which would bring a joy of happiness to everyone and in every state of India, where they would usher a bright future for their next generation, the offspring of that generation would live in a land of their own freed from the bondage of foreign rule. But alas! Everything was cut short. It was an atmosphere just after war, there was shortage of food, and a famine-like situation, people were dying in the remote region on the one hand and spray of incident of rioting was going on the other hand in the urban region. Although Jinnah's militant ML volunteers were less than 2%, they had continued the killing of Hindus. The majority of Hindus were aimless without any direction of central leadership. It was a sorry state of affairs just before partition of India and independence of India.

At that point of time, there was no commanding leader from Bengal to foresight the future of Bengal other than the emotion of religious hatred, a hatred that had been allowed to grow by the stalwart leaders like Gandhi by escaping the responsibility of giving the Muslims their proportionate representation in the power of administration, bringing an undercurrent feeling of suppression among the Muslim leaders and raising the right of majority Hindus to the extent of denying every right of Muslims.

What the northern leaders had expected, the more the religious hatred had been there in Bengal, the more was likelihood of inner fighting between these two emotionally fighting communities of Hindu-Muslim to bring destruction. Thus the leaders got their opportune moment to divide Bengal and destroy Bengal and Bengalis forever so that in future in no time the Bengalis could rise to make Bengal a centre of power. Had it not being a moment of success for the northern leaders, they would have been in fight to the last against Jinnah, the leader of ML.

[A picture was here of Jinnah and Gandhi, which could not be seen due to copyright restriction but that reflects how in the ethics of the governance of power both Gandhi andJinnah are at logger head but in public they were at close relation. Is it not a travesty of truth to betray the common man?]

But very cordially, Jinnah, Gandhi, and Nehru including Petal all together had settle the matter and had amicably settle the power of chair among themselves, who had got their power of chair and where, everything was settled amicably in a family atmosphere, the very above picture tells the truth of inner mind. Indian people are not fool, what had happened in their settlement was very much imaginable from their picture. How dearly Gandhi had embraced Jinnah! Could it justify hostility? Never! It was a win-win situation for both. They did it with full knowledge of their conscious looking to the goal of power and glory. The partition of India as well as the division of Punjab and Bengal was carried out in full knowledge of friendship and not in hostility. They never had thought of the people who had been affected by the policy of partition. Jinnah became the chief of Pakistan, Nehru became the PM of India, Petal became the home minister of India, and the post of Father of the Nation had been kept vacant for Gandhi to be filled up in the due course of time. What a wonderful solution the leaders had been founded out. The crying of millions, who were displaced, millions who were killed and many more millions whose huts and homes had been burnt in the fury of rioting did not affect them. Today they are all icons; nobody has the power to say anything against them.

[10]

The Linking Unit: The onslaught of Bengal was culminated with the distribution of power. Let us see how power was divided in the **Provisional Constituent Assembly, 2 September 1946**. The World War II was ended; all political prisoners in India who had taken part in the Quit India Movement had been released by the British. The government of British had decided to hand over the administration to Indians. Now a time has come to form a constituent assembly. Both Indian National Congress and the Muslim League had decided to take part in the election. The result was as expected—the Indian National Congress had won most of the seats, including seats in areas with a Hindu majority. The Muslim League on the other hand had won seats in areas where there was a Muslim majority.

[Here is a magificant picture of Parliament of British India to be occupied by the Indians that could not be shown because of the copyright restrictions—that signifies the dignity of the following content:
Seating in Parliament glorifies the Indian leaders but suffering of partition victims diminishes the glory of Indian icons—the facts and sufferings could be understood only by the victims and not by icon leaders, because the mind-set of icon leaders was flourishing at different heights of pleasure with the dream of occupying the status of *power*.]

Sadder Vallabhbhai Patel had held the Home Affairs; Baldev Singh, a prominent Sikh leader, was appointed as the leader of the Department of Defence;John Mathai to Supplies; and C. Rajagopalachari to Education. The Railways and Transport was given to Congress leader Asaf Ali, Jagjivan Ram to Labour, and Rajendra Prasad was given to Food and Agriculture Department.

The Muslim League (ML) also had taken part in the interim government. The Department of Finance was headed by Liquate Ali Khan, the Departments of Posts and Air was headed by Abdu Rab Nishtar, and Commerce was given to Ibrahim Ishmail Chundrigar, and the Department of Law was given to a Scheduled Caste Hindu politician Jogendra Nath Mandal.

The selection of persons for provisional assembly just before Partition by the ML had appeared that the prominent person like A.K. Fazlul Huq of East Bengal (EB) was not listed. It had appeared right from the beginning that the leaders of East Bengal were looked down every time even before the question of language had appeared prominently.

[11]

Let us know about Abul Kashem Fazlul Haque (1873–1962). It was necessary to discuss his life history that would expose the icon leaders of India, who were to what extent liberal, communal, partial, and self-centred. A.K. Fazlul Huq, having born in a village called Saturia of Barisal Division of East Bengal (EB), had qualified as BA from the prestigious Presidency College, Calcutta, and MA from Calcutta University. Lastly he was qualified as BL in 1897, from University Law College, Calcutta. His political life had started as a congress worker and he became very soon the general secretary of Congress Party for the period 1916–1918. Slowly and gradually he had realised that congress could not be his party. In 1929, he had formed a different party and named it as KPP (Krishak Praja Party). He was a strong supporter of Hindu-Muslim unity at the time of working as general secretary of the Congress Party or in the later period too. Jinnah had convinced him to join ML, although he had agreed but he did not abolish KPP.

In the Bengal election of 1937, KPP succeeded with thirty-five, while ML with forty seats. However Huq had formed the ministry with congress and became the first premier of Bengal in British India. But in the later stage during the presidency of Nehru, that might have some secret strategy; congress had withdrawn support and had pushed Huq to join ML. Even after joining ML, he was for the *unity* of Hindu and Muslim. Hague was a rarity among Muslim politicians of Bengal of his time who could look upon Bengalis as Bengalis and not as Hindus or Muslims. He had remained in Calcutta quite a time even after the formation of East Pakistan and finally went to East Bengal.

In East Pakistan he made a landslide victory in 1954 as the head of a United Front to become the chief minister of East Pakistan. The next year he had made a trip to Calcutta where he had given a speech advocating the reunion of the two Bengals. On return he was deposed probably Pakistan government did not like his statement.

He was honoured as the Tiger of Bengal. He was a stunt fighter for the independence of India. Like Suhrawardy he was also misled by Muhammad Ali Jinnah for the formation of Pakistan in the cry of a falsehood for a separate homeland for the Muslims of India inflicting the sentiment of religion having being a Pakistan in the East and a Pakistan on the West, although very few Muslims of other state went to Pakistan. The Muslim leaders of East Pakistan had realised it later that it was Pakistan for the West Punjabi people with the imposition of Urdu over Bengal. His fight for the right of Bengalis had turned him an activist of secessionist.

He was one of the senior most figures of the Indian National Congress at one time, but later he had joined the Muslim League under the prevailing situation of the country. A man like AK Fazlul Huq could not be accommodated in the congress, how the icon leaders of India could claim that congress had looked upon Muslims equally.

Congress had deprived the Muslims right from the beginning that had compelled the Muslims to take a resolution for the creation of sovereign Muslim state. If the congress was justified in their decision that proportionate right of equality was given to Muslims, then congress must strict to its decision and did not allow the ML to take upper hand in rioting and killing people. But instead the supreme leader of congress had surrender to the leader of ML. What was the reason, the reason was to preserve the fake idealism of 'NON-VIOLENCE', the glory of Gandhi being rested with it. But by the time India had experienced the effect of non-violence. It was not necessary to mention the matter of incidents, one after another, the Chinese aggression of 1962, the occupation of Tibet 1956, the war with Pakistan (four times).

The important portfolio finance was in the hands of Liquate Ali Khan, and he had shown his power of supremacy in the sanctioning of money to each and every department and had established a record in proving that the Muslims might be less in number, only of 20% and occupying less number of portfolios but no matter, one portfolio might be sufficient enough to keep a holding in all other portfolios in the power of administration because the Muslims were clever in the art of administration and will remain so in future too.

That was why probably Liquate Ali Khan was very successful to send all the Hindus of East Bengal to India befooling the Bengali Muslims just in a period of two months in the month of February and March 1950, after partition, to reduce the % of Hindus from 47 to 12, to make it completely Muslims while India could not send a single Muslims from West Bengal to East Bengal to make it Hindu Bengal in view of the partition of Bengal on the basis of religion, keeping in mind East Bengal for Muslims and West Bengal for Hindus, rather Liquate Ali had created a situation for which Nehru, the PM of India was compelled to made Nehru-Liquate Ali Pact whereby all the displaced Muslims, who had fled to East Bengal out of fear, had returned to West Bengal and thereby had raised the Muslim population even after partition and had made a threat of getting majority now in near future in West Bengal too.

Thus it could not be unjustified to say that Muslims had got East Bengal by *force* and West Bengal by the *art* of administration. Like the finance portfolio, the Muslim leader like Liquate Ali Khan can befool the Indian PM, how powerful the leader might be, who was a leader of 80% people of India, did not matter, who would not be able to apply the power because he was lacking in the art of administration, the art administration for Muslims like Liquate Ali Khan was an inherent right, a heredity right.

It also had appeared in so many occasions that congress stalwart leaders had failed to attract the talented youngsters in the party. There was something lacking in the look-out of all high commanded leaders. Liquate Ali Khan was also a strong supporter at the outset for Hindu-Muslim unity. Getting a law graduation from inner temple, London, he also had started his practice at one on the Inns of Court in London in the year 1922. After returning to India, he had arranged a meeting with Jawaharlal Nehru, to join a political party. But it had appeared that after having a thorough discussion with Nehru, his ambitions and political views had changed completely. The question was likely to arise what had happened? Most likely, it was that Nehru was lacking in the art of convincing the other leaders with opposite views or he was indifferent to Muslim rights.

The same was applied in the case of another Inner Temple genius, who was no other than Netaji. He went to congress leadership, though he was in congress, but he had never accepted the views of congress leadership, and he had accepted Chittaranjan Das as his mentor, who was a spokesman for aggressive nationalism in Bengal in the year 1923. Was it not something of lacking of congress leadership? Unity of the nation could not be build up in vacuum of leadership.

[12]

The Linking Unit: The all kinds of activity of Indian independence movement although ended in 1947, centring Gandhi and Jinnah, but the under current activity of *naval mutiny* in the background shadow of Netaji cannot be overlooked. As such a little of Indian independence and naval mutiny is describe here.

What happened with Indian independence and naval mutiny? If the independence of India would have been achieved through naval mutiny, India would never be divided, Gandhi would not get the opportunity to befool the illiterate poor Indians to fight against the mighty British through non-violence, and finally bow down to militant Jinnah and achieved Delhi chair by dividing India in secret negotiation keeping the public in the dark and giving Pakistan to Jinnah without thinking the sufferings of millions who would be in the turmoil of violence, sufferings in the struggle of displacement.

[A picture of naval mutiny was displaced here, but due to copyright restrictions, it was omitted, but that signifies in vision **partially how the public was in emotion to support the mutiny, which could not be expressed in language.]**
[RIN Revolt–March on Mumbai(Bombay) Street]

Naval mutiny was a forgotten torch of Indian freedom struggle, an uprising that had once shaken the basic foundation of the British empire, yet it had remained relatively unknown to the masses, the Royal Indian Navy mutiny or Bombay mutiny, as it was known, or the February 18 revolt as it was called for and had kept under suppression without bringing it to the knowledge of the present generation of the Indian people less the image, the only image of NON-VIOLENCE to what extent that had contributed in achieving the independence of India would have been exposed.

The INA and Netaji were not in the warfront after the downfall of 'ATOM BOMB' and surrender of Japan, but the impact of INA's heroics and naval strike was there. British rulers knew their armed forces were becoming less and less trustworthy. After suffering with Netaji's INAforce, the British empire was lost not only in the strength of its armed forces, but also in the economic front as the government was running out of funds. The situation had compelled Prime Minister Clement Atlee to think afresh, and within two months, on 16 May, Atlee's cabinet mission promulgated the plan to decolonize India that had paved the way for independence.

The declaration of Nehru was that 'India wins independence with non-violence'. What a travesty of truth! However, suppression of facts had encouraged the image of a few individuals but had demoralised the youths of the nation. The country could not forget the defeat and complete surrender to 2% militant ML volunteers to give away the unjustified demand of Pakistan and had showed the seeds of communal hatred forever in India. Who were those fools who would consider these leaders were for the good of masses? They were for the good of themselves, for the image of self, and for international prestige and image.

Let us look at the actual happenings of naval mutiny. The beginning of naval mutiny had started in the winter of 1945, when the world was just getting to terms with the effects of Second Great War. Campaign for freedom of India was at its peak, the country was in a volatile situation in a religious atmosphere of hatred due to mishandling of political rights of communities. The

Indian leaders, the so-called icons, and above all the *father* figure Gandhi all had failed miserably to find a formula of living together with a logical conclusion of a better future keeping safety and stability of the nation beyond question. Instead everyone had remained in the look-out of personal gain, personal fame, and personal glory.

Under those prevailing situation, one such Patriot, Balai Chandra Dutt, along with a small group of naval ratings dreamt of doing something for the country. Dutt was a young telegraphist of the British Royal Indian Navy and acted as trained officers engaged in communication and radar. He had got the opportunity to come in close contact with many members of the Azad Hind Sena of Netaji through a journey along with his friend covering Malay Peninsula. He was inspired on seeing the spirit of nationalism that had been burning in their mindset. Very soon he was grouped with young volunteers and had decided to raise their voice in any opportune moment. It was December first, when the navy day celebrations were on; they had decided to express their emotions through slogans like 'Jai Hind' painted on the walls of the ship. It had taken a little time for the British to realise, who was behind the graffiti and who was distributing anti-empire literature across. Finally, the

British was succeeded to identify Dutt and had arrested him then and then. The ratings were not happy with his arrest. Moreover they were not happy with the British officers since a long time as they had suffered ill-treatment and simmering with a sense of humiliation of discontent over the poor service condition of food materials.

Dutt's detention had triggered a spontaneous call for strike among the Indian ratings on Talwar. The hips of discontent had taken its exposure to all over, when several other ships had joined the strike and had turned the events of strike into a full-fledged revolt.

The sailors were in charge of wireless communication centre, the revolt had started on 18 February, in no time it had spread to other ships and establishments. The gravity of the situation had increased in many folds in the very next day as several other ships resting in Mumbai (Bombay) and other ports, notably Karachi had joined the revolt. In the evening of 19 February, the events had turned a step further in the formation of Naval Central Strike Committee (NCSC). Signalman M. S. Khan and Petty Officer Telegraphist Madan Singh unanimously had been elected as the president and vice president bestowing a sense of unity among Hindu and Muslims in the naval force unlike religious hatred among political stalwarts.

The most important striking feature was the downfall of British flag and rising of Indian flags. It was the White Ensign was taken down and had hoisted three flags tied together over the revolting ships. It was a moment of joy, workers from all walks of life, even some officers of Castle Barracks, and some residents of Bombay also had joined the occasion and enjoyed the very moment coming down to the streets.

The depth of revolt was continued to be felt on each passing days. On 22nd and 23rd, there were mass agitations on Horn by Road—today's Dadabhai Novroji Road (near Victoria Terminus). What a spirit Netaji had injected in slogan of 'Jai Hind' was unimaginable, uncontrollable. The demonstration out of emotional outburst had turned violent causing the opening of fire on the ratings. Indian people, already had been gripped by the heroics of INA, had extended their heartedly support for the strike. The impact of strike had been spread to other places too. The ratings in Calcutta, Madres, Karachi, and Vizag also went on strike, thundering the sky with the slogans 'Jai Hind'. They had been came out with a new demand of releasing 11,000 INA prisoners.

Many units of the Royal Indian Air Force and local police force had also taken their oath to participate in the strike. Naval officers had begun calling themselves Indian national Navy. One thousand RIAF men from the Marine Drive and Andheri Camps had also not left behind. By the end of the day, the love and sympathy of Baloch and Gurkhas had increased so much that they had not dare to refuse to fire on the striking sailors.

On seeing the situation, the day-to-day rising of public sympathy leading to the refusal of military command, the British government was shell-shocked. Finding no other alternative, the British government was compelled to proclaim an order to the highest commander-in-chief of the Royal Navy to clench the revolt. Finding the necessity of full preparedness, the British destroyers, stationed at Tricomalee of Ceylon (Sri Lanka) were called for, to proceed to Mumbai. The flag officer commanding the RIN, Admiral J.H.Godfrey had been asked to issue ultimatum on air 'submit or perish', British bomber planes were asked to fly over Bombay Harbour to be ever vigilant to destroy the mutineers in necessity.

The clashes between Second British Battalion and Rating had started in regards to the holding of Hindustan superstructure. The decision of Indian sailors was to hold on and fight back. They knew they had limited strength from military point of view, but they had a greater force of mass support. They were expecting political leaders would come forward in their support when a mass agitation would turn the revolt a real success; the success would bring independence for United India. Neither Gandhi with Congress nor Jinnah with ML had come forward for their support except the two persons Aruna Asaf Ali and Achyut Patwardhan who had assisted the revolutionaries on personal capacity. Rather Congress and Muslim League had supported the British government and asked the Sailors to end the strike.

The general mass population were bewildered by the statements of political leaders and as such, the situation did not escalate any longer and ended quickly with sufferings of little causality among the Indian sailors. On the evening of February 23rd, after a meeting between Vallab Bhai Patel and MS Khan, the President of (NCSC), along with Jinnah's support, the revolt was called off.

British government was familiar with Gandhi's civil revolt, non-violent revolt that never could have been affected very much in the process of administration and not to the question of security. But here it had shaken the British empire by its six-day strike as it had involved seventy-four ships, twenty fleets, and twenty-two units of RIN. The building up of the British empire was based on its navy power. Navy's strength was the centre of their pride. It was navy that had raised them as traders and then rulers around the world. This revolt had prompted the British government to hand over the power to Indians.

However, despite assurances of no punishment, there were widespread arrests after calling off the strike. The strikers had to face court-martial; many of them had been dismissed from the service. The recognition had finally come in the year 1970, the RIN Revolt was renamed as naval uprising and the mutineers were honoured by the government. The two ships of the Indian navy were named after the name of Madan Singh and B.C.Dutt. Memorials also had been built in Mumbai.

Why had Gandhi, the chief of congress, and Jinnah, the chief of Muslim League not supported the sailors' revolt was a mystery of politics. If the public memory had been taken a little behind, the picture would have been crystal clear. It was known that Netaji was qualified in ICS, employed in civil service in UK, but he had left service and had returned to India to join Indian politics. He was in congress and he was always out spoken with his youthful vigour of voice such as,'Give me blood,

I shall give you freedom'. He had never qualified Gandhi's 'non-violence'. As such there was always a clash between Netaji and Gandhi or Gandhi's supporter. And this conflict of clash had come into light in the election of president of the Congress Party in 1939. Netaji Subhash Bose was the candidate in the election, but Gandhi said,'Sitaramayya Pattabhi is my candidate; the defeat of Pattabhia is my defeat.' Netaji had won and Gandhi had to bear the brunt of humiliation.

It not only had ended here, Netaji had to leave the post of presidency. Afterwards Indians had heard the voice of Azad Hind and INA. The origin of naval revolt was the inner inspiration of INA Force. How Gandhi could tolerate the success of naval revolt?

The reason why had Jinnah not supported the revolt was different. He was in the dream of the creation of Pakistan. If a military force or naval force had risen in the Indian independent movement, then Gandhi's *nonviolence* would no longer be continued, and killing of Hindus by the militant Muslims of Jinnah to pressurise the demand of Pakistan by the division of India based on 'two religion–two nation' would not have been succeeded.

Indian independence came on 15 August 1947, after a bloody holocaust, losing lives of millions on inner fighting because independence was not a united India but a divided India based on religion. It was the belief that religion brings peace, happiness, and joy, but in India, it had brought a misery to many although it had brought fame for many in the international circle, such as Kaydey Azam. Jinnah, the president of Pakistan; Jawaharlal Nehru, the prime minister of India; and Gandhi, the Father of the Nation of India. The partition of India had not affected the other states very much as that had affected particularly the Bengal. The effect of Bengal partition was not ended even after sixty-five years. Even today, the year of 2015, the news in the paper, what is the status of Hindus of East Bengal, or East Pakistan or Bangladesh? We are in Bengali of Bengal, but Bengalis are divided. The unity of Bengalis had vanished, now Bengalis are united as Muslim Bengalis or Hindu Bengalis. Pakistan was formed with religious unity, but it had appeared now that the religious unity is also not permanent, otherwise Bangladesh would not have been formed. Jinnah's theory of two religions–two nations had been proved wrong, and Gandhi's theory of non-violence had been proved wrong because non-violence could not bring independence to United India, rather violence had succeeded to create Pakistan. But both the leaders had succeeded in one aspect, Jinnah to become the first governor-general of new nation Pakistan and Gandhi, the *Father* of the Nation of India. Both the leaders had earned the international fame at the cost of the sufferings of the people of the regions of the state. It is only the time will say when the sufferings of the common people would end.

[13]

The Linking Unit: The **Patriot** (Nikunja Bihari Goswami) was a staunch devotee of Gandhi, who worked with all sincerity and sacrificed his life for the people of his region, which was in no way less than the other great leaders, who might be internationally known for the creation of a country or destruction of a country, but he is known here very much to the people of the small regions of the district Sylhet. But his instinct of sacrifice without hankering of power and money is no way inferior to any kind of activity of any other world leaders. He born in Bengal, he worked for the people of Bengal and died for Bengal of present Bangladesh. As such how the country of Bangladesh has come into existence is very much appropriate to describe here.

Let us see the movement of Bangladesh, and what was Bengal? Let us look at the name of Bangla or Bengal (or

Bangladesh), the source of which is Vanga Kingdom that was being founded by Harivamsha Vanga, who was one of the adopted sons of King Vali. The Vanga Kingdom was also known as Banga. The Vanga Kingdom was a powerful sea-faring nation of ancient India. They had developed overseas trade relation with Java, Sumatra, and Siam (modern-day Thailand). It was believed that the Vanga prince Vijaya Singha conquered Lanka (modern-day Sri Lanka) in 544 BC. Many Bengali people migrated to the Maritime South-east Asia and Siam and had settled there.

By the time period of seventh century BCE, there exists the Nanda Dynasty that was the first historical state to unify all of the present Bangladesh under Indo-Aryan rule. Later after the rise of Buddhism many missionaries settled in the land to spread religion and established many monuments such as Mahasthangarh.

Again by the time period of 323 BCE, there exists another empire in the Bengal region, known as Gangaridai empire. In 326 BCE, the region came into prominence because Alexander the Great had started his campaign of invasion, but he withdrew his force quickly anticipating the valiant counter-attack of the mighty Gangaridai empire that was located in the Bengal region. At that time Gangaridai was the most powerful empire in India, where the king possessed an army of twenty thousand horses, two hundred thousand infantry, two thousand chariots, and four thousand trained elephants remained ever ready for war. Ancient history of Bengal consists of several kingdoms, Maurya Empire (second century BC), Gupta (fourth century AD), and Buddhist Pala empire (eighth to eleventh century). The Pala empire under Pala dynasty can be said as the golden era of Bengal. It was this period when the Bengali people reached to the extreme height of power and glory. It was the period when Buddhism spread to Tibet, Bhutan, and Myanmar. The Pala had extensive trade as well as influence in South-east Asia. This was a period of style of architecture and sculptures.

The thirteenth century Bengal was under sultanate, and subsequently the later period was starting with Babur, the first ruler of Mughal empire, who had established his holding in 1526, at Delhi but Bengal came into the domain of Mughal empire during the reign of Akbar (1556–1605) after the battle of Tukaroi, which was fought in 1575 near a village of present Balasore District of West Bengal. In 1612, during Emperor Jahangir's reign (1605–1627), Sylhet was brought under Mughal empire, and Dhaka was brought in prominence by making it the capital of Bengal. A well-known Dhaka landmark,

Lalbagh Fort, was built during Aurangzeb's sovereignty (1695–1707).

[Here was a picture of Siraj ud-Daulah in his youth, the very appearance signifies his vision of mind-set, his nationalism that a language cannot express, but due to copyright restriction, the picture is ommitted.]

Siraj ud-Daulah was the last independent Nawab of Bengal (1756–1757). It was not only the sultanate at that time, but also the Khilji dynasty, a Muslim dynasty of Turkic origin, which ruled large parts of South Asia between 1290 and 1320. It was founded by Jalal Ud din Firuz Khill and became the second dynasty to rule the Delhi sultanate of India and other parts of India. The dynasty is known for their faithlessness and ferocity, as well as their raids into the Hindu south and defending the sultanate against the repeated Mongol invasions of India.

[14]

The entry of East India Company into Bengal became possible due to Clive: The English East India Company sought to gain access to the province of Bengal because it was the most developed industrial region at that time in India. It was estimated that in 1750, India accounted for 25% of world economic production in contrast to England's 1.9%.

Bengal was at the centre of economic growth. In 1776, the Bengali city of Dhaka alone, had engaged 80,000 women to spun cotton for 25,000 weavers who produced approximately 180,000 piece of cloth. Indian textiles wove their way so gracefully into British culture that South Asian names for clothes such as bandana, calico, taffeta, etc., had been derived into English language.

In addition to textile front, Bengal's fertile soils of the Ganges River Basin had made outstanding agricultural production. Any company seeking a profit in India wanted footholds in Bengal at that time. The East India Company opened a port in Calcutta to access to the rich elite section of Bengal.

In 1717, the company could convince the weak and short-lived Mughal emperor of that time to give them a 'Farman' in Bengal—a decree that gave the company the rights to trade duty free in return for a small annual fee to the Mughal court. The British company gets a certificate to do trade in Bengal tax-free. Thereby the other European companies had failed to compete in trade with British company. The local Bengali rulers resented this privilege that deprived them of tax revenue. Despite relentless protests from the local Nawab, the British had increased their trading in Bengal. Thus a clash of conflict became evident. Though the local Nawab faced the conflict with large contingent, yet British became victorious because of their superior military technology. This was the beginning of the British to exploit the wealth of Bengal by force. Very soon the East India Company's conquest of Bengal was challenged by a new Nawab, Siraj, when he came to the throne of Bengal in 1756.

By the time French had made an incursion along the coast of Bengal at Chandan Nagar. The advance entry of French into Bengal worried the British, who began to build Fort William in Calcutta to counter act the French military might, which infuriated the young Siraj-ud-daulah, who became the Nawab of Bengal just after the death of his grandfather Alivardi Khan in 1756. According to him, 'You are merchants. What need have you for a fortress? Being under my protection you have nothing to fear.' But the British continued with the construction of Fort William. By the time the East India Company purchased the three small villages of Kolkata to make it the city of Calcutta and began the construction of Fort William to house a garrison to face the French attack in future. The city flourished, with a large volume of trade travelling down the Ganges River.

But young Siraj was not happy with development, and so in 1756, Siraj attacked Fort William in Calcutta with thirty thousand troops. The thrust of onslaught was so severe that most of the British settlers, including military commanders quickly had to evacuate the place leaving the others behind. After the Nawab's soldiers easy conquer of the fort, they crammed the British prisoners into a small dark basement, where the majority of the prisoners slowly suffocated to death. A British military officer wrote a terrifying and vivid account of how he endured the **'Black Hole' of Calcutta**. But in the end, it had created a stir back in England. The loss of British at Calcutta was a military disaster. But later the description of the treatment of the surrendered soldiers sparked off widespread public support for the subsequent conquest of Bengal.

By the turn of the time, it fell to a young company colonel, **Robert Clive**, to change the course of British and Indian history. During that time, it takes at least six months on average to travel or communicate one way between India and Britain. Fast-moving events prevented the company directors in London from efficiently communicating orders to India, and as such the 'man on the spot' was the right person to take the decision on any emergency. Since the arrival of Clive in Bengal, he dreamt of conquest right from the outset. He quickly retook Fort William and Calcutta with one thousand fighters (Indian soldiers trained by the British), along with eight hundred British troops, fourteen cannons, and keeping with the full support of naval experts. Finding the daring attack of the British in the soil of Bengal, the Nawab of Bengal returned to Calcutta from the capital of Murshidabab with forty thousand infantry, sixty thousand cavalry, and thirty cannons. The French also had offered military support to Nawab. The force of Siraj surrounded and severely outnumbered the British force. But luck mixed with a dash of treachery went in favour of Clive, turning events to his advantage at the **Battle of Plassey**.

The news of Afghan troops was in advance in the north to sack the Mughal capital of Delhi and was reportedly heading towards Siraj to plunder his palace. The attack never came, but it make Siraj so worried that he left the siege of Calcutta and actually asked for British support against the Afghanis. As the Nawab hesitated to strike back to recapture the Fort William, Clive changed his strategy and successfully turned its force to attack the French at Chandernagar, a potential European ally of the Nawab in order to eliminate the force and pushing the French out of Bengal forever. Next, he made a secret pact with disgruntled generals in the Nawab's army. The chief, Mir Jafar, agreed to betray Siraj during battle and, in return, take the place of the Nawab. The subterfuge worked.

The battle was preceded by the attack on British-controlled Calcutta by Nawab Siraj-ud-daulah and the death of British soldiers in the prison cell as was well-known as Black Hole incident was fresh in the mind-set of British fighters. The British sent Admiral Charles Watson from Madras to Bengal so as to increase the fighting strength of Colonel Robert Clive. The battle took place at Palassey on the banks of the Bhagirathi River, about 150 kilometres north of Calcutta and south of Murshidabad, the then capital of Bengal. In the battlefield troops of Nawab were present but actually the troops made no move to join the battle. As a result at the Battle of Plassey, three thousand British troops of East India Company—only one-third of them European—defeated the Nawab's army of eighteen thousand horses, fifty thousand foot, and fifty-three pieces of heavy ordnance, served by French artillery men because the commander-in-chief of the Nawab's army, Mir Jafar, betrayed Siraj. The battle ended in forty minutes. 23

June 1757 became the day of victory of the British East India Company over the Nawab of Bengal. Mir Jafar was ascended to the throne of Bengal. Siraj was soon found and killed. In the short term, the Battle of Plassey benefitted the company and its officers in Bengal at the expense of the Indians. The conquest profited the Clive as well as the company. The Mughal emperor, Shah Alam II, recognised British power by granting the East India Company the virtual ruler of Bengal.

Now on, the English East India Company shifted from a trading company to a landlord and an occupying force. The company expanded its territory all around quickly even towards North-east of India by playing tricks of agreement with local Indian princes and Nawabs. The company created puppet rulers so that it could rule territory efficiently and inexpensively. Throughout India, the company had now used his authority to disintegrate Mughal empire for political advantage. The company now engaged the local rulers to collect taxes and thereby the economic spectra of the company get changed.

For Bengalis, however, the British conquest was a tragedy. The most productive region in India was quickly reduced to poverty. Famine spread throughout the province as the British increased tax collection, decreased wages, and failed to respond to droughts and floods. In 1769, 1 to 10 million Bengalis died of famine widely believes because no official count was ever taken. In the lower parts of Bengal, the famine resulted in a population loss of between 33 and 50 percent. Even during the time of famine, the company continued to collect taxes and actually increased the land tax. The British offered no food relief for the starving people, and shockingly, some company officials made fortunes by hoarding and charging exorbitant prices for the food. Under British rule, Bengal also lost its role as a manufacturer of high-quality goods and instead became dependent on exporting low-value raw materials, such as raw cotton, opium, indigo, and tea. Trade became a monopoly business for the British company, the company forced weavers to accept extremely low wages and consequently the industry declined. Slowly by the middle of the nineteenth century, the company had effectively de-industrialised Bengal. Since 1773 British parliament took the charge of company. A regulation was brought to control the Bengali textile industry by imposing a 78% tax on imported Indian cotton to protect the incipient British textile industry. Consequently Bengali textile exports slowed down and expansion of East India Company had continued with the new and new regulations.

The English under the General Major Hector Munro at Buxar defeated the confederate army on 22 October 1764. The winning of the Battle of Buxar had given the British to collect land revenue in Bengal, Bihar, and Orissa. This development set the foundations of British political rule in India. Now Robert Clive was appointed the governor and commander-in-chief of the English army in Bengal in 1765. He is claimed as the founder of the British political dominion in India. Robert Clive also brought reforms in the administration of the company and the organisation of the army.

[15]

The Linking Unit: The Patriot, Nikunja Behari Goswami, was a man of Bengal, who was born and died in Bengal, and as such how the administration of Bengal was changed in the course of time if not described, his life history would remain incomplete. Let us see how the British entered in Bengal and ruled for a time period.

British had established British rule in Bengal in the period of 1757–1947. The greatest disruption in Bengal's history began on 23 June 1757 at the stroke of the entry of the East India Company (an English mercantile company) as the defacto ruler of Bengal by defeating the Anwar Siraj-ud Daulah of Bengal. The economic destruction of Bengal was started due to the commercialization of power by the trading company by imposing tax on the Bengal industry. As a result, the growth of Bengal industries was stopped and as such the sources of their wealth dried up. The downfall of Bengal industries indirectly contributed to the rising of new industries in England. The capital amassed in Bengal was invested in the growth of British industries and in the end the de-industrialisation had happened on the Bangladesh region. The muslin industry particularly of Dhaka virtually disappeared as a result of British rule.

The introduction of British law, a modern bureaucracy, new modes of communication, the language English, and the opening of local markets to international trade had created new horizons in the sphere of development in various sectors. New ideas originating from the West had produced new intellectual movements for the betterment of Indians as well as for mankind. British rule in Bengal had originated a division in the society, where the city-based Hindu middle class became the office bearers and village-based Muslim peasantry became a separate group of agro-producers. Thus a class of conflict between Muslim peasantry and Hindu intermediaries prevailed during the British rule.

Economic exploitation of Bengal provoked an intense reaction against the British Raj, the Hindu middle classes, who referred to keep themselves as the Bhadralok, wanted more power in administration, the immigrant Muslim (Ashraf) of state patronage wanted their aristocracy in arts and business keeping their presence along with the Uppercase Hindu, but on the other hand, they sought the political benefit of downtrodden Muslim peasant (Atraf), who were being exploited by Hindu landlords and moneylenders because they want to increase their strength of voice.

British rule of Bengal contributed to the emergence of an elite class from local Muslims in the second half of the nineteenth century, who facilitated the business in the expansion of jute cultivation in the Bangladesh region. The increase in jute exports benefited the Muslims, who were living in lower Bengal in large number who were called now (Jotedars). The economic affluence of the Jotedars encouraged the expansion of education among local Muslims. Unlike the Jotedars and Atraf, the Ashraf in Bengal spoke Urdu. The Ashraf were enthralled by Islamic universalism while the Jotedars and the Atras identified themselves with the local culture and local Bengali language.

Leadership of the Muslim community in Bengal belonged to the Ashraf, who preferred to raise the religious sentiments in arousing the passions of Bengali Muslims. Political rivalries between Muslim Ashraf and Hindu Bhadralok first surfaced when the British partitioned the province of Bengal in 1905. The Muslim Nawab of Dhaka supported the partition in hopes of gaining the patronage of British rulers. On the other hand the Hindu Bhadralok, who viewed it as a sinister design to weaken Bengal, was at the forefront of the struggle for independence. The Bhadralok class idolized the idea of 'Golden Bengal'.

Though initially the anti-partition movement was non-violent, but at the end it went ahead in terrorist activities, and in communal riots. The charismatic leader Chitta Ranjan Das was the pioneer in foresightedness for unity of Bengal. In 1923, Das signed a pact with Fazlul Huq, Suhrawardy, and other Muslim leaders, which provided guarantees for representation of Muslims in politics and administration. However, the spirit of Hindu-Muslim rapprochement evaporated with the death of Das in 1925, leading to an atmosphere of communal hatred.

Communal problems were not unique to Bengal, it was there for the strong religious belief for the Bengalis in general, however, the political leaders of Northern

India, very cleverly utilised the religious sentiment to destroy Bengal and shift the power to Delhi for their benefit. It was the reason to discuss why did Calcutta was chosen to strike against British by the mission of killing of British officials in disguise, why did Gandhi start non-violence, non-cooperation in 1930 at Calcutta, why did Jinnah start Direct Action Day, 16 August 1946, at Calcutta after convincing Suhrawardy on the basis of religious affinity.

The Hindu chauvinistic policy of Gandhi having with a religious dress contaminated the Muslim community. Finding a suitable background the political leaders utilised the religious mind-set for acquiring the power of chair for immediate benefit. As the demand for a separate Muslim state of Pakistan became popular amongst Indian Muslims under the patronage of Jinnah, the formation of Pakistan on communal lines was deemed inevitable by the middle of 1947. To prevent the inclusion of Hindu majority districts of Punjab and Bengal in a Muslim Pakistan, the Indian National Congress, and the Hindu Mahasabha sought the division of these provinces on communal lines. Bengali nationalists such as Sarat Chandra Bose, Huseyn Shaheed Suhrawardy, Kiran Shankar Roy, Abul Hashim, Satya Ranjan Bakshi, and Mohammad Ali Chaudhury sought to counter division proposals with the demand for a united and independent state of Bengal. Suhrawardy and Bose sought the formation of a coalition government between Bengali Congress and the Bengal Provincial Muslim League. Proponents of the plan urged the masses to reject communal divisions and uphold the vision of a united Bengal. In a press conference held in Delhi on 27 April 1947 Suhrawardy presented his plan for a united and independent Bengal and Abul Hashim issued a similar statement in Calcutta on 29 April.

But the Hindu leaders of Northern India including Gandhi, Petal, and Nehru, those who were in the forefront of leadership in the absence of Bengal leaders like Netaji did not agree to see a strong Bengal, who instigated Hindu Bengalis of Bengal to oppose the plan under the leadership of Shyama Prasad Mukherjee. The cry was West Bengal for Hindus and East Bengal for Muslims. Accordingly the division came into being under the command of the British Surveyor Redcliff. But again in 1950, Nehru chocked out a plan to destroy West Bengal a step further so that no leader like Netaji had ever emerged from Bengal to challenge the Delhi chair, as such he came out with Nehru Liquate Ali Pack, 4 April 1950, by dint of which he agreed to brought back the Muslims of Bengal who had left West Bengal out of fear of communal riot in 1947. Thus the supremacy of Hindus in West Bengal was destroyed and thereby Delhi was saved from the danger of Hindu leaders of Bengal.

All activity had enhanced in the division of Bengal to finish the power of Bengalis in all-India politics. Independence came to Indian soil with the formation Pakistan (1947). Nehru became the PM of India, Jinnah became the president of Pakistan, and Gandhi became the Father of the Nation, by mutual adjustment while Bengal get exploited by division where mutual adjustment did not apply. Why? East Bengal was exploited by West Pakistan, people were tortured for their Bengali voice, treated mercilessly, who were being compelled to fled the country to take shelter in neighbour India (1971), while West Bengal was exploited by Delhi government, where East Bengal refugees were accommodated in the open field of graveyards (1950), in the hilly jungles of Madhya Pradesh (1952), while the rest were sheltered in the streets of Calcutta as Hawkers.

[16]

The Quit India Movement in the form of civil disobedience movement was started by Gandhi on 8 August 1942. It was a call for immediate self-rule by Indians and against the **British policy** of sending

Indians to World War II. He asked all teachers to leave their schools, and other Indians to leave their respective jobs and take part in this movement. The principle of the movement was non-cooperation with non-violence against British rule, even though the British resorted to brutal force. Gandhi gave his famous message 'Do or Die!' for the cause of the nation. The aim of the movement was to force the British government to sit on the negotiating table.

However, almost the entire congress leadership was put into confinement in less than twenty-four hours. The British, already alarmed by the advance of the Japanese army to the India-Burma border, responded the next day by imprisoning Gandhi and kept him at the Aga Khan Palace in Pune. The Congress Party's working committee members all were arrested together and imprisoned them at the Ahmednagar Fort. The movement soon became a leaderless act of defiance, and in large parts of the country, the local underground organisations took over the movement. In many cases their activity gets deviated from Gandhi's principle of non-violence.

All the other major parties rejected the Quit India plan, and most cooperated closely with the British, as did the princely states, the civil service, and the police. Jinnah

of the Muslim League also supported the British Raj
and grew rapidly as an influential person of British
Raj. There was opposition to the Quit India Movement
from several political quarters too. Hindu Mahasabha,
Vinayak Damodar Savaekar went away of Quit India
Movement. Overall, the Quit India Movement turned
out to be not very successful and only lasted until 1943.
It eventually became a rebellious act without any real
leader and without any pre-plan strategy.

But by doing **Swedish Movement or Quit India
Movement**, a great harm was done to Bengal. Bengal
was the place of centre to start any movement as a result
industry, business, and agriculture everything was
destroyed and Bengalis had to face the brunt of poverty
and famine. The destruction of economic structure had
brought the question of survival in front. The religious
minded Bengali people had left with no other alternative
but to remember the supreme power 'God' of respective
religion. Thus political leaders came out with the weapon
of religion to cherish their goal of power. Otherwise if
C.R.Das could find out the best solution to live together
united, why Gandhi did not? It was the future strategy of
Gandhi to reduce the power centre of Calcutta and shift
the power centre to Delhi. Unless, movement, secret
killing, non-cooperation started at the city of Calcutta,

how could he think to minimise strength of Bengal as well as its power structure?

Lord Curzon was the man behind the partition of Bengal in 1905 that gave modern Bangladesh its political boundaries. The decision to affect the **partition of Bengal** was announced in July 1905 by the viceroy of India, Lord Curzon. The partition took place on 16 October 1905 and separated the largely Muslim Eastern areas from the largely Hindu Western areas. Initially Bengal was divided into two new provinces of 'Bengal'. Western Bengal comprises a province along with of Bihar and Orissa while Eastern Bengal compares a province along with of Assam. Dacca was made the capital of the Eastern Bengal.

Partition was promoted for administrative reasons because Bengal was geographically as large as France and had a significantly larger population. Curzon instigated the people by saying that the eastern region was neglected and under-governed. By splitting the province, an improved administration could be established in the east, where subsequently, the population would benefit from new schools and employment opportunities. The Hindus of West Bengal who dominated Bengal's business and rural life complained that the division would make them a minority in a province that would incorporate the province of Bihar and Orissa. Indians were outraged and termed it a 'divide and rule' policy, of British. But the British said that it is for administrative efficiency. Due to political protests, the two parts of Bengal were reunited in 1911.

As the independence movement throughout British-controlled India began in the late nineteenth century, the movement gained momentum during the twentieth century. Bengali politicians played an active role in Mohandas Gandhi's Congress Party and similarly played an active role in Mohammad Ali Jinnah's Muslim League. It exposes the opposing forces of ethnic and religious nationalism.

[17]

Let us see the role of Jinnah for the people of Bengal. Suhrawardy played the vital role in post-independent India to achieve Pakistan. He was responsible for unleashing the Direct Action Day in August 1946, at Jinnah's behest. The Direct Action Day, no doubt a black day for all Bengalis, but intention was to prove that if the Congress Party did not agree to division, all of British India would be engulfed by civil war. But after the incident, Suhrawardy was restless as he has hurt the mother of Bengal with stream of blood. He stopped talking to Jinnah, however big he was, he was thinking for a section of the Muslims only particularly of Punjab in the name of a 'Separate Homeland for the Muslims of India'. However, he was consoled by A.K.Fauzlul Huq and Abdul Hasan of Burdaman, the leader of ML. He came out with a new idea of Sovereign United Bengal, which was strongly supported by many Hindu stalwart like Sarat Bose, the elder brother of Subosh Bose; Kiran Sankar Roy; and many others. He had realised the sectarian thinking of Jinnah, who had to create Pakistan taking Punjab region into confidence and sacrificing the Muslims of other regions at the mercy of India, but that injustice also had been burning in the inner mind-set of Jinnah, which had been exposed in public when in the dying bed he said that 'I did the greatest blunder in my life by creating Pakistan'. But the action of 'Direct Action Day' already had turned Hindus and Muslim neighbours into enemies and caused a cycle of death, and emotion of revenge led to further destruction. Emotion ran high which had broken all call for unity. Thus Jinnah was finally successful to achieve Pakistan at the cost of breaking the heart of Bengal and Bengalis.

Today USA is the superpower not by sacrificing the *black* people of America, the strength of USA in military, in sports is due to the contribution of the black people of

America. The unity of USA was kept as one solid stone under all adverse by the sacrifice of one American who is no other than the brave Abraham Lincoln, the saviour of the *unity* of the Union, who was the real hero of USA, unlike Gandhi or Jinnah, who became the leader of the nation by destroying the *unity* of the Union of India.

Let us know who Huseyn Shadheed Suhrawardywas. He was a Bengali politician with full of vigour and energy. He served as the last prime minister of Bengal during the British Raj. Suhrawardy was educated at Oxford and joined the Swaraj Party of Chittaranjan Das upon returning to India in 1921, and very soon, he became an ardent follower of Chittaranjan Das as he found a spirit of love for Bengalis irrespective of religion of Hindu-Muslim or high-low cast was boiling in the mind-set of this man as if he was a true friend of Bengalis. Very soon he became the deputy mayor of the Calcutta Corporation at the age of 31 in 1924, and the deputy leader of the Swaraj Party in the provincial assembly under the patronage of C. R. Das. However, God has taken his life very soon and following the death of Chittaranjan Das in 1925, Suhrawardy began to disassociate himself with the Swaraj Party and eventually finally he joined Muslim League. Henceforth he became attached with Jinnah.

He served as minister of labour and minister of civil supplies under Khawaja Nazimuddin among other positions. He was the minister responsible during the Midnapore (Bengal) famine of 1943, but did little to relieve it. His heart cried for Bengalis, but he obeyed Jinnah for greater benefit. Why? Winston Churchill was the then wartime premier of Britain and Jinnah was obliged to hear him because after the war British would be favourable to grant Pakistan to Jinnah. Churchill's intention was in blocking relief to Bengal, in the 'scarcity of shipping' in the Atlantic. It was Suhrawardy's government, the only Muslim League government in India at that time to implement British scorched earth policies designed to counter Japanese invasion threats, policies like burning over a thousand fishing boats to block any potential movement of invading troops. These measures aggravated starvation and famine. Although his heart was burning for the Bengalis who were dying in fame, yet he had to obey the order of British Raj just to satisfy Jinnah for the cause of Pakistan in future. He did everything for Pakistan in connivance with Jinnah, but at last he had to pass a bonded life under the restriction of Pakistani military ruler. The memory of his tragedy had no end. Following the independence of East Pakistan and West Pakistan in 1947, he remained in disturbed mind-set quit a time and did not left Calcutta.

In 1947, the balance of power in Calcutta was shifted from the Muslim League to the Indian National Congress, and Suhrawardy stepped down from the chief minister ship, setting the mind-set of Suhrawardy in a state of disturb agony. He knows how he was befooled by Jinnah in the name of religion to bring destruction in Bengal. But in his inner mind, a constant fire was burning for the mistake he did by starting the onslaught on 16 August 1946, a black spot in his life, though his attempt of forming a Sovereign United Bengal had failed, but still he hopes for a better future day, when the unity of Bengal would be restored.

Unlike the other Muslim League stalwarts of India, he did not leave his hometown immediately for the newly established Pakistan. Anticipating revenge of Hindus against Muslims in Calcutta after the transfer of power, Suhrawardy thought to utilise Gandhi for the success of his secret mission. Gandhi on the other hand find that he was not successful to bring unity between Hindus and Muslims in Bengal without coming to any negotiation with Suhrawardy or Jinnah before the starting of *direct action* was rather a mistake. However Jinnah was left for Pakistan and the Delhi chair remained vacant for Nehru, but he was disheartened on seeing spray of violence. If it continues, his image as an inventor of new weapon

'NON-VIOLENCE' will die down. As such both of them Suhrawardy with a plan of greater Bengal and Gandhi with his international image of non-violence united together after the formation of Pakistan. Thus Gandhi was persuaded to stay in Calcutta and pacify tempers in Calcutta with the intention of keeping Suhrawardy sharing the same roof with him so that they could appeal to Muslims and Hindus alike to live in peace. 'Adversity makes strange bedfellows together.'However, finally Gandhi was successful to bring out negotiation with Suhrawardy after breaking of Bengal to enhance his mission of **'NON-VIOLENCE'** into success, although he remained silent at the call of direct action and breaking of Bengal. Thus Gandhi had achieved a success in two fronts, the success of bringing independence and the success of peace for the glory of 'non-violence'.

But ultimately Suhrawardy left for Dacca, the capital of new East Pakistan. On return to Dhaka, he joined Awami Muslim League that was being formed by Maulana Bhashai. In the 1950s, Suhrawardy worked to consolidate political parties in East Pakistan to balance the politics of West Pakistan.

[Here is a picture of Huseyn Shaheed Suhrawardy (left) with Sheikh Mujibur Rahman (right) of 1949 where the young Mujibur was influenced by the matured Suhrawardy, the vision of attachment of nationalism that had been visulaised in the very picture that is not possible to express or explain in the language of English that was here, but it had been omitted for the copyright restriction.]

In Dacca, along with A.K.Faziul Hug and Maulana Bhashani, he led the Bengali United Front alliance to a resounding victory in the year 1954, and later in 1956 he became prime minister and pledged to resolve the energy crises and since then the economic disparities between East and West Pakistan came into surface. In 1956, Suhrawardy became the prime minister in a matter of haste being appointed as fifth prime minister by President Iskander Mirza after the surprise resignation of Chaudhury Muhammad Ali. As prime minister, Suhrawardy took the nation on confidence giving a talk on radio, promising to resolve the energy crises and economical disparity, and promised the nation to build a massive military in an arms race with India to satisfy the West.

Suhrawardy knows the relation of Pakistan with India was not friendly in true sense because of various factors since birth. Therefore he thought it right in the eventuality of any conflict Pakistan requires a strong military force as well as an effective foreign policy. In order to do that, he extended his hand towards United States as well as towards China. He tried his best to improve the relation with USA. To improve relation with China, he visited China in 1956 and had established the Pakistani embassy in Peking.

Suhrawardy tried to increase the military strength by extending the area of military districts, and training the military with enhanced military expertise. He also tried to increase nuclear capability. In order to do that in 1956, Suhrawardy announced the nation's first ever nuclear policy. He established first Pakistan Atomic Energy Commission (PAEC) 1956 by passing an act in the parliament and also established the first nuclear power plant in Karachi, when it was recommended by the PAEC. He also assured the people of Pakistan that very soon the nuclear plant would be established and energy crisis would be eliminated.

After becoming prime minister, he faced with a controversial geopolitical programme of *One Unit*. The One Unit formula consisting of the four province of

West Pakistan concerns with the integration of Pakistan while it was not a problem in East Pakistan to bring integration and stability of Pakistan on the basis of the act of Pakistan passed in 1955. There was politics over this issue and the four provinces were engaged in a political struggle with the issue. Suhrawardy abandoned to implement the sections of One Unit formula. The four provinces retained their geographical status while the East Pakistan retained its single large geographical status of single unit. Similarly there was different opinion in regards to joint electorate system or separate electorate system in West Pakistan while the joint electorate system was very much popular in East Pakistan. In order to avoid controversy he turned his attention towards economy and encouraged small investors to set up business in the country.

Suhrawardy tried his best to remove the economic disparity between the Eastern and Western wings of the country and also tried to alleviate the food shortage in the country. But his administrative policy was not liked by the people of West Pakistan as they thought that he was doing everything such as financial allocations, aids, grants, everything for the benefit of the people of East Pakistan, and not anything for the people of West Pakistan.

Looking to economic condition of East Pakistan, Prime Minister Suhrawardy immediately suspended the National Finance Commission Program (NFC Program). He advocated for the USSR-based Five-Year Plan to centralize the national economy. In this effort, the East Pakistan's economy was quickly centralized. However all major economic planning shifted to West Pakistan. But efforts of centralizing the economy were met with great resistance in West Pakistan when the elite monopolist and the business community angrily refused to oblige to his policies. The business community in Karachi began its political struggle to undermine any attempts of financial distribution of the US$10 million CA aid to the better part of the East Pakistan. In the financial cities of West Pakistan, such as Karachi, Lahore, Quetta, and Peshawar, there were series of major labour strikes against the economic policies of Suhrawardy.

Furthermore, Prime Minister Suhrawardy tried to end the crises by calling a small group of investors to set up small business in the country. But all his action was not accepted gracefully in the four provinces in West Pakistan. His image was deteriorated further bad to worse. Many nationalist leaders and activists of the Muslim League were dismayed with the suspension of

the constitutionally obliged NFC Program. His critics
and Muslim League leaders observed that with the
suspension of NFC Award Program, Suhrawardy tried
to give more financial allocations, aids, grants, and
opportunity to the people of East Pakistan than that
to West Pakistan. During the last days of his prime
ministerial years, Suhrawardy tried to remove the
economic disparity between the Eastern and Western
wings of the country but he failed to do that. He also
tried unsuccessfully to alleviate the food shortage in the
country. But all his efforts failed.

In foreign policy, he pioneered a strategic partnership
with the United States. His thinking of nationalization
of East Pakistan annoyed the central leadership for
which he was forced to resign on 10 October 1957,
under the threat of dismissal by President Iskandar
Mirza. Afterwards he was treated badly by the central
leadership because he thinks for Bengalis, the tragedy
of his life was that he was the man, who was won over
by Jinnah by the argument of the religion of Islam, who
was he, the pioneer of establishing the base of Pakistan
by the onslaught of the Direct Action Day on 16 August
1946, was cornered by the military ruler of Pakistan,
who was banned from public life by the military junta
of General Ayub Khan. He never get relieved from the

pain of suffering of restricted life, which led him to give up his last breath after suffering a massive heart attack in Beirut, Lebanon, in 1963 remembering that he was befooled by Jinnah to destroy Bengal as he himself stroked axe in the heart of the mother of Bengal, that incident of 16 August 1946 was a black spot in his heart, which cannot go away till the last breadth.

The Linking Unit: The Patriot, Nikunja Behari Goswami, was a man of Bengal, who was born and died in Bengal, as a small village man, but he had lofty desire, a desire to do good to people. The spirit of desire is no way less than any of world leaders, who sacrificed the life remaining as a bachelor, less his desire for the service to others get hampered. He was among many of unknown, who sacrificed their lives in silence in the service of mankind. Let us discuss **'the world leaders of twentieth century'**—just to remember the service of a person for the cause of nation.

2 The World Leaders of Twentieth Century

[1]

Muhammad Ali Jinnah, born on 25 December 1876, was a lawyer, politician, and the founder of Pakistan. A nationalist Indian had been changed to a nationalist Muslim. Jinnah served as leader of the All-India Muslim League from 1913 until the creation of Pakistan on 14 August 1947.

[A photograph of Jinnah was given here to show his spirit of ability as advocate, reflected in the picture itself, and that was unparallel to explain in any other way, but due to restriction of copyright, it was omitted.]

He became Pakistan's first governor-general until his death. Muhammad Ali Jinnah was the most influential figure in Indo-Pak subcontinent's history. He was an outstanding pleader first in Bombay and later in the United Kingdom after 1930. His name was also forwarded to be one of British parliamentarian. But he returned to India and joined the All-India Muslim League in 1913 and afterwards after 1930. He is revered in Pakistan as Quaid-i-Azam (Great Leader) and Baba-i-Qaum (Father of the Nation).

To describe Jinnah's earlier life, it is to be noted that crossing the examination of matriculation, Jinnah proceeded to London to study law in 1893 and completed his studies in 1896. He became a law graduate. Thus after born in Karachi he trained as a barrister at Lincoln's Inn in London. It appeared from the life style of Jinnah that he was a person of Western mentality and he was habituated with desperation, eloquence in expressions of the West, and acquainted with etiquettes of the Mughals. Indian Independence Movement started more positively after the formation of the Indian National Congress in 1885, but significant activity took place in Indian politics only in between 1917 to 1920. Secret killings of British officials spread to Calcutta, and other places. By the time the growth of communal organisations among the Hindus had grown up in a few places. It had brought a change of mind to Jinnah. Thus a Nationalist Indian changed to a **Nationalist Muslim**.

Jinnah rose to prominence in the Indian National Congress in the first two decades of the twentieth century. In these early years of his political career, Jinnah advocated Hindu-Muslim unity, but later on he went away from unity and asked for a separate 'Home Land for the Muslims of India' on the ground that 'two religion, two nations'. The rights of Muslims became an important subject matter before independence of India. By 1939 Jinnah came to believe that rights of Muslims would be better protected in a Muslim homeland. He was convinced that this was the only way to preserve Muslims' traditions and protect their political interests. His earlier vision of Hindu-Muslim unity no longer seemed realistic to him at that time.

By 1940, Jinnah had come to believe that Indian Muslims should have their own state. In that year, the Muslim League, led by Jinnah, passed the Lahore Resolution demanding a separate nation. During the Second World War, the league gained strength as Muslim volunteers, who were asked to be trained in place to place while Jinnah maintained a close cooperation with British administration. On the other side leaders of the congress who opposed the British views were imprisoned, and in the elections held shortly after the war, Jinnah won most of the seats reserved for Muslims.

At this juncture, Jinnah was displeased with Mohandas Gandhi's stance at the London Round Table Conference in 1939 and frustrated with the Muslim League who was on the verge of merging with the National League of Congress, with the goal of participating in provincial elections and potentially conceding to the establishment of a united India with majority Hindu rule. No doubt, Jinnah was a good pleader, who could place the right of Muslims with logic and that became possible because of his long standing stay at London and passing the days in the atmosphere of Inner Temple luminaries and also for a strong desire being infused in his mind-set by the depressed Muslim community of India, who could not think equal to Hindus in the matter of right of service, in the matter of administration or in the matter of social status, to live as a Muslim, a human being the follower of Islam.

Afterwards after colliding with Jinnah, in 1942 the Muslim League adopted the Pakistan Resolution to partition India into two states. Finding Jinnah was an eloquent speaker and favoured by the British, he (Gandhi) thought it wise to talk with him in private. Gandhi had insisted that any division of India must take place by mutual consent after the British had left India. Jinnah on the other hand had insisted that partition must come before freedom because Jinnah had suspected something fishy. After seating at Delhi, the Indian congress may not agree with the demand of Pakistan. Jinnah attended all the conferences with a strong group of supporters. It appeared that although Jinnah was representing the Muslims, less than one-fifth total population of India, out of which a large section of Muslims also were not of his support, while Gandhi along with congress representing more than four fifth of the population of India, but in the conference the atmosphere had been prevailed in favour of Muslims because of Jinnah's wonderful capacity of placing the topic of problem with logic.

What had happened in Round Table Conference at London? While Gandhi, along with a group of Hindu personalities, full of the Hindutva knowledge of ancient India, thought for the rights of Hindus through the teachings of Hindu-Vadas and Upanishads. Thus tolerance and appeasement became the weapon of attack to acquire the rights of Hindus as a status of majority population of India. There were no person of Inner Temple personality, who could bring an impact in the conference, although the conference was confined in a *hall* of a British government in London, but its impact of utterances had been spread to every corner of British empire, so to say to the whole world. Thus the distress state of Muslims in the twentieth century that was kept in hanging in a state of uncertainty had been spread throughout the world by the eloquent expression of Jinnah, but on the other hand in the absence of an equal calibre of Inner Temple personality, the legitimate rights of Hindus had not been spread to the world rather a picture of Hindu chauvinism was expressed resulting the overall expression of sympathy went along with Jinnah and in favour of the rights of Muslim community. Consequently the letter of the British government that was given to the congress before the year of 1947, asking to hand over the charges of British administration involves not only India but also Pakistan.

In the year 1946, Britain sent a cabinet mission to India to outline a constitution for the transfer of power to India. Thus India was then divided into two regions India and Pakistan. But when the congress president expressed objections to implement the plan, Jinnah voted against it. Immediately after that Jinnah as planed earlier announce in connivance with the Bengal Chief Minister Suharwardy declared **'16 August is the DIRECTACTION day'**. The congress did not take any preventive action; the ML (Muslim League) volunteers were previously trained and kept ready for any action to begin with.

In the daytime meeting was held in the open field in Calcutta at the foot of the Ochterlony Monument (now known as Shaheed Minar). In the afternoon, in the absence of light rioting took place killing more than six thousand Hindus, the sparks of violence spread to different places. Suhrawardy has left a controversial legacy in post-independent India. He is perceived as responsible for unleashing, at Jinnah's behest, the Direct Action Day in August 1946 which killed thousands. The intention was to prove that if the Congress Party did not agree to division, all of British India would be engulfed by civil war. This action turned Hindus and Muslim neighbours into enemies and caused a cycle of death, revenge, and further destruction. It proves his determination as a leader to achieve his goal right or wrong. On the other hand Gandhi was hesitant in determination, neither could he be determining to a united India or a divided India. Neither he could negotiate with Jinnah nor could he stand in firm against Jinnah. He surrendered and humiliated his spirit of leadership and the spirit of youths of Indians.

Gandhi has no alternative but to come forward with the spirit of sacrifice and non-violence, Pakistan came into being. Millions killed and millions displaced. The independent state of Pakistan that Jinnah had envisioned came to be on 14 August 1947. The following day, Jinnah was sworn in as Pakistan's first governor-general. He was also made president of Pakistan's constituent assembly shortly before his death.

[2]

Who was Mao Tse-tung? Mao Tse-tung was the revolutionary who founded the Communist Party of China at the early stage of his life. Since 1949 he became Mao Zedong the founding father of the People's Republic of China who governed the country as chairman of the Communist Party of China until his death. He brought China under unified standards, which is considered as one of the most important personalities to have lived in the twentieth century.

[A picture of Mao Tse-tung was here to reflect his vision of determination, but that has been omitted because of restriction in copywriting.]

Mao acquired *power* by his own efforts. His beginning of revolutionary thought of development was started from his school life. He developed an early interest in political and international affairs. The philosophy of wider development after graduation took him to Beijing in 1918, where he studied and worked part-time in the library at Peking University, the nation's premier institution of higher education, and at that time, he was one among hotbed of radical political thinker among many of the faculty and students.

The record of history reveals that the young Mao (Mao Zedong) tried hard to bring back the past imperial glory of china by making a balance in between the China's traditional civilisation and the modern civilisation of the world dominated by the advent of advanced technology. The nations of Europe and North America had emerged with new civilisation with new technology.

He thought to build a new socialism under the influence of Chinese characteristics. Keeping the Chinese character in the mind-set Mao sparked off a country-wide nationalist upsurge directed against the European and Japanese influence in China. However he was successful to motivate the students. Their participation made the movement a success. He thought to choose an ideology. Soon after, Mao declared himself to be a Marxist-Leninist and went back to his hometown in Hunan. Then he founded the Chinese Communist Party, which was formally established in Shanghai on 23 July 1921.

As per record of history, it is found that Chiang Kai-shek for the gain of political power started a movement against the Communist Party of Mao. He gathered a large force and also a force of young students of locals and students of abroad that were studied in Moscow and adopted with the Moscow culture, who all together had undertaken a bloody coup in 1927. The combine force had effectively destroyed the Communist organisations in Shanghai and also the Communist organisations in other major cities. Finding no other alternative, Mao took shelter in the mountainous hinterland in south-central China, in Jiangxi province. Very soon Mao came down to adjacent city Hunan where Mao had been born and raised. After getting stabilised in his birthplace, Mao formed the local Communist government in this isolated base area and declared himself as the chairman of the party.

In the course of time, he transformed the party into a system of ideology. An organisation was grown up based on certain ideology, the strength of which rests with its own military force named as the **Red Army**, empowered with wings of guerrilla warfare and new recruits. However the fighting spirit of Red Army by the time was turned towards the outer foreign force in the event of invasion of China by Japan. The Red

Army remained engaged to fight against the Japanese force along with other Chinese force to save China from foreign occupation. It was the year 1937 as per record of history. The Communists emerged as a formidable competitor for state power with the Nationalists. The Communist Party became victorious. However after the end of war the Mao Communist Party came to power and rival Chiang Kai-shek's had to flee the country.

Industry came under state ownership and China's farmers began to be organised in a new set-up of groups. All opposition was ruthlessly suppressed. The Chinese initially received significant help from the Soviet Union, but relations soon began to cool down because of ideological difference. In 1958, in an attempt to introduce the system of Chinese communism, Mao launched the 'Great Leap Forward' movement. It was an economic and social campaign started by the Communist Party of China (CPC) from 1958 to 1961. The campaign was led by Mao Zedong, keeping in mind the rapidly transforming the country from an agrarian economy to a socialist through rapid industrialisation and collectivisation.

However the Great Leap ended in catastrophe. The result did not show a positive result, agricultural output declined, which led to famine. The policy was abandoned but it had made a bad name for Mao. It had caused deaths in tens of millions, estimated from 18 million or 45 million. After that Mao launched the 'Cultural Revolution' in 1966, to revive a revolutionary spirit by the destruction of old tradition. One and a half million people died and much of the country's cultural heritage was destroyed. In September 1967, with many cities on the verge of anarchy, Mao sent the army to restore order. Mao appeared victorious, thereby he was successful at last to set up the foundation of rapid development, but his health was deteriorated to an extreme end. His later years remained attached to build bridges with the United States, Japan, and Europe. In 1972, US President Richard Nixon visited China and met Mao, who died on 9 September 1976. He was an inborn fighter, he never get dishearten with immediate failure and never get away from the ultimate goal of his vision unlike other leader.

What about Gandhi, the leader of more than 80% Indians in particular, who on seeing the danger of rioting, immediately made the transformation of his vision from the goal of United India to a nation of divided India. Was it not a sorry state of affairs?

[3]

Let us know Adolf Hitler. The record of history reveals that Hitler was a military man, but later he was transformed into a German politician. He became the leader of a German political party. By virtue of efficiency, he became the chancellor of Germany and worked for the period of 1933 to 1945. The record further shows that during his period and under his guidance Germany had initiated World War II in Europe. The reason of World War II was explained by different historians in different way. But the most probable reason was first the economic exploitation of Germany by Jews, and second was the injustice done to Germany by the agreement of World War I. It is in the record of history that German initiated the war by invading Poland in September 1939.

Apart from the warfront, Hitler had shown his efficiency in the service sector as well as in the spectra of development. During this time period, unemployment ratio fell from 6 million in 1932 to 1 million in 1936. In the sphere of development, he had brought the largest infrastructure improvement scheme in the history of German leading to the construction of dams, autobahns, railroads, and other civil works. He not only made history by the invasion of Poland in 1939, but even after two years, he again ordered for the invasion of the Soviet Union. However that might have been a mistake in war strategy by dint of which German suffered defeats. Finally the war came to an end during the Battle of Berlin in 1945.

[A photograph of Hitler was kept here to reflect his personality that he was a great worrier, but it had been omited because of restriction in photocopying.]

Let us find out what were the reasons of World War II. The economy of German was not with the German people rather it was with the Jews people although they were living in Germany since a long period of time. Accordingly policy had been drawn to eliminate Jews from Germany. During World War I the joint force of Britain and France defeated Germany and snatched away the German territory. The World War II was for German to regain the lost territory of Germany. It was one of the reasons why German had initiated the war by attacking the Poland in 1939.

These actions made him the most popular man in German. Thus some long-term **causes of World War**

II are found in the conditions preceding World War I and seen as common for both World Wars. Among the causes of World War II, Italian fascism in the 1920s and Japanese militarism were also the reasons to be counted. In August 1934, Hitler became president, and since then he was preparing for the war. Hitler made the largest infrastructure improvement in German.

There was other different opinion of the World War II. Hitler made his foreign policy very aggressive and thus it became the primary cause of the outbreak of World War II in Europe. He directed large-scale re-arrangement of the territory, and on 1 September 1939, he invaded Poland, in result the British and the French declared war on Germany. In June 1941, Hitler ordered an invasion of the Soviet Union. By the end of 1941, German forces and the European Axis powers occupied most of Europe and the North Africa. Failure to defeat the Soviets and the entry of the United States into the war forced Germany to be the defensive and it suffered a series of escalating defeats and the final collapse came in Berlin on 30 April 1945.

Hitler was first a military personal, he had proved his efficiency, he thought for German how to increase its area and how to regain its lost prestige, he never deviated from his vision but fought for right till

death. He had brought immense destruction but still people would remember him for his heroism and expertise in war technique.

What about Gandhi? Did he have any remarkable proficiency as advocate; his proficiency was in the art of befooling the common people in the name of religion. Today question before many people are like this: Did he have any fixed vision of life? Did he have the courage to face Calcutta killing? No. How the people could remember him as a pride of the nation either as a man of independence movement by the division of India on the basis of religion or as a man of instrument for the millions to die or millions to displace leaving their ancestral home was a big question and will remain so all the time.

[4]

Let us know Winston Churchill. Sir Winston Leonard Spencer-Churchill was a British politician. He was best known for his leadership of the United Kingdom during the Second World War. He was a successful leader, and brought to the post of prime minister, at the middle of the Second World War. He was best known for his oratory particularly in wartime. Born to an aristocratic family in 1874, Winston served in the British military.

He worked as a writer before going into politics, and his writing won for him a Nobel Prize in literature.

[Here was a picture of Winston Churchill, a man of strong personality what was very much evident in the face of the picture, which cannot be expressed by any literary expression but omitted here because of the restriction of copyright.]

He was a man of Conservative Party, but because of party squeal, Churchill switched to the Liberal Party in 1904. He was elected a member of parliament in 1908 and was appointed to the prime minister's cabinet as president of the Board of Trade. Churchill served as minister of war and air and colonial secretary under Prime Minister David Lloyd George in the period of 1919 to 1922. But again due to fractures in the Liberal Party he had to face defeat in contest as a member of parliament in 1922. However, he rejoined the Conservative Party.

World War II was the design of Hitler. The military ruler Hitler of Germany became a threat to other nations of Europe, because of the strength of military. But Churchill never dared to express his resentment against Hitler in British parliament. By 1938, as Germany began its occupation in controlling its neighbours, Churchill had become a staunch critic of British Prime Minister Neville Chamberlain's policy of appeasement toward the Nazis. In 1938 Chamberlain returned from Munich proclaiming 'peace for our time' after sacrificing Czechoslovakia to Hitler. Churchill was furious.

German very soon unilaterally occupied the vital Norwegian iron mines and seaports. It was in a debate in parliament on the Norwegian crisis led to a vote of no confidence toward Prime Minister Chamberlain. By May 1940, Britain and her allies were losing the war. In the face of the Nazis' relentless march across Europe, Chamberlain bowed to pressure and resigned as prime minister. In no time King George VI appointed Churchill as prime minister and minister of defence. Immediately the German army began its Western offensive, invading the Netherlands, Belgium, and Luxembourg. Hitler invaded Poland on 1 September 1939. Britain was once again at war with Germany.

On 3 September 1939, the day that Britain declared war on Germany. Hitler could not tolerate the declaration of aggression of French and Britain. Two days later, Hitler applied his war skill and allowed his forces to enter France. Britain stood alone against the onslaught. Quickly, in order to form a unity among all, Churchill formed a coalition cabinet consisting of leaders from the Labour, Liberal, and Conservative parties and led the country to face war by placing intelligent and talented men in key positions.

The year 1940, Winston Churchill became the prime minister of Britain. He was successful to lead a successful Allied strategy with the United States and Russia during World War II to defeat the Axis powers and craft post-war peace. Politically he was a lonely figure until his response to Adolf Hitler's challenge brought him to leadership of a national coalition in 1940. On 18 June 1940, Churchill made one of his iconic speeches to the House of Commons, warning that 'the Battle of Britain' was about to begin. Churchill was immediately recalled, again becoming First Lord of the Admiralty. The war was going badly and Lord Halifax, the foreign secretary, urged Churchill to negotiate peace terms with Hitler.

March 1941 was important for Churchill. Churchill kept all out resistance alive to stop Nazi advance and continued negotiations to form an alliance with the United States and the Soviet Union. Even in the 1930, Churchill had an opportunity to make a relationship with US President Franklin D. Roosevelt. Thus in the hour of crisis, he was able to secure vital US aid through the Lend Lease Act, which allowed Britain to order war goods from the United States on credit by March 1941. After having been success to bring the United States along with him in World War II, in December 1941, Churchill became confident that the Allies would eventually win the war.

In the months that followed, Churchill worked closely with US President Roosevelt and Soviet Union leader Joseph Stalin to forge an Allied war strategy and post-war world. Thus he led his country from the brink of defeat to victory. The British Expeditionary Force was facing encirclement in France. Churchill, though, was resolute and overruled Halifax, hundreds of thousands of allied soldiers were evacuated from Dunkirk. France surrendered. On 22 June, French leader Marshal Pétain signed an armistice with Germany, when France would be occupied.

Now standing alone, Churchill's speeches stirred Britain to continue fighting until the US and USSR joined the war in 1941. On 6 June 1944, US, British, and Canadian forces invaded Nazi-occupied France. D-Day had arrived. More than 150,000 troops were landed on French soil in the biggest ever seaborne invasion. On 7 May 1945, Germany surrendered. Though Japan would continue fighting until September, the Allies had won. Churchill had led the nation to victory.

After holding meetings in different places, Churchill collaborated with the two leaders to develop a united strategy against the Axis powers, and simultaneously attempts have been made to work united under the shadow of United Nations after the war. But very soon he had noticed the aggressive war threat from USSR.

In March 1946, after the breakdown of the alliance he alerted the West to the expansionist threat of the Soviet Union, while on a visit to the United States, without keeping anything hidden in mind, he boldly made his famous 'Iron Curtain' speech, warning of Soviet domination in Eastern Europe. He also advocated that German remain independent from European coalitions and maintain its independence. Churchill's fortune turned back. In the general election of 1951, Churchill returned to government. He became prime minister in October 1951. His performance made the Britons brave and proud.

If we look to the performance of Gandhi what we could see, a man of poor fellow was begging for everything without any ability, without any determination. Winston Churchill saved the nation

from the point of collapse under the bombing stroke of Hitler keeping the nation hanging for more than a year while the weak leader Gandhi claiming the leader of more than 100 million people of India did not have a mental stamina to keep the nation at least for few months but not to surrender to watch the situation to save the nation from disaster of breaking into pieces. Will his performance made the Indians brave and proud?

[5]

Let us know Franklin D. Roosevelt. Franklin Delano Roosevelt became president in a very critical period of time. It was a period of time of worldwide economic depression and a time of war. He was democratic and most revolutionary. Because of his outstanding capacity of leadership he won wars in two fronts, in one he helped America to get out of the depression by the progressive norms and policies, and in second he also created a Social Security system that helped senior citizens. He remained as president for the period 1933–1945 bypassing the establishing norms of two times president.

[A picture of Franklin D. Roosevelt brings inspiration in the heart of every individual, but omitted here for photocopy restriction.]

Franklin D. Roosevelt was a polio patient at the growth of his youth, but under all obstacles he became the thirty-second US president in 1933 and was the only president to be elected four times. He was president of United States under the most difficult period. Roosevelt led the United States through the most turbulent period of Great Depression and World War II. However Roosevelt died in Georgia in 1945.

Franklin D. Roosevelt was a Democrat, and he dominated his party for many years as a central figure in world events during the mid-twentieth century. His program for relief, recovery, and reform, known as the *new deal*, involved a great expansion of the role of the federal government in the economy. As a dominant leader of the Democratic Party, he built the New Deal Coalition that brought together the united labour unions, big city machines, white ethnics, African Americans, and rural white Southerners in support of the party. The coalition significantly realigned American politics after 1932. He had brought a system of confidence in his government by the policy of American liberalism throughout the middle of the twentieth century where white ethnics, African Americans, and rural white Southerners raised no objection to live together and work united.

He entered into politics, but his greatest setback was that he was a polio patient. He was stricken with polio in 1921, which cost him the use of his legs and put his future political career in jeopardy. But due to his strong determination, God had given him a new life in his attempt to recover from the illness and founded the treatment centre for people with polio in Warm Springs, Georgia. Recovery of illness tempted him again to return to politics to serve the people. Roosevelt, at Smith's behest, successfully ran for governor of New York in 1928. During his office period from 1929 to 1932, he served as a governor, bringing a drastic change in promoting the enactment of programs to combat the Great Depression besetting the United States at that time.

Roosevelt successfully defeated incumbent Republican president Herbert Hoover to win the presidency of the United States. Having been succeeded in the endeavour of winning over polio, he turned to social work with great optimism keeping within a renewed national spirit.

He brought legislation under a New Deal and made everybody happy and satisfied.

In 1935, after the economy had begun to show signs of recovery, Roosevelt asked congress to pass a new wave of reforms, known as 'Second New Deal'. These included the Social Security Act, which included Americans with unemployment, disability, and pensions for old age, on the other hand, high taxes on large corporations and wealthy individuals. Thus the law of 'Repeal Prohibitions' and the 'Second New Deal' helped him to win re-election by a landslide victory in 1936. Now Roosevelt was faced a new challenge, an international challenge how to save the nation as well the globe from the disasters of war.

Franklin Roosevelt was the president of the United States of America during the period of World War II. He was in a state of mental dilemma, how to lead the country either to keep the country away from the warfront or to take part in it. However he was constantly hammering by his onetime close friend Winston Churchill, the prime minister of United Kingdom, the country was being severely bombed by the force of Hitler. At the beginning he kept the country away from the warfront, although he was supplying the war materials to the Allied Forces. The record of history reveals that Japanese bomber destroyed Pearl Harbor on 7 December 1941. The incident compelled the president to tell the country man that USA was no longer could remain away from the warfront.

USA joined the Allied Force with men and materials taking the army and navy in full military command to defeat the Axis powers of Germany, Italy, and Japan. Having been an army man, he developed a strategy for defeating Germany in Europe through a series of invasion apart from the supply of abundant war materials. He first attacked North Africa and then turned towards Sicily and Italy in 1943, and finally towards Germany of Europe to carry out the final victory of invasion.

A whole generation of Americans cannot forget the President Franklin Roosevelt for his leadership for long twelve years. His remarkable leadership during wartime had increased the American prestige in the world. His leadership in economic front had not only pulled the country from the state of depression but even lifted the economy to the highest in the world to lead the country to the status of superpower.

Franklin D. Roosevelt was a man of exceptional quality of character and he was a man of necessity for the nation in the period of crisis. What about

Gandhi, a man of exceptional character no doubt, but that was something unnatural to befool the people and mislead the nation to disaster without any leader like vision of determination. Does it signify a healthy state of mind?

[6]

Mohandas Karamchand Gandhi was made Father of the Nation by Nehru. It was circulated by Nehru, the first PM of India, who had been made the PM by Gandhi himself by debarring Petal, the selected candidate of the congress with a motive. That had been revealed later on in public by the subsequent events. Gandhi had been thrown to the stature of the Father of the Nation single handedly by Nehru without taking the consent of the Indian public.

[Gandhi's photograph has been given here, which reflects his religious mind-set and not a statchu of photograph that reflects a leadership character for all sections of the people. But photocopy retriction prevented to display the photograph.]

Not only that Nehru hurriedly declared India wins independence by 'non-violence' whereas nowhere that act of non-violence had succeeded; it turned to violence in every event. But to glorify Gandhi, Nehru kept the song of non-violence at high esteem and after independence spread this message to every country and everywhere.

2 October 1869 is the date of birth of Gandhi. He was successful to cross over the schooling in India and reach to London Inner Temple to get LL.B but failed to apply the knowledge of LL.B in proper place. Anyway his success lies in becoming a popular leader in India by joining the Indian independence movement in British-ruled India. Knowing his weakness in the application of the strength of mind, he had chosen the application of the weakness of mind in the struggle against the British. To win the heart of illiterate Indians, he took the help of all mischief of Hindu religion and projected himself a man of saint by passing a simple life and dressed as a common poor Indians. He very tactfully utilised the ethics of Hindu religion AHINGSA (non-violence) and the art of sacrificing anything remaining in FAST and became a popular leader particularly in rural areas of India.

The city or town area was confined to a limited place and that was also being developed under the British administration otherwise the whole of India was covered with jungles and temples here and there without any communication of road or any common language of communication. Thus his voice of non-violence movement in village area makes him most popular and thereby he became a leader of mass people without any militant force behind. He started with non-violent civil disobedience. It is known to the world that Gandhi led India to independence and inspired movements for civil rights and freedom across the world. But the record of history says the 1942 DO or DIE movement of Gandhi was not completely non-violent, Gandhi and other leaders all were in jail, there was nobody left to guide the movement and it had turned violent in many cases. Moreover the declaration of British Prime Minister Attlee at Calcutta in 1946, that British had no force to rule India any longer as most of the British fighters were killed by Azad Hind Fauj of Netaji as such the declaration that India wins freedom by non-violence became a subject of question. However, the rural people have made him a mass leader and people called him Bapu (papa or father).

Looking to history, it is found that in 1888, Gandhi left India to study law in London, in England. When he returned to his homeland in 1891, he had difficulty finding employment as a lawyer, so in 1893 he travelled to South Africa, where an Indian firm had given him a one-year contract to do legal work. In South Africa, which was then under control of the British and the Dutch (known as Boers), he, like other Indians there, encountered frequent discrimination. This mistreatment prompted Gandhi to begin campaigning for the civil rights of Indians in South Africa, and he eventually developed his concept of 'satyagraha' ('firmness in truth'), or nonviolent resistance. Despite being arrested and imprisoned multiple times, Gandhi remained in South Africa until 1912. Afterward, he returned to India, where he became a transformative figure and led the non-violent social action movement for his homeland's independence.

Gandhi first started non-violent civil disobedience as an expatriate lawyer in South Africa, for the resident Indian community's struggle for civil rights in South Africa. Finding people's response, he thought to return India and become a mass leader. But very soon he had realised that he could not be a mass leader by the method of non-violence in India unless he could bring religion in the movement as the majority people were the ardent devotee of Hindu religion. Thus a religion-based movement based on the love of humanity and love of God is playing in his inner mind. After a few days in India in 1915, he set about organising peasants, farmers, and urban labourers to protest against excessive land tax and discrimination. Getting the opportunity of leadership of the Indian National Congress in 1921, Gandhi led nationwide campaigns for easing poverty, expanding women's rights, building religious and ethnic amity, and make all out effort for ending untouchability existing in the Hindu society and behind all these the desire of achieving the supreme power without occupying any executive post by achieving Swaraj or self-rule remain inherent at the back of his mind. He knows he was lacking in the spirit of the vision of violence. Finally it came to his mind here too he should start non-violence like South Africa taking the advantage of the religious weakness of Hindus towards 'tolerance'.

Gandhi famously led Indians in challenging the British-imposed salt tax known as Dandi Salt March in 1930, and later the Quit India movement in 1942. He was imprisoned several times in the attempted practice of non-violence. His failure in most of the cases resulted with the success of gathering of mass in large number.

Everybody knows the violence is not our principle of movement as directed by our leader Gandhi; the non-cooperation movement under the principle of non-violence is our path of movement, where the people are ready to face the police torture. But in how many cases the people remained non-violence is yet to be counted, let it be the Quit India Movement or 'Do or Die' movement. Gandhi had to remain in the palace of Agha Khan, other congress workers were in jail, how many others had remained outside to see how the principle of non-violence worked, after all it was a human passion and vision of mind, and everywhere violence, violence in the railway station, violence in the railway track, violence in the communication of telegraph, police action and reaction had continued, but the real fact was the disturbances everywhere, in street, in office, and in industries but not by Gandhi's principle of non-violence, but by violence under out of inner calls of mind and passion.

But the true fact was that the message of non-violence had gathered the people together. It was said that he was one of the most pacifists, the belief that disputes should be settled by peaceful means, and that war and violence are unjustifiable, which was nothing but a misnomer, but if it really true, why did he fail to settle the dispute with Jinnah and why did he allow Jinnah to strike out at Calcutta by the name 'Direction Action Day' to kill thousands of innocent people while he kept himself in hiding? Today, the question in front of the public, **was it for any secret motive**?

What? Was it in his mind-set let the Bengal go down by killing and rioting so that no other leader like Netaji had emerged from Bengal to challenge the power of Delhi? Gandhi was ready to discuss with Jinnah in secret at Jinnah house, not with the sharing of Delhi chair, but with the regional areas of Pakistan, how to keep him away so that Delhi chair remain free that could be decided afterwards to be posted in time by his favourite.

He was successful in his endeavour, Nehru became the PM and he became the Father of the Nation but what kind of father's duty he had done for the people, the people could not have found to be seen to be benefited by him particularly in Bengal. Rather all the Indians are suffering with the pain of hatred of Hindus and Muslims that the seeds of hatred that Gandhi had sown in the soil of India by bringing the division of India on the basis of religion. This was surprising to see how Gandhi had made his place among the most influential people in history. He had done nothing extraordinary like any of the world leader, he was not an outstanding pleader like

Jinnah, who was called to enter British parliament, he was not like Mao Zedong, a revolutionary, who brought China under unified command, he was not like Adolf Hitler, a dictator, he was not like Winston Churchill, an outstanding orator, he was not like Franklin D. Roosevelt, to device policies to get out of economic depression, but still he was an icon of the twentieth century.

Why could Gandhi not do anything to save the lakhs of people who were dying in famine, or provide social security to elderly people, or by any ways and means to diminish the hatred between Hindus and Muslims? But still he was one of all outstanding personalities, how was that possible? Definitely, it was due to intentional circulation on the part of the government of India at that time by hiding the real truth. Gandhi's leadership was outlined as the most pacifists. But that had been proved wrong because he had failed to keep the country *united* and settle the matter peacefully rather he had created a situation by dint of which millions had to die and millions had to migrate.

His simple life and simple dress befooled the Indians to stand behind him with all faith, who would do everything good for them. They never had thought that at the end he would create a situation for which the country would be divided on the basis of religion. A situation of Hindu-Muslim communal clash would be created, which would never been ended in their life time nor probably not even afterwards. He devised a new excitement in the rural mass of making self-made traditional Indian working cloths by woven with yarn hand-spun on a machine of Charkha to give a spectacular stern to the common people to win over the common people very tactfully and skilfully.

To win the heart of faithful Hindus, he used to take simple vegetarian food, and also undertook long fasts, as it was the tradition in Hindu society to take simple food and keep the body under fast to make the mind bright and pure before offering something to the deity of God.

Gandhi's vision of an independent India based on religious pluralism was not liked by a Muslim leader Jinnah, who challenged it in the early 1940s by a new Muslim nationalism which was demanding a separate Muslim homeland to be carved out of India. Eventually, in August 1947, Britain granted independence, but the British Indian Empire was partitioned into two dominions, a Hindu-majority India and a Muslim-majority Pakistan. As many displaced Hindus, Muslims, and Sikhs made their way to their new land of security, religious violence broke out, especially in the Punjab and Bengal. Avoiding the official celebration of independence in Delhi, Gandhi visited the affected areas, attempting to provide peace without going for killing of violence to bring back the message of non-violence to make himself in glory as he failed in the leadership either in negotiation by the knowledge of inner temple of London nor by the force of art of war as preached by Krishna in asking Arjun to fight for right in the battle of Kaurav-Pandav as depicted in the Epics of Hindu-Mahavarata.

In the following months, he undertook several fasts unto deaths to promote religious harmony. The last of these, undertaken on 12 January 1948 at age 78, and also pressurized Indians to stop rioting in Delhi, vacate the Majids being occupied by the Hindu refugees at Delhi, to pay out some cash assets to Pakistan and nothing was said to Pakistan or nothing about the killing of Hindus in Punjab and in other areas of Pakistan. Some Indians thought Gandhi was too liberal to Pakistan but very harsh to Indians, why? Is it for his non-violence at the cost of the lives of Hindus only to keep him in glory? A Hindu nationalist, Nathuram Godse could not tolerate it anymore; he assassinated Gandhi on 30 January 1948 by firing three bullets into his chest at point-blank range.

[7]

Why was Gandhi shot dead by a fellow Hindu?
Gandhi was shot dead by a Hindu nationalist named
Nathuram Godse. The gunman blamed Gandhi for
the partition of British India on the basis of religion.
However after partition, communal riots broke out
across India in between the two religious communities
where Muslims are killing the Hindus and Hindus
killing the Muslims. Godse believed that even after the
partition of India on communal lines, Gandhi indirectly
favoured the Muslims to kill Hindus. All such activity
of Gandhi made him angry when he lost his temper and
that caused him to shot Gandhi. However Godse was
quickly apprehended and hanged for the crimes.

**Gandhi was a man of peace, but why did he not
get the Nobel Peace Prize?** Gandhi was nominated
for a Nobel Peace Prize several times, but he was not
awarded with Noble Peace Prize. The reason might be
genuine because he was known for the movement of
non-violence, but behind the activity of non-violence,
there was hidden violence, otherwise millions of Indian
people would not lost their lives during partition or
after partition of British India. But instead, in the year
1964, Nobel Peace Prize was given to American civil

rights leader Martin Luther King Jr who acknowledged Gandhi's work in his acceptance speech because there was no violence. Again in the year 1989 Nobel Peace Prize was given to Dalai Lama, who called his award a tribute to 'my mentor, Mahatma Gandhi'. Here too there was no secret plan of violence behind that act of non-violence. Gandhi could not bring peace in India, where **millions were died** and millions were displaced although his movement was non-violence. How could he been assigned with *peace*?

Mohandas and Indira—are they related? Despite sharing a last name, Mohandas Gandhi and Indira Gandhi were not related. Indira was the daughter of Nehru, the first prime minister of India, while Gandhi belongs to a different family of Gujarat. However Indira Gandhi was assassinated by her bodyguard. After her assassination, her son Rajiv Gandhi succeeded him. Afterwards he too was assassinated by the attack of bomb and bombing. This was a record of the history of tragedy of Nehru dynasty. At present Rahul Gandhi, son of Rajiv Gandhi, is in continuation of political activity as per the tradition of the family's political dynasty, who might have been a candidate for PM from the Congress Party of India if not from the general public.

After a long struggle at last, independence came to India in 1947. India became a secular democratic country and Pakistan became an Islamic country. By the time many years have passed, what was seen in India, was it justified enough that a true democracy had prevailing in India, if not what ideals Gandhi have left for India, let us look into it.

Let us talk of Gandhi's democracy. India is a failed democracy in compare to other nations of the world as the ideals set by Gandhi was not democratic in heart and soul. It has reasons because the icon leaders of India had failed to think for the future democracy of India. Gandhi was such a popular leader, that no one of present generation could think of. He was such a great or a bigger leader, who could convince the whole nation for anything and for any movement for the betterment of people, but why he had failed to satisfy the Muslims? Why had he made the Muslims the enemy of Hindus? Why had he sacrificed Khan Abdul Gaffer Khan, who was no less than Gandhi? Is it because he was a Muslim? These are the questions floating in front of the present generation of Indian people. In USA black and white people could live together, in India the people are not different in colour, taste, or amusement, why could the people not live together? Is it the efficiency of leadership to be honoured with title 'Father' of the Nation bypassing the constitution of India? Why? Are the Muslims not the citizens of India? What do we mean by democracy, it is equality, fraternity, and brotherhood? Where is equality in India when we send our candidate as Dalit, as a Hindu, or as a Muslim?

Is there any logic in thinking that the Indian Muslims who are leaving in India are secular, while the Indian Muslims who are leaving in Pakistan after partition are non-secular? Everybody is secular or everybody is non-secular, it reflects the love and affinity among the people. Here lies the failure of leadership, the farsightedness of the leadership. It is now more than sixty years Hindus and Muslims are fighting openly in between India and Pakistan and sometimes fighting in disguise in dark of night. In total Gandhi had failed to bring true democracy and destroyed the fabric of the country by the act of religious division. Who were the individual leaders compel the people to think in terms of religion?

Gandhi utilised religion in politics to carry out the movement. His intention was to bring the common Hindu people in the non-violence movement in large number. The majority people of India are Hindu and the common Hindu people are very much religious minded.

All these consideration tempted Gandhi to introduce the religion of tolerance in the form of non-violence to the process of movement against the British India government. In course of time, if the Muslims join the movement, it would be something a miracle and a threat to government, no doubt. His movement was 'non-violence' as he was against any kind of violence. It was nothing but tolerance of Hindu religion. Anybody can say Gandhi had befooled the Indians by his mystic, but the fact of the matter was just to turn the attention of the common people towards the movement against the British government. It is also true; there was nothing in the world that has been fulfilled by non-violence. But his movement was nothing but protest. It was not for achievement at the outset. It is true violence had given the world many, many things. It was violence in USA, civil war between black and white, but behind violence, the nation of USA came into being as a nation of superpower, it is revolution in French, but behind violence, the real democracy evolved out of autocracy, atom bomb used out of violence but behind atom bomb, nuclear energy came to light, space rocket, computer science came into the earth. By Gandhi's non-violence, India achieved a mass protest. Every action has a reaction; the result of reaction of mass protest might be good or bad. Sometimes it depends upon the destiny.

Here it has given the birth of violence, a miss fortune; and thereby the unity of the country was destroyed.

Today India is insecure because of the creation of Pakistan, because of the Muslims, who were made enemy, however good of Hindu-Muslim is said, no matter, a Muslim always think, I am a Muslim; I am different from Hindus of India and I have been kept away from Hindus. Is it not the creation of great leader Gandhi? Is it not the outcome of the religious movement of 'non-violence'? The ideals of democracy could not be preserved during the protest carried out by Gandhi against the British. Yet Indian people showed their highest respect to Gandhi because he could accumulate a large mass of people to join the non-violence movement and compel the British government to come to terms with the Indian congress.

Who knows it might be because of the weakness of Hindus, the weak religious ethics have been introduced into Hindu religion. Many people saying the weakness of Hinduism is destroying the Hindu mankind. Originally this kind of weakness was not present in Hinduism. Krishna, the Hindu god or king, said to Arjun, take arms and fight for right. But Gandhi said opposite don't take arms, never fight for right, rather sacrifice. Is it Hindu religion or a twisted Hindu religion to protect India?

However, the non-violence movement in India had made Gandhi an international icon.

A country that has no vision cannot survive with democracy. Where is democracy, where we know in Assam or in Bengal every year 3 lakh matric candidates in general course and 2'5 lakh candidate in Madrascourse—why? Is it the goal of equality or democracy? Sanskrit for Hindus or Arabic for Muslims could not be a subject in the general course and treat them all equal. Without a vision, a country cannot survive, similarly a man without ethics of justice cannot be a leader of mankind. A man without a stable vision cannot be a popular leader of a country.

However, apart from earlier mistake, the country is running under a democratic process as the election is carried out at regular five-year intervals. By the time India had achieved a progressive leader Modi, who had prevailed an atmosphere of equality not only in India but even in outside as he is talking of equality globally, and it is believed that in future Modi will not be afraid of to take drastic action for the sake of equality and follow the Prime Minister Sheik Hassina of Bangladesh who had set the record in the world by hanging many that the guilty would be punished and elected government would never go away or never be afraid of to hang the culprit in time and set the rule of law supreme under all circumstances to make the country great.

[8]

The Linking Unit: The **Patriot**, Nikunja Bihari Goswami, a silent worker, who had sacrificed his life keeping the ideals of Gandhi in his mind. Now time has come to give a rational thinking of discussion of the contribution of Gandhi in compare to other world leaders, as such the discussion such as '**compare the role of Gandhi with other world leaders'** is enclosed here.

Let us compare the role of Gandhi with other world leaders. Let us see few of the outstanding world leaders of twentieth century one by one. The achievement of Gandhi was the independence of India not by violence but by non-violence. The result was a divided India; the basis of division was religion. It created two countries with inborn animosity killing millions to die and millions to displace. Does it justify the greatness of great leadership?

Gandhi vs. Roosevelt: Let us compare Gandhi with Roosevelt. After 1932, Franklin D. Roosevelt had brought a system of confidence in his government by the policy of **American liberalism** throughout the middle third of the twentieth century where white ethnics, African Americans, and rural white Southerners raised no objection to live together and work united. After 1946, Mohan Das K Gandhi did anything like **Indian liberalism** like that of American liberalism to unit Hindus, Muslims, and Dalits, where a system of confidence would have been prevailed to work together and live united. Gandhi could not establish anything of Indian liberalism like that of American liberalism.

A leader is born with certain objective; the fulfilment of the objective makes him immortal forever. The objective of Franklin D. Roosevelt was to make United States a strong country, strong in economy as well as strong in military. A leader is known by his work, the problem of the country is the challenge to an ideal leader, whoever who can solve the problem, remain immortal as hero of the nation. American people cannot forget Roosevelt as he had solved the economic as well as the military problems.

1940 Franklin D. Rooseveltwas faced with two problems, on the one hand he has to fight to remove the economic depression, and on the other hand he has to face the warfront with strategy of success. He solved the economic depression by taking **SEAL DEAL** to make every individual happy and in the warfront by breaking the isolation of United States and taking the country along with French, Britain, and Russia and China. Roosevelt enlightened the Americans about the war's atrocities and convinced the Americans that it is not the time to remain in isolation. The sentiment of isolationist diminished. Roosevelt took advantage, standing firm against the Axis powers of Germany, Italy, and Japan. With the support of congress, he expanded the army and navy and increased the flow of supplies to the Allies. Hopes of keeping the United States out of war ended with the Japanese attack on Pearl Harbor on 7 December 1941.

During World War II, Franklin Roosevelt was a commander-in-chief who worked with army executives and sometimes around with his military advisors. He helped to develop a strategy for defeating Germany in Europe through a series of invasions, first in North Africa in November 1942, then Sicily and Italy in 1943, followed by the D-Day invasion of Europe in 1944. At the same time, under his strong support Allied forces rolled back to Japan in Asia. During this time, Roosevelt also promoted the formation of the United Nations. On the afternoon of 12 April 1945, Roosevelt suffered a massive cerebral attack.

He had led the United States through an economic depression and the greatest war in human history. A whole generation of Americans had grown up knowing no other president. His role during World War II established the United States leadership on the world stage. His twelve years in the White House set a precedent for the expansion of presidential power and redefined liberalism for generations to come.

On the part of India, Mohan Das K Gandhi similarly faced with two problems in 1946, one was the 'economic depression', during wartime Gandhi has no power to do anything and the people were allowed to die under the sufferings of famine in Bengal, and the other one was the declaration of 'DIRECT ACTION DAY' (16 August 1946) for Pakistan as he failed to establish **Indian liberalism** like that of **American liberalism**, now the immediate challenge was the thrust of communal riot started by Jinnah. But the activity of a leader lies in his afford to face the challenge and solve the problem boldly. At that time there were two options left to Gandhi; one was to solve the problem by negotiation with Jinnah under all circumstances keeping the unity of the country at the top, and the other one was to face the open rioting with opposite force. Well, there might be civil war, no matter; the existence of a country is superior to the killing and torture of few lives. There is no point of total surrender of a leader (Gandhi) of 98% people to a leader of 2% militant leader (Jinnah). The weakness of Gandhi was non-violence, by virtue of which he had made the youths of India defenceless and cowered.

Franklin Roosevelt under the threat of Axis force, never think to surrender rather expanded the army and navy. Gandhi was more concerned with the glory of non-violence rather than the unity of United India.

Considering the FORCE of Axis that might be bigger, he made a war strategy and accordingly he was thinking to join with France, Britain, and other forces, but did Gandhi thought of anything like this? Well he might have advanced the independent movement by the art of non-violence, but as soon as it faced with the threat of *direct action*, did he think of any other option other than surrender? Gandhi might have realised his mistake in taking the path of non-violence for independent movement, but instead of surrender, he could face it with *force* of 98% Indian supporters. Even if he thinks the *force* is not trained and competent enough, why did he not break his isolation by joining with SriLanka, Bhutan, Nepal, and Burma as they were no other country other than India at the beginning? If **Franklin D. Roosevelt** can join France, Britain, and Russia, for the safety of

United States, why did Gandhi not join other forces? A leader should have a future outlook, a broader outlook how to make the country big and prosperous and live with a greater mass of covering a greater area instead of thinking narrow of living in a smaller area with a community as good as a family.

Gandhi vs. Churchill: Let us compare Gandhi with Churchill: **It was the most critical time for Briton**, the country was about to collapse to Hitler's Nazi force, but it was **Winston Churchill** who was being made the prime minister by removing Chamberlain to save the country. It was his courage, iconic speeches, and the judgment of war strategy that brought him success. Let us see how he did it.

Hitler invaded Poland on 1 September 1939. By 3 September, Britain was at war with Germany. Two days later, German forces entered France. Britain stood alone against the onslaught. The year 1940, Winston Churchill became the prime minister of Britain officially. He is thinking the Allied strategy with the United States and Russia during World War II how to defeat the Axis powers. On 18 June 1940, Churchill made one of his iconic speeches to the House of Commons, warning that 'the Battle of Britain' was about to begin. The war was going badly. Lord Halifax, the foreign secretary, urged Churchill to negotiate peace terms with Hitler.

In the months that followed, Churchill worked closely with US President Roosevelt and Soviet Union leader Joseph Stalin to forge an Allied war strategy. The British Expeditionary Force was facing encirclement in France. Churchill, though, was resolute and overruled the advice of foreign secretary Halifax; hundreds of thousands of Allied soldiers were evacuated from Dunkirk. By the time France surrendered and on 22 June 1940, French leader Marshal Petain signed an armistice with Germany. Britain was about to fall.

It was Churchill's courage and determination that he continued the war alone by giving encouragement to the soldiers. Churchill's speeches stirred Britain to continue fighting until the US and USSR joined the war in 1941. On 6 June 1944, US, British, and Canadian forces invaded Nazi-occupied France. D-Day had arrived. More than 150,000 troops were landed on French soil in the biggest ever seaborne invasion. On 7 May 1945, Germany surrendered. Thus he led his country from the brink of defeat to victory.

The most critical time for India was 16 August 1946, 'THE DIRECT ACTION DAY' calls for Pakistan by

Jinnah under the direction of Suharwardy, the then chief minister of Bengal. Did the Indians find any role of Gandhi to face the situation other than surrender? How can it be a courageous step for the independence of United India? French surrendered on 25 June 1940, Briton was about to fall but Churchill continued with the war till 6 June 1944, till D-Day had arrived. Churchill continued four years in a state of surrender, while Gandhi within a period of few months of rioting succumbed to the pressure of Jinnah and agreed to give Pakistan indirectly. Gandhi did not went to Jinnah house again and again but communicated in absentia with his trusted people to give Pakistan to save Hindu leaders rather than Hindus, because Hindu leaders were defenceless as they have not kept any militant volunteers. Muslim leaders were full of defence because of their militant groups. Muslims do not know appeasement, they know how to rule, how to occupy territory, how to fight for the right of existence.

Winston Churchill's controversial remarks became a subject of discussion in India. Churchill was dead against of giving Independence to India. He had strong views on the man (Gandhi) now widely respected for his work in advocating self-determination for India. According to Churchill (1931),'It is alarming and nauseating to see Mr Gandhi, a seditious Middle Temple lawyer, now posing as a fakir . . . striding half-naked up the steps of the vice-regal palace.'

He further said,'Gandhi should not be released on the account of a mere threat of fasting.' Churchill told the cabinet on another occasion, 'We should be rid of a bad man and an enemy of the empire if he died.' At the time of handed over the power, what was quoted in the Indian press attributing to Winston Churchill.

'Power will go to the hands of rascals, rogues, freebooters; all Indian leaders will be of low calibre and men of straw. They will have sweet tongues and silly hearts. They will fight amongst themselves for power and India will be lost in political squabbles. A day would come when even air and water would be taxed in India.'

Churchill's remark will hurt every Indians but the fact of the matter is partially true. It may be a tough word on the part of Churchill, which would hurt every Indians, but when something is said, it appears a little true if not 100%. He said Gandhi a 'half-necked Fakir', because the dress of Gandhi appears like that, As Churchill words such as 'Power will go to the hands of rascals, rogues, freebooters'; although not correct but it appears to be partly correct. And that Indians have seen in the last almost fifty years, who are ruling the country, scam and corruption are the news of the nation. If they are not rascals in the language of Churchill, but they are rogues, they are looters. Let us look at the first part of the administration of independence of India, the Nehru period.

Nehru as prime minister of India: When the United States won their war of independence, some people suggested that George Washington to be declared as king. But Washington chose to become president. He also chose to step down after two terms. That became the norm, however that norm was broken during the time of Franklin Roosevelt, because of the situation of war.

Contrast to Jawaharlal Nehru who ruled like a king till death. He ruled from 1947 to 1964 and stagnated up to the end. There were ten ministers in the Nehru-Patel cabinet. Six of those rebelled against Nehru and quitted. Even Indian Governor-General C.Rajagopalachari rebelled against Nehru and formed the Swatantra Party. While the founding fathers of America ruled their country in turns, Nehru behaved like a dictator who chased away party talent. This leadership style continues till this very day in the congress. Does it not justify what Winston Churchill said,'They will fight amongst themselves for power'? Nehru's daughter Indira Gandhi (with a brief three-year gap) also ruled till death.

Not to speak of economy, Nehru thought of the economy of congress and Congress Party. If not Forex reserves cannot be non-existent and Prime Minister Chandra Shekhar would not have been in compelling situation to selling the country India airlifting sixty-seven tons of gold to the Bank of England and the Union Bank of Switzerland to raise an amount of $600 million.

It is also not worthy to speak of the condition of defence and security of the nation, even when China attacked, Nehru looked the other way. At that time the Indian Air Force was superior to the China's Air Force, but Nehru was too scared to use it. The non-aligned movement was also a joke more so because India was closely aligned with the USSR, which was not a democracy but a communist dictatorship. In 1991 Indian defence forces had problems with spares when the USSR collapsed.

Who created Nehru-Gandhi dynasty? Some people try to defend Nehru by saying that Nehru died in 1964 and Indira took over in 1966 and he had nothing to do with the dynasty taking root. This was not correct in true sense. Nehru made Indira congress president in the 1959 Delhi session and always indicated that she was his choice as a successor. Are these not in consonances with what the **Winston Churchill** said?

What **Winston Churchill** left for Britons after saving the country from the brink of defeat to victory, a democracy, an ideal democracy, a democracy that preserves individual liberty, the rule of law, mutual respect, tolerance of those with different faiths and belief, a country of little space of 93,410 sq.mi., bounded by a population of only six cores but a country of human civilisation that was being emerged from the civilisations of networks of cities emerged from pre-urban cultures, and also being defined by the economic, political, military, diplomatic, social, and cultural interactions among all while **Mohandas Karamchand Gandhi** left a divided India, an India, seventh largest in the world, destined to be the world superpower partitioned based on narrow thinking of religions submerging the greatest value of humanity and sowed the seeds of hatred, destroying his all endeavour in keeping the every creatures of India in the bond of unity of love, who is said to be the international leader of humanity?

Gandhi vs. Adolf Hitler: Adolf Hitler was a German politician who was the leader of the Nazi Party and chancellor of Germany from 1933 to 1945. He initiated World War II in Europe. He invaded Poland in September

1939 and initiated the war and the Holocaust, **but why?** It was because of his love for his own people. It was because a great injustice being done over German in the post–World War I. It was Britain and France, who brought restrictions over Germany, snatch away the German territory by dint of their strength in World War I. At his initial first six years in power, he brought a rapid economic recovery from the Great Depression, and then he turned his attention towards the injustice and the restrictions imposed on Germany and German people. He tried up to the last breath of his life to get back territories that were once the homes of millions of ethnic Germans. These actions made him the most popular and immortal in German.

Adolf Hitler could not win the war, but he had made the people happy and proud by his double stroke action. By one as in the Economic Front, he was successful to overcome depression and to make people happy by reducing rate of unemployment from six million in 1932 to one million in 1936, by second in the warfront he fought for justice making the Germans great and sacrificed the life for the nation although he was defeated.

On the other hand **Mohandas Karamchand Gandhi** in the Economic Front could not remove the famine like situation, due to which lakhs of people died in Bengal, and on the rioting front as good as the warfront, he could not save the killings of millions, but finally agreed to the demand of division with humiliation making the country men unhappy making himself a victim of bullet. Who is the man dearest to the country with honour and dignity, Gandhi or Hitler?

Gandhi vs. Mao Tse-tung: The spree of love for the people, and love for country was so much that the poverty of the common people could not be tolerated by his mind-set that tempted him to go along with Chiang Kai-shek to crush the warlords in the period of 1927, who were those to keep the wealth at their custody depriving the poor. But the change of mind of Chiang Kai-shek threatened him and compelled him by undertaking a bloody coup in the spring of 1927 effectively destroying the communist organisations in Shanghai and other major cities, forcing them to find refuge in Jiangxi province, in the mountainous hinterland in south-central China but again called him back in the invasion of Japanese onslaught in 1937 but revolted again after 1949, but here by the time he himself was compelled to flee to the island of Taiwan.

Mao Tse-tung never went back from the mission of goal, the goal of bringing development for the poor and industrial revolution in the rural sector, which he completed by launching the cultural revolution in 1966. It merged as a source of revolutionary spirit that brought the development by the destruction of old tradition. One and a half million people died, and much of the country's cultural heritage was destroyed.

However he was successful to build bridges with the United States, Japan, and Europe to bring the development of the West to the Land of East to the land of China, the linking of bridge being brought by the US President Richard Nixon in 1972 to make trade relation with China. His object was China's development and an honourable position of China in the economic front in the international arena. He was happy, the people of the Republic of China were also happy to see before he took leave of this world in 1976.

On the part of Gandhi in India, the movement of independence was going on under the spirit of non-violence although the cry rose by Netaji 'Give me blood, I will give you freedom' was popular once, but that had been doomed down after his leaving the country to fight with Azad-Hind-Fauj. There was no scheme how to fight with poverty and famine. There was dearth of literate, intellectual people in India at that time, but there were plenty of devoted people to worship in the premises of temples asking peace and pleasure.

Mohandas Karamchand Gandhi, an inner temple barrister of London, found it easy to win over these people by the dress of a Fakir and projecting himself as saint. Eighty per cent people had been living in villages. As Gandhi was looking like villagers, he was liked by all village people that made him a leader of the mass people of India. Gandhi looks like a saint or monk, but his intention was not to act like any monk but to work as a politician to get the British out and to think how to capture the power of chair at Delhi. He could not bring the spirit of revolution in the minds of the millions of youth like that of Mao Tse-tung to lead the country from the poverty to the one of the greatest rising economy of the world, but he led the country to face the British Raj with the spirit of sacrifice of non-violence in getting the independence by the sacrifice of a part of India and separating a part of its citizen because they are of different faith, which was not known to the world ever before that people of different faith cannot live in one country. His decision could not make the people happy, and so his death came under the fire of a bullet. Gandhi is now an international hero but not with honour because his simple life, a dress of Fakir could not bring the wishful result. Hindus and Muslims are now living in different countries, but after a certain period of interval, the incident of killings are coming in the news of India as they could not forget their past-time closeness of hatred.

Gandhi vs. Jinnah: Jinnah was asking for Pakistan to fulfil the aspiration of Muslims of India, while Gandhi, was asking for the United India for the people of India including the Muslims. But Jinnah was successful to create an atmosphere that the Muslims have lost their faith over Gandhi and Gandhi have understood that he was no longer a leader of Hindus as well as of Muslims as he failed to keep them together in United India. Moreover Gandhi failed to convince Jinnah at any cost to come to the term of a united India just before granting independence to India.

The atmosphere was already created by Jinnah in the favour of Muslims in the Round Table Conference. How it happened? Gandhi represented the conference along with a group of Hindu personalities, full of the Hindutva knowledge of ancient India, thought for the rights of Hindus through the teachings of Hindu-Vadas and Upanishads, where Hindu personalities talked of tolerance and appeasement of negotiation. There were no person of Inner Temple personality, who could bring an impact in the conference by giving a logical argument in favour of the rights and safety of the Muslims in the independent united India, although the conference was confined in a hall of a British government in London, but its impact of utterances had been spread to every corner of the British empire, so to say to the whole world.

Thus the distress state of Muslims in the twentieth century with respect to the safety and rights of the Muslims in the Hindu-majority British India was kept in hanging in a state of uncertainty. This distress state of affairs of Muslims had been spread throughout the world by the eloquent expression of Jinnah, but on the other hand in the absence of an equal calibre of Inner Temple personality, the legitimate rights of Hindus had not been spread to the world rather a picture of Hindu chauvinism was expressed resulting the overall expression of sympathy went along with Jinnah and in favour of the rights of Muslim community. Consequently the letter of the British government that was given to the congress before the year of 1947, asking to hand over the charges of British administration involving not only of India, but also of Pakistan.

Gandhi lost to Jinnah in the Round Table Conference in the demand of a united India from the law point of logic, and again lost to Jinnah to stop the rioting after the call for DIRECT ACTION on 16 August 1946 by the spirit of NON-VIOLENCE. He could not get satisfaction by the independence of India because of partition. He himself was dissatisfied by his performance, how he could give consolation to other Indians, but his last wish was rested with the prayer to almighty to do good to Indians but the last wish was not accepted by the public, which was resulted in his death by a bullet under the barrel of a gun.

On the other hand Jinnah might be happy for the logical point of view for the cause of Pakistan and also to liberate a part of India as a sovereign country of Pakistan for the Muslims of India, but his happiness definitely would die down on remembering the Indian Muslims, the number being more than the number of liberated Pakistan, who had been left behind for no fault of them. Probably these sufferings of pain in his shadow of mind compelled him to utter at the bed of his death that 'I have done the greatest blunder of my life by dividing India'.

As such neither Jinnah is great nor Gandhi because both were dissatisfied with their ultimate results of achievement. But from satisfaction point of view on the part of public, Jinnah had brought a satisfaction to Muslims by giving them a security of their own making Islam as their democracy or rule of law without any danger from any other religious community as the origin of the state is based on religion, while Gandhi could not give any kind of satisfaction to the Hindus because Gandhi could not give the rest of India to Hindus only as it is now a secular country, a country for all nor the security as the number of Muslims are rising in every state bringing the same kind of threat as it was before the partition. Thus the contribution of Jinnah appears to be more than Gandhi in respect of the benefit of their respective religious community.

However, in the respect of benefit to the human community, the contribution of Gandhi might be more and because he had set the example in the world history that the art of 'non-violence' is supreme as it has compelled the mighty British to give independence to India (if true) and leave the country. It is also great as, the art of non-violence rests behind the art of 'sacrifice'. Gandhi has sacrificed a part of land to Jinnah to form Pakistan, if this art of sacrifice continues and India could give its other parts to the neighbouring countries such as Pakistan, Nepal, Bhutan, Myanmar, Sri Lanka, and Bangladesh, which were once in the part of British India and left with nothing, then Gandhi would be the first and the only one world leader to culture 'non-violence' cum 'sacrifice' for the best cause of humanity, when nothing would be left with India, then Indian would be vanished with space of universe, but Gandhi would survive as a spirit of universe of 'sacrifice' and 'non-violence'.

Gandhi vs. Lincoln: Let us see how Gandhi conducted Indian independence movement and got independence by the division of the country on the basis of religion bringing economic devastation and human slaughter while Lincoln enhanced the unity of black and white by abolishing the rule of slave and bringing economic prosperity for United States.

Born in Hodgenville, Kentucky, Lincoln grew up on the western frontier in Kentucky and Indiana. Largely self-educated, he became a lawyer in Illinois. In 1857, the Supreme Court issued its controversial decision in the matter of a suit of Scott v. Sanford, declaring African Americans were not citizens and had no inherent rights. Lincoln decided to challenge the decision. This was the beginning of his fight with the issue of slavery. It had led him to politics. In 1860, political operatives in Illinois organised a campaign to support Abraham Lincoln for the presidency.

Lincoln was the sixteenth president of the United States, serving from March 1861 until his assassination in April 1865. Lincoln led the United States through its Civil War—its bloodiest war and its greatest moral, constitutional, and political crisis. In doing so, he preserved the union, and abolished slavery, and also strengthened the federal government, and modernised the economy. The American Civil War continued for the period 1861 to 1865. The union faced secessionists in eleven Southern states known as the Confederate States of America. The union won the war preserving the unity. Abraham Lincoln is regarded as one of America's greatest heroes due to both his incredible impact on the nation and preserving the union from disintegration.

Similarly Gandhi started his education at Samaldas College, at the University of Bombay, and proceeded to London to finish the study of law at Inner Temple, London. Returning India, he went back to South Africa. After coming back to India, he joined politics and became a very popular mystic person under the cover of saint. His popularity lies in his Fakir dress and non-violence movement. But he failed to preserve the unity of the Indian union by non-violence and failed to enhance its economy unlashing millions to die due to famine and rioting unlike Lincoln, who preserved the union by carrying out Civil War and enhanced the economy of the union by modernising the status of its economy.

American Civil War is the bloodiest war, no doubt, but it had brought a bright future for the union, where Lincoln is regarded a hero of America, while the non-violence movement was not bloody at the beginning, but it had created a ground where the movement turned to a state which was in no way less bloodiest than American Civil War, killing and displacing millions. Lincoln became a hero by Civil War even after assassination, because of economic progress while Gandhi could not be a hero after assassination by non-violence because it turned to violence in the end bringing misery to the people and bringing thrust of famine.

The Linking Unit: The **Patriot**, Nikunja Behari Goswami, a silent worker, who had sacrificed his life keeping the ideals of Gandhi in his mind, but in the end, he was frustrated with the ideals of Gandhi. At the end of his life, how he was treated by the Pakistani government in the liberation struggle of Bangladesh is described here as '**Liberation of Bangladesh**'.

3 Liberation of Bangladesh

[1]

Let us highlight here an outline of earlier history.
A.K.Fazlul Hug was the premier of United Bengal
who moved the Lahore Resolution and later became
the governor of East Pakistan. The All-India Muslim
League was formed on 30 December 1906. It looked
for Muslim rights in the future nation of independent
India. However, in 1940 the Muslim League passed
the Lahore Resolution, which envisaged one or more
Muslim majority states in South Asia. The resolution
was moved in the general session by A.K. Fazlul Hug,
the then chief minister of Bengal, and was adopted on 23
March 1940. The new viceroy Lord Mountbatten wanted
a graceful British exit. Sectarian violence in Noakhali
and Calcutta sparked off. At the last moment Huseyn
Shaheed Suhrawardy and Sarat Chandra Bose came up
with the idea of an independent and unified Bengal state,
which was endorsed by Jinnah under compulsion. This
idea was vetoed by the Indian National Congress.

British India was divided into India and Pakistan in 1947; the region of Bengal was also divided along religious lines. The predominantly Muslim Eastern part of Bengal became East Pakistan and the predominantly Hindu western part of Bengal became the Indian state of West Bengal. Most of the Sylhet district of Assam pushed to East Pakistan following a referendum discarding 5 lakhs Hindu votes of Sylhet.

Pakistan's history from 1947 to 1971 was marked by political instability and economic disruption. In 1956 a constitution was adopted at last, making the country an 'Islamic republic within the commonwealth'. The republic was faced with military intervention in between 1958 and 1962, and again between 1969 and 1971. Almost from the advent of independent Pakistan in 1947, frictions developed between East and West Pakistan, which were separated by more than 1,000 miles of Indian territory. East Pakistanis felt exploited by the West Pakistan in linguistic, cultural, and ethnic differences.

Language movement: One of the most divisive issues confronting Pakistan in its infancy was the question of what should be the official language of the new state. The demand of refugees from the Indian states of Bihar and Uttar Pradesh was that Urdu should be Pakistan's official language. The different regions of West Pakistan have different languages such as Punjabi, Sindhi, Pushtu, or Baluchi. In East Pakistan, the dissatisfaction quickly turned to violence. The Bengalis of East Pakistan constituted a majority (an estimated 54%) of Pakistan's entire population. Their language is Bengali. Urdu and Bengali are the two languages that have different scripts and different literary traditions.

Jinnah visited East Pakistan on only one occasion after independence, shortly before his death in 1948. Speaking in Dhaka to a throng of over 300,000 on 21 March 1948, he announced that, 'Without one state language, no nation can remain tied up solidly together and function.' Most of East Pakistani political thinkers did not like it, but they showed their restrained in order to exhibit tribute to the founder personality of Pakistan. However serious resistance on this issue broke out later on after his death. In 1948, the government of Pakistan introduced Urdu as the sole national language. It sparked off extensive protests among the Bengali-speaking majority of East Pakistan. Facing rising sectarian tensions and mass discontent with the new law, the government outlawed public meetings and rallies. But the student unrest continued throughout East Pakistan. On 21 February 1952, the movement reached its climax when police killed student demonstrators on that day. The deaths provoked widespread civil unrest. The movement was led by the Awami Muslim League, later renamed the Awami League. After years of conflict, the central government relented and granted official status to the Bengali language in 1956.

Jinnah and Liaquat: The two forceful personalities of the founders of Pakistan, Jinnah, the governor-general popularly known as the *Quaid i Azam* (Supreme Leader) and Liaquat Ali Khan (1895–1951), the first prime minister, popularly known as the *Quaid i Millet* (Leader of the Community) were the persons to keep the two wings of Pakistan together. There were no limitations on Jinnah's constitutional powers. In the 1970s in Bangladesh Sheikh Mujibur Rahman became powerful because of being the leader of East Pakistan people. He was permitted to enjoy much of the same prestige and exemption from the normal rule of law, although he has often been criticised in many quarters of being autocratic.

When Jinnah died in September 1948, the seat of power shifted from the governor-general to the prime minister, Liaquat Ali, who subscribed to the ideals of a parliamentary democracy. But he was trying to fulfil the wishes of the country's religious spokesperson who championed the cause of Pakistan as an Islamic state, by seeking a balance of Islam against secularism for a new constitution when he was assassinated on 16 October 1951.

Early 1968, Agartala Conspiracy Case was filed against Sheikh Mujib and thirty-four others, with the allegation that the accused were planning to liberate the East Pakistan; however, but the public protested against this accusation and demanded to free all the prisoners. Meanwhile, on 15 February 1969, the government compelled to withdraw the case on 22 February. The mass uprising subsequently culminated into another historic uprising. On 25 March 1969, there was a change of power, General Ayub Khan handed the state power to General Yahya Khan, subsequently all sorts of political activities in the country were postponed by the new military president.

Later in 1969, Yahya Khan announced a fresh election date for 5 October 1970. The result was spectacular. The Awami League won all the East Pakistan seats as well as majority of the Pakistan's National Assembly in the 1970–71 elections. West Pakistan government changed its thinking and opened talks with the East on constitutional questions about the division of power to be handed to the provinces, to be govern by a national government headed by the Awami League. The league leader Sheikh Mujibur Rahman presented his right of claim to the president of Pakistan to form the government. The leader of the Pakistan People's Party, Zulfikar Ali Bhutto, refused to yield the premiership of Pakistan to Mujibur. President Yahya Khan called the military and asked to suppress dissent in East Pakistan.

As soon as the National Assembly was postponed by Yahya Khan on 1 March, the dissidents in East Pakistan began to target the ethnic Bihari community, who had supported West Pakistan. In early March 1971, three hundred Biharis were slaughtered in rioting by Bengali mobs in Chittagong alone. For the cause of 'Bihari massacre' the government of Pakistan deployed military in East Pakistan, when it initiated its Operation Search light. The fight for disarming East Pakistani soldiers and police began and simultaneously mass arrests of dissidents continued although strikes and non-cooperation continued in the city of Dhaka. The next operation was carried out just to kill the intellectual elite of the East. The talks proved unsuccessful.

On 2 March 1971, a group of students, led by **A. S. M. Abdur Rob**, student leader of Dhaka University, raised the new flag of Bangladesh. On March 7, there was a historical public gathering in Suhrawardy Udyan where Bangabandhu Sheikh Mujib, the frontier leader of movement said remember our struggle is for our freedom and our struggle is for our independence.

The military crackdown by the Pakistan army began during the early hours of 26 March 1971 **Bangabandhu Shiekh Mujibur Rahaman** was arrested and the political leaders dispersed, mostly fleeing to neighbouring India. Sheikh Mujibur Rahman gave a hand note of declaration of independence to the press, which was widely reported throughout the world. Major Ziaur Raman, under the direction of Bango-bondhu Mujibur Rahman declared that Independent People's Republic of Bangladesh has been established. He said we shall fight to the last to free our motherland. Liberation war started forming an army force established under the name 'Muktifoujo'. Later it was named 'Muktibahini' (freedom fighters) under the command of M.A.G.Osmani.

The Indo-Pakistani War of 1971 was the direct military confrontation between India and Pakistan leading to the liberation of Bangladesh. Looking to the Indian army at the boarder Pakistan launched pre-emptive air strikes on eleven Indian airbases on 3 December 1971. India entered into the war of independence in East Pakistan on the side of Bangladeshi nationalist forces. The war lasted only for thirteen days, it is considered to be one of the shortest wars in history. The training of the Mukti Bahini was supported by the Indian people and India government. As fighting grew in between the Pakistan army and the Bengali Mukti Bahini an estimated ten million Bengalis, mainly Hindus, had sought refuge in the Indian states of Assam, Tripura, and West Bengal. The crisis in East Pakistan produced new strains in Pakistan's troubled relations with India. The two nations had fought a war in 1965, mainly in the West, but the pressure of millions of refugees escaping into India in autumn of 1971 as well as Pakistani aggression reignited hostilities with Pakistan mainly on the eastern side.

Indian sympathies lay with East Pakistan, and as such India intervened on the side of the Bangladeshis that started the war known as the Indo-Pakistani War of 1971. After the tragic events of March, India became vocal in its condemnation of Pakistan. An immense flood of East Pakistani refugees, between 8 and 10 million according to various estimates, fled across the border into the Indian state of West Bengal. In April, an Indian parliamentary resolution demanded that Prime Minister Indira Gandhi supply aid to the rebels in East Pakistan.

On 4 December 1971, the Indian army, far superior in numbers and equipment to that of Pakistan, executed a three-pronged pincer movement on Dhaka launched from the Indian states of West Bengal, Assam, and Tripura, taking only twelve days to defeat the ninety thousand Pakistani defenders. The Pakistan army was weakened by having to operate so far away from its source of supply. The Indian army, on the other hand, was aided by East Pakistan's Mukti Bahini (Liberation Force).

At the beginning Indian and Pakistani forces clashed on the eastern and western fronts, but the war effectively came to an end after the eastern command of the Pakistani armed forces signed the Instrument of Surrender. Mukti Bihini of Bangladesh won the war with the help of Indian support. Pakistan army surrendered. The surrender of Pakistan took place on 16 December 1971 at the Ramna Race Course in Dhaka, marking the liberation of Bangladesh.

About 90,000–93,000 Pakistanis were taken as prisoners of war by the Indian army. A new nation Bangladesh came into existence. When the Instrument of Surrender was signed by Lieutenant General A.A.K.Niazi, commander of Pakistani forces in East Pakistan and handed over the document to Lieutenant General Jagit Singh Aurora, general officer commanding-in-chief of eastern command of the Indian army, the surrounding crowds on the race course began shouting anti-Niazi and anti-Pakistan slogans. It was a great moment of victory for the people of Bangladesh as well as for the Indian military. It is estimated that between 300,000 and 3,000,000 civilians were killed in Bangladesh. As a result of the conflict, a further eight to ten million people fled the country at the time to seek refuge in neighbouring India.

On 26 March 1971, Ziaur Rahman, a major in the Pakistani army, declared the independence of Bangladesh. In April, Awami League leaders formed a government—inexile in Meherpur. Bangladesh force, namely, Mukti Bahini (Regular Force) and Gono Bahini (Guerilla Force) was formed under the commander-in-chief (C-in-C) General Mohammad Ataul Ghani Osmany to fight for the liberation of Bangladesh.

[2]

India and Mukti Bahini: The Pakistan army conducted a widespread genocide against the Bengali population of East Pakistan, **targeting** particularly the minority Hindu population. Approximately 10 million people of East Pakistan had taken shelter in the neighbouring Indian states. Indian government opened the East Pakistan–India border to allow refugees safe shelter in India. The central government instructed West Bengal, Bihar, Assam, Meghalaya, and Tripura to establish refugee camps along the border. The resulting flood of impoverished East Pakistani refugees placed an intolerable strain on India's already overburdened economy.

A propaganda war between Pakistan and India ensued in which Yahya threatened war against India if that country made an attempt to seize any part of Pakistan. Yahya also asserted that Pakistan could count on its American and Chinese friends. At the same time, Pakistan tried to ease the situation in the East Wing. Belatedly, it replaced Tikka, whose military tactics had caused such havoc and human loss of life, with the more restrained Lieutenant General A.A.K. Niazi. A moderate Bengali, Abdul Malik, was installed as the civilian governor of East Pakistan. These belated gestures of appeasement did not yield results or change world opinion.

General Tikha Khan earned the nickname 'Butcher of Bengal' because of the widespread atrocities committed over Bengalis. His display of stark cruelty was so merciless that as if he is raiding an enemy and not dealing with his own misguided and misled people. Prime Minister Indira Gandhi on 27 March 1971 expressed full support of her government for the independence struggle of the people of East Pakistan. Prime Minister Indira Gandhi thought that instead of taking in millions of refugees, it was economically justified to go to war against Pakistan. On 28 April 1971, the Indian cabinet asked General Manekshaw to go with war along with Mufti Bahini of Bangladesh.

By November, war cry was heard such as 'Crush India' in the political march in Lahore and also across West Pakistan. India responded by starting a massive build-up of Indian forces on the borders. Pakistan flew no more than fifty planes to India. Prime Minister Indira Gandhi held that the air strikes were a declaration of war against India and the Indian Air Force responded with initial air strikes that very night, but in the next morning, these air strikes were expanded to a massive scale as retaliatory air strikes. This was the actual beginning of the Indo-Pakistani War of 1971. Prime Minister Indira Gandhi ordered to launch a full-scale invasion. This involved Indian forces in a massive coordinated air, sea, and land assault. According to the information gather from Delhi, in the very first day of the conflict the Indian destroyer 'Rajput' had sunk a Pakistani submarine with deep bombing. On 4 and 9 December, the speed boats of India had destroyed and damaged ten Pakistani battleships and vessels by Soviet anti-ship P-15 missiles. In addition twelve Pakistani oil storage were burned in flame. The objective of the war on the eastern front was to capture Dacca and on the western front was to prevent Pakistan from entering Indian soil.

The theatre of war in the naval sector: On the 4 December, in the Eastern sector, the Indian Eastern Naval Command, under Vice Admiral Krishnan, completely isolated East Pakistan by a naval blockade in the Bay of Bengal, trapping the Eastern Pakistani Navy in the ports, and subsequently the aircraft carrier INS *Vikrant* was placed in right place and its Sea Hawk fighter bombers were allowed to attack the coastal town such as Chittagong and Cox's Bazar.

On the night of 4–5 December in the Western sector, the Indian navy, under the command of Vice Admiral S.N. Kohli, successfully attacked Karachi's port and destroyed Pakistani destroyer PNS *Khyber* using missile boats. In response, Pakistani submarines moved out towards major Indian warships. But result was the loss of 720 Pakistani sailors and loss of reserve fuel and many commercial ships.

Again on the night of 8–9 December, in the name of Operation Python, Indian missile boats attacked the Karachi port, resulting in further destruction of reserve fuel tanks and the sinking of three Pakistani merchant ships. In response, Pakistan countered the threat by sending the submarine PNS *Ghazi*, but unfortunately that sank in the coastal area under mysterious circumstances. But on 9 December, the Indian Navy suffered its biggest wartime loss because the frigate INS *Khukri* sank in the Arabian Sea due to the strike of Pakistani submarine PNS *Hangor*, resulting in a loss of 18 officers and 176 sailors

In the naval warfront in both of Indian and Pakistani side, there was loss, but the loss on Pakistani side was more. It was almost half of the naval force of Pakistani side (according to a military personal) was destroyed.

The theatre of war in the air front: After the initial pre-emptive strike, PAF adopted a defensive stance in response to the Indian retaliation. As the war in progress, the Indian air force continued to strike the PAF over the zones of strategic importance, but the number of sorties flown by the PAF gradually decreased day by day. **In view of t**he Indian four thousand air sorties, the PAF offered little in retaliation, that partly because of the deliberate decision of the PAF High Command to cut its losses as it had already incurred huge losses in the conflict.

In the East, there prevailed Indian air superiority because the small air contingent of Pakistan air force kept in zone sector 14 was totally destroyed by Indian air force putting the Dhaka airfield out of commission.

Role of USA, Russia, and China: Looking to the Pakistani army torture over the innocent people of East Pakistan including men and women, young students, boys and girls, and in result arrival of floods of refugees in India, Indira Gandhi, the Indian prime minister, in those times decided to tour most of the Western capitals to prove Indian stand and gain support and sympathy for the Bengalis of East Pakistan. On 4 and 5 November she met Nixon in Washington. Nixon straight forwardly told her that a new war in the subcontinent was out of the question.

The Soviet Union sympathised with the Bangladeshis and supported the Indian army and Mukti Bahini during the war. According to Soviet Union, it was a support to the voice of humanity. It was also in the inner mind that the independence of Bangladesh would be a strategic gain as it would weaken the position of the United States and China. The USSR gave assurances to India that if a confrontation with the United States or China developed, it would take the necessary counter-measures. This assurance was enshrined in the Indo-Soviet Treaty of Friendship and Cooperation signed in August 1971.

President Richard Nixon and his secretary of state Henry Kissinger refused to support India in civil war in East Pakistan. Rather the **United States** was sympathised with Pakistan and supported Pakistan both politically and materially because of two factors, firstly, Pakistan belonged to American led military Pact, CENTO, and SEATO; secondly, US believed any victory of India will be considered as the expansion of Soviet influence in the parts gained by India with the victory, as it was believed to be a pro Soviet nation, even though they were non-aligned.

Pakistan was a close formal ally of the United States and was also on good terms with People's Republic of China, with whom Nixon had been negotiating a rapprochement and where he intended to visit in February 1972. Nixon was afraid to see that an Indian invasion of West Pakistan would mean total Soviet domination of the region, and that it would seriously undermine the global position of the United States and the regional position of America's new endeavour along with the new ally, China.

A resolution in the UN Security Council calling for a ceasefire and the withdrawal of armed forces by

India and Pakistan had been introduce by the then US ambassador to the United Nations George H.W.Bush, who later became the president of the United States. However it was vetoed by the Soviet Union. It was the following days the Soviets were on great pressure of Nixon-Kissinger to get India to withdrawn from the war, but Russia never succumbed to the pressure. Here lies the success of Indian diplomacy.

As a long-standing ally of Pakistan, the People's Republic of China came in support of Pakistan true, but China never agreed to mobilise its armed forces along its border with India to threaten India although encouraged by Nixon because China did not want his country to face the danger of turmoil for the fact that unlike the 1962 Sino-Indian War when India was caught entirely unaware, this time the Indian Army was prepared and had kept eight mountain divisions to the Sino-Indian border to guard constantly against such an eventuality. Soviet Union had also threatened China that, if they ever opened a front against India on its border, they will receive a tough response from the North. China instead threw its weight behind the demands for an amicable solution bringing immediate ceasefire. The idea of Nixon was that the concentration of Chinese army at the border would bring an adverse effect over India when the Indian military might collapse in tensed situation caused by fighting in three different fronts (East, North, and West). Nixon's game plan collapsed.

In the next strategy of Nixon was not only to encourage China to increase its arms supplies to Pakistan, but also to encourage countries like Jordan and Iran to send military supplies to Pakistan, knowing fully 'genocidal' activities of the Pakistani army in East Pakistan. It has also been documented that President Nixon requested Iran and Jordan to send their F-86, F-104, and F-5 fighter jets in aid of Pakistan. It was because global power is more important to USA than the human slaughter like genocide being committed by his alley Pakistan. However, there was widespread criticism and condemnation both by the United States Congress and the international press for the support of America to Pakistani government for the heinous crime of killing innocent people of East Bengal for their democratic views.

In the war, India skid off Pakistan of more than half of its population and with nearly one-third of its army in captivity, clearly indicating a military dominance of India in the subcontinent. In spite of the magnitude of the victory, India was surprisingly relived from the burden of 10 million Bengali refugees, who would be returning quickly to their homeland. By announcing the Pakistani surrender, Prime Minister Indira Gandhi had brought a clamour of joy of brave Indian military in the Indian Parliament. She said Dacca is now the free capital of a new nation—Bangladesh. We hail the people of Bangladesh in their trump of triumph in the display of bravery. All nations who value the spirit of humanity will recognise it as a significant milestone for the Bengali people of East Pakistan in the quest of liberty.

According to a Russian documentary, when Pakistan's defeat in the Eastern sector seemed certain, Nixon deployed Task Force 74 led by the aircraft carrier USS *Enterprise* into the Bay of Bengal. The *Enterprise* and its escort ships arrived on the station on 11 December 1971. The United Kingdom deployed a carrier battle group led by the aircraft carrier HMS Eagle to the Bay of Bengal. On the other hand, Russia, the trusted all time friend of India, had taken appropriate step to strike the enemy in necessity. On 6 and 13 December, the Soviet navy dispatched two groups of cruisers and destroyers and a submarine armed with nuclear missiles starting from Vladivostok, they trailed US Task Force 74 into the Indian Ocean and kept ready a nuclear submarine to help ward off the threat posed by the USS *Enterprise* task force in the Indian Ocean.

Reaction at Pakistan: For Pakistan it was not only a loss of half of its population and a significant portion of its economy and a setbacks to its geo-political role in South Asia, but above all, a humiliation of defeat and that too at the hands of intense rival India. Pakistan feared that the two-nation theory was disproved and that the Islamic ideology had proved insufficient to keep Bengalis part of Pakistan, showing the love of mother tongue is superior to the love of religion. Pakistan further had to borne the brunt of humiliation of accepting their 90,000 prisoners of war (POWs) released by India only after the negotiation and signing of the Simla Agreement on 2 July 1972.

The Pakistani people were not mentally prepared to accept defeat, as was evident due to spontaneous demonstrations and mass protests in the streets of major cities in West Pakistan. Demoralised and finding him unable to control the situation, General Yahya Khan surrendered power to Zulfiqar Ali Bhutto who was sworn in on 20 December 1971 as president as well as the chief martial law administrator, a civilian shattering the prestige of the Pakistani military. On the other hand, the Indian army chief of the 1971 war, Sam Manekshaw had achieved the highest respect for fighting bravely and skilfully against the Pakistani army.

Reaction at Bangladesh: Mujibur Rahman **became** the first president of Bangladesh and later its prime minister after being released from a West Pakistani prison, who was returning to Dhaka on 10 January 1972 as the spark of fire of astounding victory of liberation. Thus Bangladesh became an independent nation, the world's fourth most populous Muslim state.

On seeing the signal of defeat around 14 December, the Pakistani army began to kill systematically a large number of Bengali doctors, teachers, and intellectuals, and particularly the Hindu minorities who constituted the majority of urban-educated intellectuals, including the young men and women and especially the students, who were seen as possible rebels as most of the students were the strong supporter of Mukti Bhini Force. As the Pakistan force of army could not bring any kind of victory, they had preferred to finish their strength of frustration in the killing of innocent Bengalis, because at that very moment they had lost all sense of humanity. Although the extent of casualties in East Pakistan is not known but other sources of estimation place the death toll not lower than three hundred thousand. Bangladesh government figures state that Pakistani forces aided by collaborators killed three million people raped two hundred thousand women and displaced few millions.

Pakistani army at the beginning started its operation in East Pakistan to curtail the movement and anger among the Bengalis, but simultaneously it was also reported that the army was involved in mass killing of public and mass rape of women. In May, Indira Gandhi wrote to Nixon about the 'carnage in East Bengal' and asked for sharing the burden of India for the flood of refugees being sheltered in the border areas of India. L. K. Jha (then the Indian ambassador to the United States) had also warned Kissinger that India might have to send back some of the refugees as guerrillas, Nixon commented, 'By God, we will cut off economic aid to India.'

Role of Gandhi for the people of Bengal: The role of Gandhi in the sphere of non-violence and civil disobedient movement in Bengal was very much exciting and eliminating to speak of. Gandhi was the leader of Swedishi movement to raise voice against the British, but again he was the man to bring Hindu-Muslim unity, which had been polluted by the poison of hatred due to misunderstanding and ill advice of few power-hungry leaders. He was a man to say there is no Hindu-Muslim difference because all are the children of God, but again he was a man, who was compelled to say goodbye to Jinnah by giving Pakistan in order to stop bloodshed. It was because he was dead against bloodshed, no matter friend or foe. It was against his personal ethics of law. Jinnah was a successful lawyer, but Gandhi was not. Jinnah was not a mass favourite leader but Gandhi was. Again it was nothing but the destiny of fortunes that he was unsuccessful to win over Jinnah. Had he been successful the country would not be divided into two. People say something different. His inner desire was to see Nehru in the chair and not Jinnah. But the formation of Pakistan has given a chair to Jinnah too. Nobody can alter the writings of the destiny.

The state Bengal was the number one state in economic front before partition, but it became the last number of state in economic front after partition so far the Bengal (West Bengal) state of India is concerned. It was the reason why the millions of refugee Bengalis struggling hard to survive in the street of Calcutta as Hawkers. The fight among political parties had continued to give a better life to Bengalis, the Bengalis of West Bengal in India. While the Bengal state of Pakistan (East Bengal) is concerned, it became a number less state without any economic front because it became a state to be squeezed by the West or West Pakistan. It was the reason to liberate Bangladesh at the cost of the death of the millions.

At the beginning of the Gandhi's political carrier to start with non-violence after return from Africa in 1912, he was unsuccessful in three places, first in Champaran district of Bihar in 1917, second in Kheda district in Gujarat in 1918, and third in Gorakhpur district in UP in 1922, but at last he was most successful at Calcutta in the thrust of movement against the British in 1930 under the patronage of C.R.Das, the leading barrister of Bengal. C.R.Das was also mesmerised at the beginning by his Fakir Dress. C.R. Das was using clothes cleaned in French, but very soon he could judge his inner mind, and then he went away from Gandhi as well as from congress because he could realise his intention how to exploit the present situation of Bengal for the benefit of Delhi leaders. However he had formed a separate party in the name 'Saraj Party'. It was C.R.Das who had realised the future of Bengal and as such joined hands together with all Bengal leaders such as Suhrawardy, A.K.Fazul Hag, and many other and discussed openly how to accommodate equal representation and so on to bring peace and tranquillity in Bengal. But unfortunately Bengal lost such a versatile outstanding leader very soon in the year 1925. There was no leader left in Bengal after that time to look to the interest of Bengal. Afterwards, the subsequent events were framed as such that the effect of the result goes in favour of Delhi leaders and against the benefit of Bengal.

Thus Gandhi was successful to keep the two parts of Bengal apart by the passion of hatred of religion bypassing the united efforts of Suhrawardy to keep it economically down so that anybody of the powerful Bengal could dare to look to the power of chair of Delhi, but Gandhi could never be successful to keep apart the mind-sets of two Bengal as the songs of Amar Sonar Bangla of Rabindra nath Taghore is indivisible. Lord Curzon did it in 1905, but it gets reunited in 1911. Now in 1947 Gandhi again divided Bengal to get Jinnah out of power of India and made Nehru the PM, it is the future time nobody knows when it would come to get the two Bengals united. It was the Gandhi's success to keep the Bengal leaders out of power to decide the fate of Bengal. Suharwardy and Sarat Bose was for a united Bengal, at last Jinnah agreed for a united Bengal, but Petal and Nehru who worked under Gandhi never agreed for a united Bengal, because they were the leaders of Northern India, their underlying fear was anybody of Bengal leader, not the question of Netaji, who might proceed to Delhi one day to challenge the power of Delhi chair, thus in the end formation of two Bengals was written in the fate of Bengal. No doubt Gandhi made a name by bringing independence to India by violence or non-violence no matter, and Nehru single handedly glorified Gandhi first by declaring India achieved independence by **non-violence** even though the British Prime Minister Clement Attlee just before independence came to Calcutta to meet the then governor and declared that British could no longer hold on with the administration of India because a lot of British army personnel had died in the war fighting against Netaji's Azad Hind Fouj. Secondly, that was by declaring Gandhi the 'Father' of the Nation without taking the consent of the people of India.

Thus AHIMSA (non-violence) and *sacrifice* are the two basic principles of Hinduism, people used to preach to get peace and mental peace. Hindu people carry out their Pujas in every house as well as in temples for the cause of mental peace. Sometimes people remain in fast to purify themselves and then prefer to go temples to offer something in the name of Pujas, what is nothing but sacrifice to almighty for the satisfaction of mind and heart. They never thought that idealism of AHIMSA (non-violence) would be utilised in the achievement of political goal. The fasting would be utilised to befool the people to forget to exert their right of existence. If he was a super human being thinks for mankind irrespective of caste creed or religion, then why did he fail to convenience the Muslims of India? If he was a saint, free from power of administration, and self-glory, thought that his advice is not acceptable to all then he should retire from politics but instead he continued to remain in power centre . . . Why? Definitely a motive was working in his inner mind but even then how could he think of to create a situation **(the creation Pakistan)** due to which millions of people would be displaced and millions would be killed. Is it a saintly work or an inhuman work? Gandhi's mystic befooled the Hindus by carrying out the movement against the British using religion in a twisted way. The ethics of Hinduism is to sacrifice as nothing would be left in this world after sometime, and tolerance should be the virtue of human beings. He transformed the virtue of tolerance into 'non-violence' and befooled the common Hindus. The ethics of Hindu religion dictates the mind-set that if anything to be offered to the 'Almighty' must be offered with pure and purified mind-set. Thus it had brought a system of purifying self by remaining in fasting and then offering something to the 'Almighty'. Gandhi had used the 'fasting' in the movement to befool the people to accomplish his hidden desire.

What he did only to befool the Hindus, he knows Muslim religion never believe in the virtue of tolerance or non-violence or fasting? As such Gandhi kept the movement confined to Hindus only. He was an Inner Temple law graduate; he was a lone genius to see the future of India and the future of Bengal. His movement of non-violence in the way of 'non-cooperation' or 'civil disobedience movement' although had tested the gravity of the movement earlier in other places, where it could not brought effective results, it got fruitful result with huge participation of Bengali Hindus only in Bengal. Why did he avoid the Muslims in the movement? He designed the movement 'non-violence' based on the ethics of Hindu religion 'tolerance' very carefully to bring segregation between Hindus and Muslims. Thus his success of movement in Calcutta and in other places of Bengal had encouraged him to proceed with his vision of doing harm to Bengal, harm to Bengali leaders by loss of faith of Hindus over Muslims and vice versa and shifting of power centre from Calcutta to Delhi. The vision of Gandhi was to diminish the power of Bengal through communal violence. Either before or after the period of violence or rioting, Gandhi never had approach the Muslim leaders with logic of reasoning to stop the massacre.

East Pakistan did not last for more than twenty-two years as the country was emerged as a new nation of Bangladesh in 1971. Sheikh Mujibur Rahman became president of the newly formed Bangladesh. The new constitution was written. The constitution proclaims Bangladesh as a secular democratic republic. The constitution further proclaims nationalism, democracy, socialism, and secularity as the national ideals of the Bangladeshi republic. But again the founding father of the nation was assassinated along with the whole family except two daughters in 1975. The subsequent events would explain how the Silent Patriot had to pass his life in the service of the society for the cause of the helpless people.

[3]

Answers to few questions with respect to Gandhi circulated in the air: Let us see what the questions were and what the answers were. If Mahatma Gandhi was not assassinated, and had he lived for another twenty years, then what change he would have brought to India?

If Gandhi had been alive in India the condition of Hindus would had been bad to worse. If he would have reached to Pakistan, he would have been killed brutally. The record of history says he was about to kill in Naokhali had the local Hindu volunteers not saved him in right time, however his goat, which he carried with him, had been killed. Gandhi was a good man but not a good politician. Moreover his vision was not wide, but circumstances compelled him to change his ideas and thoughts time to time.

What he was, he was an LL.B graduate from Inner Temple, London, and somehow, he returned to Bombay to practice but failed to get a single client, while the case of Jinnah was opposite, where he was flooded with suits. He went to South Africa, not very comfortable there, not happy at home due to disobedient son, also not happy in outside because he was humiliated in the travelling bus, as well as in white restaurant, moreover, he was not popular very much in his profession there too. Finally he came back to India, here also he get frustrated because no client. Finally he came across with Motilal Nehru; there he found some sort of mental stability and happiness. There he thought of doing something under the shadow of Nehru family, then onwards his love for Nehru had grown up. His thought was how he could make himself expose as a saint, or as a politician, or as a Fakir to win the heart of common people. Since then it appeared that two factors were playing in his mind, one the glory of Nehru family and the other the public sympathy which he had seen at the time of his torture period in South Africa.

He started his experiment of sympathy movement in Champaran district of Bihar in 1917, Kheda district in Gujarat in 1918 and again in Gorakhpur district in UP on 5 February 1922 against the Rowlett Act, everywhere he failed even he was imprisoned. His idea changes to a different angle since then. At that time, his attention turned towards Calcutta where violent struggle was going on against the British. Killing of British in secret mission was a regular feature at that time in Calcutta and the hanging of the culprit or sending the culprit to Andaman jail (cellular jail) was the hot news of the day at that time. The agony of the parents of these children has no end. The sympathy of the public for those sacrificing boys has crossed all limits. The speeches of elderly persons for the sacrificing boys bring tears to everybody's eyes. The speeches of young for the sacrificing boys bring thunder of excitement and thrust of revolution.

Gandhi's attention now positively turned towards Calcutta. It was his thinking how to bring Nehru and Nehru family in the forefront because he thought it wise to bring Nehru family in front of Indian politics, which will make him the great. He knows Bengalis were cultured and most religious minded. He thought of an idea, a religious movement to win the heart of common Bengalis, particularly the Hindus, and bring a sort of misunderstanding between Hindus and Muslims. Why? It was because unless the maximum harm had happened in Bengal, the top most economy went down, the power centre of Calcutta get shifted and Bengali's leadership get polluted by Hindu-Muslim misunderstanding, the chance of occupying the power of chair at Delhi would never been opened up for Nehru.

He thought of a religious movement which was nothing but 'non-violence'. Tolerance is in the ethics of Hinduism, he twisted it to non-violence. When it was proposed in Nagpur session in 1930, it was objected by Jinnah, but Gandhi remained adamant to his decision bypassing Jinnah's objection because he cannot expose his inner thought to a Muslim leader. He changed his dress, became a Fakir, because it was necessary to befool the Hindu Bengalis. He became a saint in appearance as living simple, dressed as simple Fakir, although he was not doing the activity of a Fakir, but doing politics behind the shadow of a Fakir. In 1930, he started non-violence in the form of civil disobedience movement in all throughout of Bengal including Calcutta befooling most of the congress leaders except few such as Rabindranath Takur, C.R.Das, and few others. Hindus were mad to join the movement as if it was started by the messenger of God, Gandhi, due to their religious belief and faith over Gandhi. He mesmerised the Hindu masses like a magician. No Muslim joined the movement, what he had wanted to bring mass agitation against the British, first by Hindus as the Hindus were the majority. It was in his inner mind to bring the Muslims afterwards when the situation would compel them to join the movement. That was the first success of Gandhi to bring Nehru in the chair by reducing the power of Bengalis.

The subsequent part is better not to write, how the atmosphere of violence and hatred prevailed in Calcutta, Gandhi was not in the picture, and religious violence was everywhere. It was 16 August 1946, Jinnah convinced Suhrawardy, the then CM of Bengal to start direct action. It was declared by ML 16 August was the Direct Action Day; it was the Calcutta killing day, if Pakistan was not given. Gandhi remained silent. Neither had he made peaceful negotiation nor any preparation to stop the senseless killing. It was because the inner voice of Gandhi was not to speak with anybody when he was in the emotion of violence. Now after massacre and after Pakistan somebody saying he was preparing to go to Pakistan before his assassination to bring peace there, why? Did he shown his desire of negotiation with Muslims in Calcutta before the onslaught of 16 August for the creation of Pakistan? There were different views. Some were in favour of Gandhi and again some were against the opinion of the Gandhi.

However it was his afterthought. Before the creation of Pakistan, he was anti-Muslim in the secret of his mind of action. He talked of Ram Rajya keeping Nehru in the chair. But after completion of division, he openly became a spokes person of Muslims, because of two reasons: (1) the Muslims were well prepared by their ML volunteers to carry out massacre anywhere everywhere, and (2) his goal of glory lies in non-violence.

Now he was in Calcutta just after Pakistan to save the Muslims in Bengal. His weapon was again a religious weapon the *fasting*, which is generally undertaken by the Hindus at the time of offering something to God at the time of doing Pujas. Again by his saintly activity he befooled the religious Hindus to stop anti-Muslim activity, thus Muslims remained in peace in West Bengal even after the formation of Muslim East Pakistan. Thus today we find Muslims in East Bengal (now Bangladesh) as well as Muslims in West Bengal.

After his success he went to Delhi, to clear the MAJIDS of Delhi, which were occupied by the refugees who had arrived here from West Punjab losing everything and in most of the cases half of the family members. Gandhi did not stop here, he asked Nehru, Petal to give cores of money from Indian treasure to Pakistan for running Pakistan administration. Now to satisfy the Hindus, he was spreading the message that he would go to Pakistan to stop the killing of Hindus by Muslims there. How funny it was? Is there any time that he was successful to befool Muslims? Never, he was successful to befool the Hindus because of religious instinct. Muslims never believed him because he was after Ram Rajya. God was favourable to him that was why today he was an international icon and placed along with other international icon of twentieth century like Winston Churchill, Roosevelt, Hitler, or Moa-Sa-Tang. Abraham Lincoln sacrificed his life for the unity of America, unity of white and black, while Gandhi became an icon by dividing India and creating a permanent hatred in between Hindus and Muslims and also killing millions of Punjabis and millions of Bengalis and also displacing millions from their ancestral home.

Gandhi favoured Nehru many times that had been exposed in public. He was happy by making Nehru the president of the congress party, but he was not happy with Netaji being inducted as president in 1938. In 1939 he openly opposed Netaji by posturing SitaRam Pattavia, but unfortunately he was defeated against Netaji. Does it indicate his simple life with simple mind or a simple life with dishonest mind? Not only that he had discarded Sadder Petal being the selected candidate by the Congress Party, as first PM of India, and he replaced Petal by Nehru, why? Did it indicate his honest or saintly behaviour?

Indians don't know whether India won independence by the act of Gandhi's non-violence, but what the Indians know or what the Indians have seen that he has done the greatest harm to India to live as a great nation. Had his vision was not limited to Nehru and really think equally for all to create a great country and a Ram Rajya, he could do that. But his idea remained confined in limited area of community, personality, and above all in religion. A national leader is always above religion in every country and everywhere. The formation of India-Pakistan on the basis of religion is first in the world.

Afterwards Gandhi realised his mistake in carrying out non-violence movement, while Jinnah carried a violent movement under trained ML volunteer, where 2% militant voice prevailed over 98% neutral cum non-violence voice. To rectify its effect, Gandhi followed the policy of appeasement towards Muslims. After Gandhi, congress followed the same policy of appeasement; thereby Muslims have consolidated their position not only in Pakistan east or west but also in India. Pakistan became one country, one law while India became one country but different law, one law for Hindus and another law for Muslims. Muslims got Pakistan and prevailed Muslim right but in India also they prevailed Muslim right in every state of India bypassing Hindu right in many cases on the basis of Muslim's personal right of personal law by the act of their political maturity.

Gandhi never thought of the development of the economy that could build a united solid foundation as that had been happened in Japan and USA or UK, but Indian leader Gandhi in particular always think of religion and power of chair. Today the cry is for 'Muslims Free India' as said by one of BJP worker, Shakhi Maharaja if it was not mistaken. Why? The situation was created by Gandhi that indicates his little power in foresightedness. Pakistan became an enemy country, why? It was because of Gandhi and non-violence activity, the activity of appeasement and surrender to militant force. A country is ruled by its strength and not by the policy of surrender and sacrifice.

Today Modi is speaking in front of American dignitaries that terrorism is the enemy of humanity and the country who are nurturing the art of terrorism are the enemy of humanity pointing finger towards Pakistan, why? It was because of Gandhi. Modhi is asking for action, asking for cooperation of all country, not asking for non-violence. The man, Gandhi, who had done the greatest harm for the present, for the past, and also for the future, but the Indians are honouring him now, every year in Gandhi Jyanti, in every state in India as well as in foreign soil. The Indians honouring him even in Indian currency giving his picture. Why? It was because the first PM of India Nehru had made him the 'Father' of the Nation bypassing the writings of the constitution and spread the message all over the globe. In summary his contribution was very little in preserving the unity of the country, who had created a dark India having a dark future, a future calling the Babur to come to India as it was once predicted by Jinnah that one day Indians will call the Muslims to rule India because the Indian Hindus do not know how to administer a country because it existed in Muslim blood, who ruled India more than the Hindu kings.

In congress regime Gandhi's idealism was spread in every country, but could India have preserved it in its own soil. It failed to preserve it with China, had it followed the same principle, India had to give off the whole of Arunachal and even the whole of North-east, had it followed the same principle with Pakistan in the last four wars, in that case, it had to give off Kashmir, Bangladesh, and half the territory of India. Should the Indians will follow non-violence or discard non-violence forever? Only the unknown power of God will save India if Indians follow and preserve Gandhi's idealism of non-violence with the same spirit of Gandhi.

Why did Gandhi fail in uniting Hindus and Muslims?
Gandhi was a clever man ever born in India. He has little vision for United India; he has only one vision to make Nehru the PM as he was attached with Nehru's father, Motilal Nehru. He thought of his success only with Nehru family and Nehru dynasty. His long-time strategy had been seen in the transfer of Gandhi title to Nehru dynasty.

To achieve his success, he (Gandhi) required to shift the power from Calcutta to Delhi, he required to divert the attention of the leaders of Bengal, because it was only the leaders of Bengal who could challenge Nehru to occupy the chair of power at Delhi. To complete his mission, he tried his level best to bring an atmosphere of friendship between Hindus and Muslims, but it turned into communal hatred at Bengal. How? He had chosen the path of movement as non-violence, to start the civil disobedience movement, a movement that attached with Hindu religion to attract the Hindus, thereby a kind of hatred might have been produced in between Hindus and Muslims in Bengal at the beginning, but what he thought the participation of the people in large would bring a change of heart that would lead to a bond of friendship and brotherhood. Thus it was in his mind-set the initial hatred would transform into a bond of love and peace so that he could proceed with his secret plan. The ethics of Hinduism is always to sacrifice while the virtue of Hinduism is nothing but tolerance. He had twisted the virtue of tolerance to non-violence intentionally; thereby he had made all the Bengali Hindus of Bengal a follower except a few such as C. R. Das, Rabindranath Thakur, and a few others. It was truly a Hindu movement of civil disobedient movement in 1930, what was started to pull the Hindus in the movement in large numbers. Muslims did not participate in the movement but even than his belief was that the participants of large numbers would attract them or compel them to join the movement. Gandhi did not enquire or interested to talk with any Muslim leader because mere talking does not produce result. The action produces results. It was because of that he started the movement under the principle of non-violence to bring the Hindus in large numbers first followed by the Muslim. The initial hatred would transform into a bond of love and peace what was his belief. Otherwise he would not proceed with the movement as he knows his initial proposal in Nagpur session was objected by Jinnah.

But again Gandhi did not have any importance to other's view, which might be logically correct. This is one of Gandhi's mischievous characters. He was also an advocate like other law graduate, but he was behaving like a magician as a mystic, using a Fakir dress as if to all Hindus he was a messenger of God. It was done with a purpose to win the hearts of all Hindus. Thus all Hindus were mesmerised by his saintly behaviour although he was not doing any activity of saint rather he kept himself busy with politics of its own way without taking into account the other's view to think for a better future. He had something in mind never disclosed to second man or discussed. It was he who had his own secret plan. He started his movement to bring Hindu-Muslim unity after all in Bengal, but it turned into communal violence or killing, and in the end division, where in the opportune moment Jinnah utilise the emotions of hatred for the formation of Pakistan actually for Punjabis, but the formation East Pakistan was a bonus point for him. Any political movement requires public participation that he did it through the movement of non-violence, but the result of the movement always remains uncertain. Here the results had turned the nation to divide in order to bring peace. But again had the two country India and Pakistan would remain in an atmosphere of peace, the relation might have been a set of example of brotherhood as if the division of house was carried out in between two brothers.

Gandhi never came forward to stop the declaration of 16 August either by talking with Muslim leaders nor by opposite force. Gandhi knows any talk in a moment of emotion of violence does not produce any result. He was to wait till the cool atmosphere prevailed. Violence is not in his ethics of law. So the question of force against force does not apply to Gandhi. He wanted peace in his inner mind, but he prefers to wait to bring back the atmosphere of peace to talk. Definitely he was interested with independence and Delhi chair, who should be the prime minister of the country, such a big country it is! Every moment is important for the country. He never wanted division, and so he was less interested with the question of divided India or undivided India. Under circumstances, he was under compulsion to agree to the question of the division of India as well as the division of Bengal. It was painful and sad to see the millions to death, and millions to leave their ancestral home and hearths.

He was living as a poor man, talking much like that of poor people; all activities were to increase his so-called saintly character to bring more people with him because no political party can be a strong force of voice without the support of the common people. He encouraged Hindu-Muslim unity directly and thought for a strong and happy India as we find in the description in our religious book called Ram Rajya where the ethics of administration was given in the religious book of Gita and Mahabharata. It should be the character of a leader to know the character of administration available in any of religious book or in any of administrative set-up of an ideal country. The division of India and Bengal in particular was a matter of concern to him. Although Indian's concern was the capital Delhi, still any state is not less important. That was why today the importance of India lies with the Indian people and the country. After all above ifs and but Gandhi is the **Father, Gandhi is the glory of India in every country and everywhere.**

If there was no Mohammad Ali Jinnah, would India and Pakistan have remained together? It is not true if there is no Muhammad Ali Jinnah, there would not be any Pakistan; rather the opposite is true, if there is no Gandhi, there would not be any Pakistan. Why? Gandhi had little foresightedness; Gandhi had a great vision to make Nehru the PM, after the independence of India, as he was the most etiquette person of India at that time. He was little careful in the case of united India or divided India, otherwise he would not agree to divide India, to kill millions and displaced millions till the last breath. If the contribution Abraham Lincoln is 100% in keeping the country of USA of black-white together by recognising the right of slaves, the contribution of Gandhi was little in keeping the country of India United. Gandhi might be pious in personal life but not so in any activity such as in the case of achieving the personal vision of making Nehru the PM.

In 1914 Jinnah represented congress at the discussion with British at London. At the Lucknow session at his speech the congress called him an ambassador of peace of Hindu- Muslim. But after 1930, he became anti-congress. He left India and used to live in UK, it is young Iqbal and Rahamat Ali, who compelled him to come back to India for the survival of Muslims. Had Gandhi thought for the poor and the countrymen, he should first think for economy of the country in cooperation with the British, when millions of the people are dying in famine in Bengal? He was neither a good lawyer nor a visionary with strong farsightedness. He could not stand at Bombay unlike Jinnah; he could not do well at South Africa, rather humiliated in travelling bus or in entering white restaurant. On the other hand Jinnah made a name in London in the British atmosphere and even he had been offered once with a place in the British parliament.

After coming back to India, he faced the same problem, no client for practicing law. He came under great lawyer Motilal Nehru. He was saved here and thought something high under the shadow of Nehru family. That was the reason why he was after Nehru, who became PM and Gandhi the Father of the Nation and as such the glory of Gandhi was spread in every country and everywhere. To bring Nehru in the chair of power, he designed a plan, how to reduce the importance of Calcutta, how to shift the power centre from Calcutta to Delhi, he designed how to downgrade the power of the leaders of Bengal, who were the only leaders in India, who could challenge Nehru. He designed the plan how to reduce the economy of Bengal by bringing unrest in Bengal and he designed the plan how to defame

Bengal leader by bringing the logic of misunderstanding between Hindus and Muslims, he designed how to bring ethics of religion in front by the act of movement of non-violence. All kinds of activity lead to one point a sort of misunderstanding between Hindu and Muslims leading to communal violence in order to reduce political power of Bengal leaders.

He designed the outline of the movement, a religious movement, what he called non-violence movement. The Hindu religion is based on two ethics, sacrifice and tolerance. He converted the virtue of tolerance into non-violence. He passed a resolution at the session of Nagpur to start the independence movement under the shadow of non-violence, such as civil disobedience movement in spite of the objection from Jinnah. He did not hear the Muslim voice; he came to Calcutta to start the movement only with Hindus. Muslims did not join the movement. Gandhi did not care for that because his intention was to bring some kind of violence against the British government first. For any movement people's participation is necessary. To bring the Hindu people in large number as Hindus are the majority of India, he thought to start the movement under the cover of the virtue of Hindu religion 'tolerance'. The other form of tolerance is nothing but 'non-violence'. His intension was first to start the movement with Hindus, and later with Hindu-Muslims. It was his belief that the Muslim views or Jinnah's view would change with the huge participation of Hindus. This was his first success to bring huge population although mainly Hindus to the street to protest against the British. According to him at that time, it was only Nehru, the right person to be thought of for the post of prime ministership of India after British. He discarded the opinion of other giant luminaries, C.R. Das of Bengal, Motilal Nehru of UP, or BalGanga Tilak of Maharashtra because his lookout was the participation of people in large number, because without people's participation, a movement could never be successful. So he was with non-violence movement.

At the extreme the Declaration of Direct Action on 16 August 1946, Gandhi did neither talk with any Muslim leader nor prepare any force to counter the act of violence. It was the inner voice of Gandhi not to disturb anybody when he was in full bloom of violence. Let the violence subsides on its own. The question of applying force does not arise because violence against violence is against his ethics of law. If nothing was understandable, then division was the natural phenomenon to subsidize the emotion of violence. The division of India will keep Jinnah away, and the division of Bengal will reduce the power of Bengal Hindu leaders no doubt when there might be nobody to challenge Nehru. All these are the facts of nature. Some facts of nature remain beyond the power of human beings to explain. Of course people differ in opinion. According to others, if Gandhi's vision was wide and farsighted, he could make India strong economically, because when people become happy economically, the narrowness of religion, communal hatred would go away as we could see in USA where people of different religion and people of different colour are living together and living happily.

Japanese boys went to United Kingdom after the devastation of Japan by atom bomb, they learn science, they converted the nuclear atomic energy into nuclear reactor and utilise this energy for the development of technology, and within fifteen years, Japan became an economic giant, whereas Gandhi remained busy with communal violence and fasting. He was looking for poor, giving messages of Gita and Mahabharata. He became a saint. According to many other Indians who differ with Gandhi in their opinion said differently. According to them, a saint cannot design the future of a nation. His narrow thinking had not only destroyed India, but also the future of Hindus in India. That was why even after division in India the Hindus are in fear of Muslims and everyone is thinking in near future the new Babur will arrive in India to establish the new Mughal empire, because the art of ruling exists in the blood of Muslims.

Sheikh Mujib Administration (1971–1975): The new Awami League government gave attention on relief, rehabilitation, and reconstruction of the economy and society because economic conditions remained as bad to worse. War criminals were treated by a general amnesty in 1973. The continuing economic deterioration brought a mounting civil disorder. Despite some improvement in the economic situation the progress was slow, and criticism of government policies became increasingly centred on Mujib. On 15 August 1975, Mujib, and most of his family, were assassinated by few mid-level army officers. The God-gifted fortunate daughter, Sheikh Hasina, was out of the country and escaped from the inhuman nature of slaughter. A new government, headed by former Mujib associate Khondaker Mostaq Ahmad, was formed. Let us see what happens next.

Two army uprisings on 3 November and 7 November 1975 led to a reorganised structure of power in Bangladesh. A state of emergency was declared to restore order and calm. Very soon Lieutenant General Ziaur Rahman took over the presidency in 1977. President Zia reinstated multi-party politics, introduced free markets, and founded the Bangladesh Nationalist Party (BNP). At that situation of multi-party politics, former Awami League was reorganised. Zia's rule of tenure ended when he was assassinated by elements of the military in 1981.

4 Role of Silent Patriot for the people of Bangladesh

[1]

29 August 1993 was the last day for Nikunja Bihari Goswami to take the last breath of his life in this world. Large streams of people gathered in his funeral procession. A large section of Hindus and Muslims expressed their sentiment of heart in remembering his sacrificing life.

Samsur Rahaman of Sylhet said, in the language of poet Rabindranath Tagore, 'Hey, Hero, your seat is empty today, who will fill up your seat', his service to the society will never die down. There are many poor, very poor, young students, boys and girls, who had completed their learning staying in his student home (Chatra-Bas), and established in life remaining in the struggling stream to survive in the newly formed Bangladesh would never forget him in their life. The veteran Goswami had established the hostel with public donation particularly due to the donation of a hostel premise and a house consisting of three rooms by the sons of Umesh Chandra Das of Sylhet.

Samsur Rahaman said he had the opportunity to get with him for a few hours only in Sylhet, but how he was charmed by his sweet talking full of love and vision of light is beyond his boundary to express. Goswami was a selfless social worker, a fighter of independence struggle against British, a follower of idealism of Gandhi although Gandhi left him alone by dividing the nation on the basis of religion for his inner motive where the mankind would never forgive him.

Goswami born in the land of Sylhet of present Bangladesh and he was determined not to leave his place even in the thrust of communal flare-up as that was very much evident at the time of partition. During the period of tension when people are leaving the country, he advised many of them not to leave the mother land because no land is superior to mother land, and his determination kept him in Sylhet till death. Although he was mentally hurt by seeing the destruction of houses, temples, and throwing away the ideals of Hindu goddess, yet he never had said that anybody hurtled him mentally because he kept human beings at the top of everything and allowed the human souls to cherish whatever way it desires to get peace and happiness in mind.

It was 1973; Indian Prime Minister Indira Gandhi felicitated him and Suhashini Das, another lifelong social worker of Sylhet in Red Ford at Delhi and requested him to stay at India or at Delhi, the rest of his life. But he could not accept her offer. It was because his inner mind is saying,'How you can leave the land of your birth as if you are promised to live here and die here?' The land of Sylhet is pure and pious to him than any other land of the world. Thus Sylhet was in his mind and the people of Sylhet in particular were in his heart. Thus the land of Delhi, however great, and however famous was nothing to him as his heart was with the land of Sylhet.

[The felicitation picture of N.B.Goswami, Suhasini Das by Indira Gandhi, at Delhi, cannot be shown here as the actual photo from the Charta-Bas could not be procured because of the absence of authority in charge.]

The foot note of Kamal Bhusan Roychowdhury. Men is mortal but still he could not find any reason why did this life long bachelor, strong and stable healthy strongman, full blown with brightness and beauty, left all of us suddenly as if not believable. However like the fact of life, the fact of death has to be accepted by each and everyone.

In 1971 East Pakistan had been liberated as an independent nation, calling it a secular nation of Bangladesh, that being liberated by the efforts of Indian army by the sacrifice of many regular army personal particularly of naval commanders and a large number of sailors due to the drowning of Indian fright INS*Khukuri* by the attack of Pakistani submarine, PNS*Hangar*, the nation that had been converted into Islamic state from secular nation in 1988 jeopardising the hopes and aspirations of many of non-Muslim people and made them a second-class citizen. Although Bangladesh have stabilised the rights of Muslims a step ahead, but it had brought an undeclared set-back in the progress of development as well as a question in sphere of security for Hindus. About three cores Hindu people have lost their hope for a better future and also lost their spirit of dedication for the growth and progress of the nation. In view of the expression of protest, some outside organisations of Bangladesh instigated the ordinary common Muslim citizens against the Hindus of Bangladesh in the name of Islam since 1989 to 1990 at different places of Bangladesh causing irreparable loss to many Hindus.

It was estimated that about 2,500 worship places and many houses were destroyed and burnt to ashes. Realising the huge destruction, and flashing of such news in the outside world, the government in power came out with a package of reconstruction and in few cases, few temples were reconstructed. The nation of Bangladesh becomes weak as the Hindus were denied the full right of equality. Had the American blacks were not taken into full confidence giving the full right of equality, America today would not be a superpower. But the government could not like to learn anything from that rather they prefer to confine themselves under the cult of religion forgetting the greater world of humanity of mankind.

6 December 1992, Babri Mazid was demolished in India for the cause of power politics, but in Bangladesh, 47 district out of 64 districts was affected by communal flare-up where the ordinary innocent Hindu people became the target. Three thousand six hundred temples, the worshipping places of ordinary Hindus were destroyed and the valuable materials of the temple were taken away, 28,000 houses, and 2,700 business centres were attacked, either burnt or demolished. Even women of different ages nearing 2,500 were humiliated and tortured. The loss was not less than 200 cores. The

regrettable thing was that most of such kind of activity had happened in front of law enforcing force, who was no other than the spectators. The government machinery was silent in all these affairs as if nothing had happened.

Two lakhs men and women Hindus became the resident in open air under the sky in the night of winter without any covering of cloth. Not the question of help, even not the sympathetic words from anybody found to be visible. People of this subcontinent had seen communal flare-up many times, but they have never seen the religious flare-up, whereby the people forget the minimum faith and dignity of humanity. They have seen the religious affinity, the culturally adverse Punjabis were became once the inseparable partner, the thrust of religious affinity took them to the madness of Calcutta killing, the killing of own origin, the origin of the same mother of Bengal, where the mother has given them two lessons to read, one for GITA and the other for QURAN. Bengal's origin has not gone to demolish Babri Mazid, Bengal's origin has not called for Calcutta killing, it was unknown power, the power of religion, and Bengalis were befooled by the power of intelligence of the man of politics.

The Bengalis of East Pakistan had realised it after a lapse of twenty-three years, the cry for religious affinity shattered and the liberation of Bangladesh came with the cry of my language, my mother's language 'BANGLA' and not URDU. But the incident of Babri Mazid again bringing back the religious affinity forgetting that who are those tortured victims, they are no other than the children of the same mother. The poison impinged in the minds of the Bengalis by the division of Bengal on the basis of religion is irreparable, the spirit of liberation of hundreds of Bangladesh might not be sufficient to remove the poison of hatred, otherwise, the same origin of mother Bengal could not dare to bring these hundred and thousands of mother and children to open sky in the winter time compelling the daring Nikunja Bihari Goswami, the all-time servant of society, who never thinks for self or self-prestige to move out in search of all-out effort with his volunteer force for the rescue in the supply of shelter, clothes, and food with special protection to babies with baby food for all those children of mother Bengal.

Was it not too much? The people could not thought out that they are no other than the Bengali, or Bengali of Bangladesh. It was because the religious hatred which was imposed in the mind-set of ordinary people by the non-Bengali people of India at the time of partition, Jinnah for the cause of Pakistan for Punjabis, and Gandhi with other northern leaders for the cause of shifting power from Bengal to Delhi and to destroy the influence of people like Suhrawardy, Netaji, C.R.Das, or Fazulal Haq, which was so much that could not be understood even after the formation of Bangladesh as if Bengalis are killing the people of their own. By the division of India and particularly of Bengal, the leaders were successful to capture the chair of Delhi for the people of their favourite. The hatred of Hindu-Muslim, the hatred between two religions became the guiding force for them to capture the power of Delhi, nowhere existed in the world.

They knew the flame of hatred will never die down, that was being seen even after sixty-five years in Mauzafferabad the communal flare-up with the eruption of violence, burning of houses, killing of men and children, and scene of dying of small kid in the cold of winter in camps under Manmuhan Sing government in India. But nothing had deter the leaders to finish the Hindu-Muslim hatred in finding an amicable solution for living together peacefully because the leaders of both the party were in the win-win situation to carry out the division and capture the respective power of chair. No matter with the common people as the people was dying at that time due to the prevailing situation of famine. The power of chair became dearer than the lives of human beings, though apparently one looks as a *saint* as well as a lawyer of Inner Temple, London, others a giant lawyer with of Inner Temple, London, but sword in hand. However, India got independence, and Jinnah succeeded to achieve Pakistan at the cost of Calcutta rioting of 16 August (1946), but Bengali of Bengal lost their united Bengal. Rich Bengal had turned into beggar's Bengal, this part or that part, the age-old love, friendship, and bond of attraction diminished to zero under the cloud of communal flare-up being infused in a tactical way taking the sentiment of religion by the intelligence of political leaders of non-Bengal regions. The intelligent Bengalis became a watch dog of fools. What a travesty of truth?

The Bengali people never could realise that every act of communal flare-up was with only one destination to destroy the political power centre of Calcutta, although the same was thought by British a little earlier due to which the capital was shifted from Calcutta to Delhi in 1911, that was why Gandhi had started his non-cooperation movement along with C. R. Das in 1930 at Calcutta to destroy the economic base of Bengal, Jinnah convinced Suhrawardy to start DIRECT ACTION DAY, 16 August 1946, at Calcutta instead of Punjab, the strongest military base of ML. Thus Bengal was destroyed, economy destroyed, Bengalis engaged in killing each other, but who has benefitted, the people of Northern India, the leaders of Northern India. The leaders of this Bengal such as C.R.Das, Netaji, and leaders of that Bengal Suhrawardy, Fazulal vanished from the scene in the course of time, but even now Bengalis could not succeed to discover who is friend and who is enemy.

On 16 December 1971, Lt. Gen. A.A. K.Niazi, CO of Pakistan army forces located in East Pakistan, signed the Instrument of Surrender and the nation of Bangladesh was finally established. Over 90,000 Pakistani troops surrendered to the Indian forces, making it the largest surrender since World War II. The new country changed its name to Bangladesh on 11 January 1972 and became a parliamentary democracy under a constitution. On 19 March Bangladesh signed a friendship treaty with India. Bangladesh sought admission in the UN with most voting in its favour, but China vetoed against as Pakistan was its key ally. The United States, also a key ally of Pakistan, was at last accorded recognition to Bangladesh. Accordingly in 1972 the Simla Agreement was signed between India and Pakistan. Pakistan recognised the independence of Bangladesh and India in exchange released more than 93,000 Pakistani POWs.

Nikunja Bihari Goswami had broken his silence on the thrust of breaking the temples and idols of Hindu god, on that day, he called all the Hindu leaders and said it was not the time to remain in silence, and it is time to protest, if you have to die, die with protest. The government became bound to respond to the roaring voice of the old aged fighter, the lifelong fighter against the British, fighter for the down-trodden, fighter for the human right. The roaring voice of a peace-loving man attracted many souls of Hindus as well as Muslims and slowly restored the peace.

Nikunja Bihari Goswami is no more today, but he would be remembered as the genius of the district of Sylhet and a great sacrificing Bengali of Bengal. He started his school life along with the teachings of scout training. A learning lesion was there:'Do every day something for the good of others'. He had started to follow the ideal of this lesion right from the beginning of his life.

A fight for social status for the Hindu people of Bangladesh, a new beginning of a new struggle had emerged in the mind-set of the veteran Goswami. A service centre was opened with lots of volunteers, and arrangements were made to supply the essential materials to the devastated Hindu families, who had lost everything in the communal flare-up. A peace committee with peace-loving people was formed, a newspaper 'Jana-Sakti' by name had been published from Sylhet to preach the ideals of brotherhood and attempts have been made to maintain an atmosphere of communal harmony utilising the writings of intelligent and progressive minded people of majority Muslim community. A working committee for service was formed, trained, and sent to different villages to enhance the development of villages in different sector, to help in the construction of the rest house for the protection of helpless children, to create learning centre for helpless women, and also to create student home for the poor students. His later life remained busy in doing all these well-fare works. His service to the society remained up to the last breadth of his life.

[Nikunja Behari Goswami]

[2]

Land Gift Movement: He involved himself in many other voluntary works. In 1964, he went to different places along with Vinoba Bhave to join the land gift movement. The mission of the movement was to persuade wealthy landowners to voluntarily give a percentage of their land to the landless people. Vinoba Bhave walked across India on foot to persuade landowners to give up a piece of their land. The landless labourers were being given a small plot of land on which they can settle, as well as grow some of their own food. The government accordingly also passed Bhoodan Acts, which generally stipulated that the beneficiary had no right to sell the land or use it for a non-agricultural purpose. The beneficiary should use the land for agricultural cultivation to secure his own and family's daily bread.

In 1964, he established a press 'Gita Press', but during the time of India-Pakistan War, his activity of Gita Press was not looked favourably and he was arrested and kept in jail for six months. Even after release from jail, he was kept confined in his student home for another two years.

In 1971, during the time of Bangladesh liberation war, the student home was attacked by the Pakistani army; he fled away to India and had taken shelter in Cachar. By the time he also had travelled to Tripura and the different places of Assam to see the conditions of the Bengali people of East Bengal, who were accommodated in different camps by the India government. However in 1972 after the liberation of Bangladesh, he returned to Bangladesh and had started again the well-fare activity in the service of the ordinary people. In 1973 he was facilitated by the Indian prime minister Indira Gandhi and requested to stay in India the rest of his life, but he returned to Bangladesh and had decided to serve the people in different well-fare works till death.

He found the depth of his social activity has increased tremendously, because Pakistani army had not only destroyed the Hindu houses, but also particularly destroyed the Temple of Worship of Hindus, burned the houses of worship, and destroyed Hindu goddess. So he engaged himself very much in the reconstruction process. After losing own living houses, losing every essential materials of the life process, the every Hindu family lost their self-respect in the society. Looking to the helpless condition of Hindu society, in 1975, he arranged a grand Hindu Bengali gathering at Narayanganj, near Dacca of Bangladesh under the patronage of late advocate Benoy Krishna Roy, making Mahanam brata Brahamchari as the president. However Sri Debash Chandra, the judge of supreme was made the chief guest. About four hundred representatives from all over Bangladesh came here to attend the gathering to decide the future of Hindus in Bangladesh. The representatives included the Hindu minister, deputy minister, government executives, and people of important Hindu leader, Hindu intellectuals, social workers, and Hindu religious leaders. The association of gathering had continued continuously for three days, discussed the various problems of Hindus, and finally came to the decision how to solve the problems. A committee was formed making Mahanambrata the president and advocate Binoy Krishna Roy, the general secretary, and Goswami himself the chief organising secretary. It was a non-political committee, but of universally Hindu religious organisation what was formed for doing good to the society.

Who is Mahanambrata? Mahanambrata began his schooling in a nearby Pathshala primary school in 1909 but gave up further study as he remained attached with the service of his father, who had lost his eyesight at that time. After the death of his father in 1922, his mind was in search of Almighty, he came to Angan, Faridpur to take sanyasa of Mahanam Sampradaya, the association dedicated for the propagation of teachings of Prabhu Jagadbandhu, who was considered an incarnation of Sri Chaitanya. Sripad Mahendrajee, the chief Sebait of Prabhu, brought Mahanambrata close to the Prabhu who he considered his guru. But Sripad Mahendraji, the then spiritual master of Mahanam Sampradaya, asked him because of his youth to return home, pass the matriculation examination first, and there after think of Sanyasa. His eagerness for ascetic life prompted him to sit for the matriculation examination in 1923, when he came out with success having obtained the district scholarship. Then he left home for good, came to Sri Angan, Faridpur, and was initiated into Sanyasa by Sripad Mahendraji with the name of Mahanambrata. But again Mahendraji asked him to take admission in Rajendra College, Faridpur, for further studies. After performing various duties of the Ashram and attending college classes, he had hardly any time for other studies, however despite all other difficulties, he continued study and he came out with a BA degree after appearing in BA examination in 1928 with honours in Sanskrit. He continued further study and finally obtained MA in Sanskrit from Calcutta University in 1931, keeping his name in the list of first class in first position.

Mahendraji as president of Mahanam Sampradaya received an invitation from the president of World Fellowship of Faiths, Chicago, USA, to send a delegate to its conferences. He sent Mahanambrata Brahmachari to represent the sampraday in the USA. Brahmachari obtained a PhD in Vaishnava Theology from the University of Chicago. While there he had many discussions with religious thinker such as Thomas Merton, who had showed his interest in learning Hinduism. However he advised him to explore his own Christian tradition and spiritual roots rather than learn more about Hinduism. In his later life, Merton acknowledged the role of Brahmachari in making him discover Catholicism.

After the partition of India and Pakistan in 1947, he remained in the then East Pakistan (now Bangladesh) in order to safeguard and protect the religion and culture of minority Hindus of his motherland. After the atrocities Hindus faced at the hand of the Pakistani army, he set up Devasthali Samskar Samity to raise funds for reconstruction of temples and reinstallation of deities. He tried his best in the reinstallation of temples at different places such as Dhaka, Narayangonj, Brahmanbaria, Sylhet, Sunamgonj, Faridpur, and Chattagram of Bangladesh. In 1975, in the gathering of Narayangonj, he founded the non-political Sanatan Dharma Mahamondal and became the president for the service of society.

There were three-fold activities for the committee: (1) the first and foremost principle of the committee was to preserve the sanctity of the Hindu religion avoiding the prejudices which was prevailing in the society since a long period. The religion is also polluted with the emergence of innumerable preachers, what should be rectified by bringing all the preachers under the shadow of one institution. (2) The religion must be made free from un-touch-ability and sartorial division of splitting and the religion must be brought under the shadow of one undivided Hindu religion. (3) The committee would look after the problems of Hindus of Bangladesh so that they can live in their motherland with full right, dignity, and respect performing their religious rituals and festivals as usual.

[3]

What are the teachings of Hindu religion? Western scholars regard Hinduism as a fusion or synthesis of various Indian cultures and traditions including the historical Vedic religion of Iron Age, the Harappa cultures and also including the traditions of Srimana of North-east India. Hinduism co-existed for several centuries with Buddhism, to finally gain the upper hand at all levels in the eighth century.

The Bhagavad Gita is one of the greatest religious spiritual book of Hindu religions. Its teaching has long been influencing the people not only of India but also of other places of the Earth. As sage Ved Vyasa is known for writing Mahabharata, as also of Gita being a part of it. In the epic Mahabharata, when cousin brothers Pandava and Kaurava are about to fight among themselves for the throne of Hastnapur, Pandava prince Arjuna find himself weak in the battleground on seeing his relatives, teachers, and friends in the opposition with full arms, Lord Krishna gave him advice what is known as 'Gita Gyan'.

Teachings of Bhagavd Gita show the path to the lost, answer to the confused and wisdom to all. The primary purpose of the Bhagavad Gita is to illuminate for all of humanity, the realisation of the true nature of divinity. What are the substances of realisation—we came to this world empty-handed. We have made everything here relations with love, and respect or love out of money, knowing well that we cannot take anything with us when we die. As everything would be left over here, so we should not do evil of anything when it comes to the question of our duty of respect, nor should we be really concerned about making as much of money and enjoyment as possible. We should be satisfied with what we have as everything would be left over here in this material world. Thus the teachings of Gita Gyan will bring peace of semblance in the mind-set of the oppressed Hindus in Bangladesh.

The Linking Unit: The Patriot, Nikunja Behari Goswami, a silent worker, who had sacrificed his life keeping the ideals of Gandhi in his mind. He was a Hindu, who was born as a Brahmin, and his forefathers were once the custodians of the Hindu religion, but today why has the religion reduced to a religion of destitute and poor? Let us discuss here the reasons with the title **'The Hindu Religion of Past and Present'**.

Let us see the Hindu religion of past and present: The Indus River Valley Civilisation is also a part of Hindu religion. The so-called Indus Valley civilisation (also known as the 'Harappan civilisation') is thought to have originated as early as 7000 BC and to have reached its height in between 2300 to 2000 BC, at which point it encompassed over 750,000 square miles and traded with Mesopotamia. In Indus Valley civilisations two major cities have been uncovered, Mohenjo-Daro and Harappa, which has given us the alternative name of Harappa culture. These cities housed about 40,000 people who enjoyed quite a high standard of living with sophisticated water systems.

Vedic period began by the decline of Indus Valley culture around 1,800 BC. It can be concluded that 'Vedic period' refers to the period when the Vedas were composed. What was Hinduism was a debatable subject quite a time. Firstly, in a strict sense there was no 'Hinduism' before modern times, although the sources of Hindu traditions are very ancient. Secondly, Hinduism is not a single religion but embraces many traditions. Thirdly, Hinduism has no definite starting point. The traditions which flow into Hinduism may go back several thousand years and some practitioners claim that the Hindu revelation is eternal.

However in Hinduism there is an emphasis on personal spirituality. Hinduism's history is closely linked with social and political developments, such as the rise and fall of different kingdoms and empires. The period of Hinduism is difficult to date with certainty; however, the following list presents a rough chronology.

Before 2000 BCE:	The Indus Valley civilisation
1500–500 BCE:	The Vedic period
500 BCE–500 CE:	The Epic, Puranic, and Classical Age
500 CE–1500 CE:	Medieval period
1500–1757 CE:	Pre-modern period + Islamic period (1100CE–1850 CE)
1757–1947 CE:	British period 1947 CE–the present: Independent India

The Epic, Puranic, and Classical Age (500 BCE–500 CE): This period, beginning the time of Buddha (400 BCE), saw the composition the Dharma Sutras and Shastras through the two Epics, the Mahabharata, and the Ramayana and subsequently the other Puranas. The famous Bhagavad Gita is part of the Mahabharata. The idea of dharma (law, duty, truth) which is central to Hinduism was expressed in a genre of texts known as Dharma Sutras and Shastras.

The Epic and Early Puranic period, starting from 200 BCE to 500 CE, saw the classical 'Golden Age' of Hinduism, which merges with the Gupta empire. These texts were composed in Sanskrit making a collection of poetic hymns used in the sacrificial rites was the criteria of Vedic priesthood. The Medieval period roughly 650 to 1100 CE forms the late Classical period or early Middle Ages in which classical Pauranic Hinduism was established. With the collapse of the Gupta empire, regional kingdoms developed which patronized different religions, such as Jagganatha in Puri in Orissa, the Shiva temple in Chidambaram in Tamilnadu, and the Shiva temple in Tanjavur, also in Tamilnadu. All of these temples had a major deity installed there and were centres of religious and political power.

There is a period of the emergence of poet-saints and gurus who were not only famous in religious literature of Sanskrit but also in vernacular languages, particularly Tamil. Most notable are the twelve Vaishnava Alvars (sixth to ninth centuries), Shankara (780–820) travelled widely, and who had established prominent seats of learning throughout India. He tried to re-establish the traditions of known Vedanta. The Vaishnava philosophers, Ramanuja (1017–1137), had propounded new theologies and similarly Shaivism was developed by philosophers such as Abhinavagupta (975–1025). These were the development of Hinduism.

The Pre-Modern period (1500–1757 CE): In India Muslim conquests took place between the eight and the fourteenth century, mainly in the north of India but also in the south to a little extent. It was noticeable that during Mughal period Islam was spreading from 1100 CE to 1750 CE under the patronage of Mughal rulers while in Hinduism there was increasing prominence of the bhakti movement, which has an identical phenomena found in present Bangladesh. In front of aggressive religion, Hinduism by virtue of its principle of Ahimsa (non-violence) and sacrifice, it increases its bhaki movement to win the heart of the people of other religion.

The development of Hindu traditions was widespread spreading widely in the south, the religion Islam was spreading on the other hand in the north making the Muslims a political force in India. The new religion of Islam had reached Indian shores around the eighth century, via traders plying the Arabian Sea and the Muslim armies gradually had conquered the northwest provinces. During this period, a further development in devotional religion (BHAKTI) took place. The tradition of good qualities transformed into the elements of bhakti, meditation, or yoga.

Thus it is seen that during the rule of Turkish sultanate, the Muslim religion spread towards Europe, but the spread of Islam was prevented by the Christian. There were nine crusades in between Muslims and Christians, Muslims could not enter Europe, but towards north of India, the Muslim religion spread without hindrance as the Hindus fought against Islam with the principle of BHAKTI. Thus the history says BHAKTI could not stop the spread of Islam, similarly Gandhi's movement of AHIMSA (non-violence), could not stop Muslims from rioting, as such Pakistan was formed. If the Hindus follow the same principle, a day might come when Hinduism will vanish from India.

British period (1757–1947 CE): At first, the British did not interfere with the religion and culture of the Indian people, allowing Hindus to practice their religion unimpeded. Later, however, missionaries arrived preaching Christianity.

[4]

Hindu reformers:

In the history it is recorded that Hinduism is the oldest religion although the record does not show how older it was. But it was a belief that Hinduism has come to this world about two thousand years before of Christianity. However in the modern world it was observed that Hinduism was suffering because of its lacking of preacher. It is believed that Hinduism evolved on its own and time to time God-like superman comes to this Earth to guide the people to follow the path in the life process to reach to the destiny of heaven. There were many superstation found to be seen in the religion of Hinduism. There was a time a 14-year-old girl became a widow as she was married with a high-class Brahmin of seventy years, forced to sacrifice her life along with the burning fire of her husband at the time of cremation, what was known as 'Sati-Dohoo'. Raja Ram Mohan Roy a reformer who was born on 1772 and died on

1833, fought throughout his life for the removal of such kind of prejudices. The nineteenth century was as such considered a century of reform. It was outlined as 'The Development of the Hindu Renaissance'. It was in this period of time there were many intellectuals had born in Bengal to bring a change in the society by removing the prejudices of the Hindu religion. Raja Ram Mohan Roy brought a radical change in the Hindu religion and founded the Brahmo Samaj.

Again during this period another man, Dayananda Sarasvati was preaching against the prejudices of Hindu religion. He advocated for original Vedic religion, the law of 'eternal law' or the law of Sanathan Dharma, what was followed by Arjya Samaj and what was called the Dharma of Hinduism. Both of these reformers tried their best in different way to get rid of the superstition of Hinduism. They were the pioneers in sowing the seeds of Indian nationalism. Since then there was sea change in the ideals and ethics of Hinduism that lead to Hindu missionary movement, the depth of which even spread to the West exceeding all corners of India.

The birth of giant figure Paramamahamsa Ramakrishna of nineteenth century and his teachings were in no way less than anybody else, who declared that Hinduism is the unity of all religions. His disciple **Vivekananda** went to Chicago in USA in 1893 to attend the international gathering where he established with logic that the source of all regions rests in ideals of Hinduism. Vivekananda was the man who brought the idea of United India, which was based on the unity of religion being of equal ideals. The people of India might have speak differently leaving in different distant region, but their way of thinking, their nature of custom, and nature of amusement are all alike and as such why they would not be thinking to live together and united.

These ideas were utilised by Gandhi (1869–1948), who was instrumental in bringing mass uprising by his mystic of Fakir dress to expose himself as a saint. The same ideals were utilised by Krishna who was succeeded to win the war for Pandavas while Gandhi had failed to win over Jinnah because his power of mystic was not as sharp as that of clever Krishna. Moreover he was not supported by any mighty force as a king was always protected by force. Gandhi failed to come out with a negotiated agreement of independence as his voice had no force. His large forces of Hindu volunteers were useless at the time of crisis, at the time of rioting in the open street, because Gandhi had made them useless by the teachings of non-violence. Gandhi had no alternative but to surrender to Jinnah. Country was partition,

Jinnah became dictator and Gandhi became a person to obey. Thus Gandhi humiliated the 80% strength of Hindu youth to 2% militant volunteer Muslim force of Jinnah. However he was succeeded to make Nehru the PM and also succeeded in keeping a place for himself as the future head of the nation under the cloud of humiliation and rioting and displacement of millions. But the extreme public bitterness was exposed by his assassination in 1948.

[5]

Independent India (1947 CE): Gandhi is no more; he was pious, his thinking was always for human beings as well as for humanity. But what he thought and what he did became the opposite. He thought for unity of India after independence, but it resulted with a divided India. As the partition happened on the basis of religion, it became a divided entity based on religion and created hatred between Hindus and Muslims. People blame Gandhi by saying Gandhi was a man of saint, but he sowed the seeds of hatred. The partition of India in 1947 resulted through the streams of blood shed although it had been started with 'non-violence'. Initially nationalistic thinking wanted to make India 'a Hindu country';'a Hindu Rashtra' of Hinduism however afterwards constitutionally made it a secular democratic country. Under the atmosphere of violence stray incidents of rioting continued here and there sometime, but a little bigger incident happened in 1992 by the downfall of Babri mosque in Ajodhya on political ground.

Hindus in the West: Under long suffering of political turmoil, Hindu movements find its root into the West, bringing wide migration of Hindus. It had raised the questions about the exact nature of Hindu identity. From the 1960s onwards, many Indians migrated to Britain and Northern America. In the late 1960s, transcendental meditation achieved worldwide popularity. Perhaps the most conspicuous was the Hare Krishna movement. They built many magnificent temples, and such has the Swami-narayan Temple in London. However happy they were in the West, their mind-set always turns them back to their roots in India.

Thus AHIMSA (non-violence) and *sacrifice* what are the two basic principles of Hinduism become the good ideals of mankind and spirituality of humanity but not good for neither the existence nor the expansion of Hinduism. Unless a drastic change is made in the basic ideals of Hinduism, the existence of Hinduism is bound to vanish. Gandhi's AHIMSA (non-violence) movement should be eye-open awakening for the survival of Hinduism in India if not anywhere else.

Chaitanya Vaishnavism (1486–1534): In the Eastern India particularly in Bengal, Hinduism in the form of Vaishnavism under the guidance of Chaitanya Mahaprabhu came to light. Vaishnavism meaning 'the worship of Vishnu'. He teaches the people of this world the process of Bhakti (love of God) and how to attain the perfection of life. Six other co-workers who were Rupa Goswani, Sanatana Goswami, Gopala Bhatta Goswami, Raghunatha Bhatta Goswami, Raghunatha dasa Goswami, and Jiva Goswami devoted themselves in spreading the process of Bhakti. Sixteenth century was the century of Chaitanya Dev.

Chaitanya Mahaprabhu was born as the second son of Jagannath Mishra and his wife Sachi Devi, who lived in the town of Dhaka Dakhhin, Srihatta, now Sylhet, Bangladesh. Srila Bhaktisiddhanta Sarasvati Thakura, who founded sixty-four Gaudiya Matha monasteries in India, Burma, and Europe getting grant from the then British government existed in India at that time. The teaching of Vaishnavism is to worship Vishnu (Krishna) and that by chanting God's names, the soul can be reawakened to original spiritual knowledge, so as to live peacefully in this life and to return to the spiritual realm, or Vaikuntha, the place of no anxiety, at the time of death.

In the twentieth century the spread of **Vaishnavism** is found to be prominent very much in USA. In 1965, at the age of 69, a spiritual master, A.C. Bhaktivedanta Swami Prabhupada went to Boston, USA, to spread Lord Krishna's message in the West. By 1966 Srila Prabhupada was living in New York City and had begun regular weekly lectures on Bhagavad-gita, along with public chanting sessions, kirtan, in Tompkins Square Park. On that year, he established a society, named as the International Society for Krishna Consciousness (ISKCON) in New York City, envisioning that soon there would be many centres around the world. That was the beginning of spreading the message of love through ISKON. In the period of 1966 to 1968, many more spiritual seekers became attracted to Krishna consciousness; as such he opened ISKCON temples in New York, Los Angeles, San Francisco, Seattle, Montreal, and Santa Fe, New Mexico. To spread the love to mankind in 1967, the first Ratha-yatra festival outside of India was held in San Francisco. This festival is now regularly held by members of ISKCON in cities around the world.

But in India on the other hand the growth of Islam was found to progress with quite a speed because of two factors of the principle of the religion: (1) the equality among all, rich or poor, big or small, all are equal in the eye of Allah because all have to do prayers in the same ground under similar way; and (2) the easy method of conversion, anybody can take up Islam at ease without any hindrance, but in necessity apply of force to create fear psychology if it helps in the conversion is not an offence.

By the tenth century Mahmud of Ghazni defeated the Hindu-Shahis, and thereby effectively removed the Hindu influence and also vanished the self-governance ruling of Buddhist across Central Asia, as well as the Punjab region. In most of the cases shrines and temples were destroyed. Facing danger to life many Buddhists had taken shelter in Tibet. In the fourteenth-century another war-lord Timur, the founder of the Timurid empire, came in Asia who destroyed Buddhist establishments in and around Western India and Central Asia.

The record of history shows that Hinduism based on AHIMSA (non-violence), sacrifice, Bhakti (love of God), and Vaishnavism is good for peaceful life and good to return to the spiritual realm, or Vaikuntha, but not for safety, protection and expansion of Hinduism in India. The study of the consciousness of soul might have succeeded a few individuals to reach to **Vaikuntha** but left the general mass in disarray, which lost the consciousness of strength and vigour.

The loss of consciousness of strength and vigour, of Hinduism as well as of Buddhism had made the mass people of Northern and Western India including Pakistan and the vast regions of Buddha, a sub-ordinate to Mughals, who lost mental strength to rule over the region. The teachings of Hinduism have eliminated the Hindus from the path of administration. It was the reason why did most of the rulers were Muslims in the vast Indian subcontinent starting from the end of Gupta period till the entry of British subtracting few Hindu kings who were also being under the command of Muslim rulers under the agreement of alliance. Is it not **Hinduism** that spoiled the mental strength and energy of Hindus, which had been diverted to the 'Consciousness of Soul towards Krishna Consciousness' to reach to the place of peace of 'Vaikuntha' keeping a greater mass of Hindus in distress and despair. Gandhi followed the teachings of Hinduism and Geeta, the principles of AHIMSA (non-violence) in the independence movement of India, but what was the result, misery for Hindus (millions displaced and killed), and happiness for Muslims(Islamic country).

ISKCON AND ITS FUNCTION: Now in the twentieth century under the endeavour of A.C. Bhaktivedanta Swami Prabhupada, ISKCON has emerged in NY, and today it is more American citizen who is in the enlightenment of 'Krishna consciousness'than the Indians. The reason would be clear if one looks to the history of the formation of United States of America reaching to the state of superpower and compare to the history of the formation of India reaching to the state of independence of India.

America achieved her independence only in the eighteenth century by declaring independence and fighting against British after a battle of long seven years with arms and ammunitions. They were divided in between black and white, but finally their leader Abraham Lincoln make them united and America became one nation one country. We the Indians achieved our independence in the twentieth century in 1947 although the struggle for independence had started in the nineteenth century after the formation of Indian National Congress (INC) in 1885 and that struggle was not with arms and ammunitions but with the ideals of Hinduism of AHIMSHA (non-violence). Indians were divided in between Hindus and Muslims, but finally Indian leader Mohandas KaramChand Gandhi made the country divided and thereby one nation of India became two nations with two ideologies.

In America, with the progress of time the difference between black and white began to diminish, the separate schools for blacks and whites abolished, the economy progressed, the country reached to the state of superpower, while in India even after the separation of a land for Muslims (Pakistan), a larger number of Muslims left in India declaring the country a secular democratic country. With the progress of time, the difference between Hindus and Muslims began to increase, the result was the outbreak of communal clashes time to time with the loss of property and lives, the economy went down till 1990, the country reaches to a lowest state of economic bankruptcy. The people lost faith on the basic principles of AHIMSHA (non-violence) as preached by Gandhi during independence or Bhakti (love of God) as preached by **Chaitanya Vaishnavism.** Finding little progress of Vaishnavism even in Bengal, the birth place of Chaitanya Mahaprabhu, an expeditious journey was under taken by Swami A.C. Bhaktivedanta in the city of NY of America in 1965 to open a new gate for the spread of **Vaishnavism,** which is now exposed as the study of the consciousness of soul or Krishna consciousness and where he was successful to come out with a society in the name as ISKCON in New York City. The speed with which it is spreading in USA, with that speed it is decreasing in India. Why?

America became a superpower; America gave its people the highest pleasure of life, pleasure in economy, pleasure in entertainment, and pleasure in all aspects of life. But peace of mind all the time does not rest on pleasure of life. The basic principle of **Vaishnavism** is to find peace of mind through the study of the consciousness of soul or Krishna consciousness. So a class of American people, who wants to forget the pain of pleasure, prefers to join ISKCON, where they believe chanting of God's names, or chanting of Krishna would lead them to Vaikuntha, the place of no anxiety, at the time of death.

But in India, the economic condition of the common people is just the reverse. Their pain of life is not due to the economic prosperity but due to economic scarcity. Their thinking is more in the search of earning money and not in the search of the consciousness of soul or Krishna consciousness. They find little time to practice **Vaishnavism** that was the reason why there is less number of people in the study of Chaitanya Vaishnavism and tends to practice under ISKCON in the search to reach to **Vaikuntha**.

Future of Hinduism: It is astonishing to hear that Hindu Dharma is not a Dharma; as such it is called Sanatan Dharma, a Dharma which is evolved by its own. The powerful man came in the history and modified the Dharma in its own way. It is a Dharma without a teacher. A child can learn something only when he or she goes to school and learn from teacher. Hindu Dharma has no teacher, as if it is the student, who has chosen his lesion, and he has chosen the method how to learn the lesion. It was the reason why Hindu Dharma could not give anything to mankind in respect of right to live, right to security of life, right to property, and right to peace except right to beg and right to sacrifice on the ground that nothing will be left for you after sometime. It also coincides with the quoting of Swami Vivekananda.

Quotes by Swami Vivekananda: 'As different streams, having their sources in different places, all mingle their water in the sea, so, O Lord, the different paths which men take through different tendencies, various though they appear, crooked or straight, all lead to Thee.'

It was framed by few people, who proclaimed himself the God, the supreme if supported by powerful king. It was Krishna who motivated Arjun to fight for right, later it was Buddha who changed the philosophy that was not to fight for right, but to follow the rule of AHIMSA, he was supported by King Asoka, Krishna became a god for the support of King Pandavas, similarly Buddha became god (Vishnu) for the support of King Asoka, then came Chaityna with Vaishnavism, love of god with AHIMSA and sacrifice, Chaityna or Nemai became god for the support of British, who were obliged to favour Hindus as they were afraid of Muslim power, then came Gandhi with AHIMSA (non-violence), but he could not be God as he was not supported by any mighty force. Similarly we are hearing everyday names of so many gurus, who proclaimed himself god.

This is not in other religion, they follow one person, Muslim follow Hazrat and Sariat Law, Christan follow Jesus, law of church, Hindus has no fix person, God comes time to time, and law changes time to time. If we believe Dharma is for people and people are not for Dharma, then Dharma must look to the future of disciples. Krishna has made the Dharma for Khatriya to fight for right but Buddha, Chaitinya, and later Gandhi has changed the Dharma to surrender (sacrifice) and follow AHINSA (non-violence) and had make it a Dharma of weak and distressed people if not cowered.

God has given you mind and strength. If you preach your mind by meditation, or by doing yoga, then why did you not preach your strength by the action of violence if necessary for the cause of right as done by Krishna?

Thus Hindu Dharma was sometime at the time of Krishna but something different at later time. It was because the god or guru of Hindu Dharma changes time to time and the philosophy of ethics changes. Is it time now to think for Hinduism to modify the ethics of law of Hinduism as it is modified time to time since its birth, to think how to protect the right to live, right to security of life, right to property, and right to peace if it is a Dharma for Hindus or mankind. In the period of Krishna it was the religion to protect your right by virtue of your strength, but subsequently it had been changed to tolerance and sacrifice. Since then the number of Hindu people are decreasing and also the Hindu territory. Is it that the common people are thinking; if a religion fails to protect its right, there is no point to keep attachment with that religion. In addition Hindu religion brings classification among the society such as Brahman, Khurtya, Baishya, or Sudra that might be another reason of discarding the religion.

Unless Hinduism fails to provide right to security to life and right to equality to every individuals, and above all right to unity, Hinduism has no future, its number will go on reducing, its territory will go on decreasing, the crying of tolerance would lead to non-violence as is done by Saint Gandhi. The preaching of non-violence would lead to a state of no return but to sacrifice as is done by Gandhi in the creation of Pakistan. Very soon a day would come to the Hindus of India not the question to any other country but to India itself, the place of birth of Hinduism, when nothing would be left off to sacrifice. By the greatest contribution of Gandhi (by the act of division of Bengal) and Nehru (by the act of Nehru-Liquate Pact) that state of sacrifice that 'nothing would be left off' had already arrived to West Bengal for the Hindus of Bengal. It is now better for Bengal to live with a single religion where Bengali can live like a tiger of Bengal not as a pussycat, and the Hindus of West Bengal would no longer live under the mercy of other leaders like Gandhi and Nehru in future, when no more Nehru-Liaquate Pact would be necessary for Bengal.

If we look to the last 1–1500 Christian era, it the Muslims who ruled India most of the time. It is surprising to see the population of Muslim was insignificant compare to Hindu population in India, but the administration was in the Muslim hands most of the time. In search of reason it could be simple to think that the Hindus were busy with religion and religious activity such as Puja, or worship, meditation, prayer, and yoga. As it is the teachings of Hinduism which is that 'know thy self' because after sometime nothing would be left in this world for you. Sacrifice and tolerance is best teachings for the mankind. As such it appears that Hindus either have no time nor Hindus are not interested with the administration. Everybody was in search of almighty to reach to Vaikuntha (the place of heaven) so that no one needs to return to this sinful earth. Is it not that the religion is self-centred and the teaching has made the Hindus selfish? How can it be a strong religion?

Muslims were interested with administration that is why in spite of their small number they were in administration in India most of the time in earlier time, their religion teaches them to live in unity, even pray to Almighty together as it is seen in the Namaz. The religion is concerned with community and not self-centered like Hindu religion. The unity has made the religion very strong. It might be one of the reason why did day by day the people are addicted towards Muslim religion and the Muslim population is increasing disproportionately with the expansion of territory turning it to the second highest in the Earth in the short span of time starting with AD 600 in compare to Christianity and not the question of Hinduism.

[6]

Early life of unknown Patriot: The Silent Patriot, Nikunja Bihari Goswai, had spent a better part of his life in Rangarkul Ashram and Chalibandar-UmeshChandra-Nirmala-Chatrabas (student home), as such let us have a historical record of these two centres.

Rangalkur-Ashram: (It is also called Kulawra Ragalkur Ashram.)

This unknown village boy was an inborn **Patriot**, the spirit of sacrifice, if compared, which could have superseded many political stalwarts. Even people like Gandhi, the present Father of the Nation of every human being of India might have been lacking in certain respect if compared. Such as Gandhi, how far superhuman being as he was, he too could not get away from the love of a married life. In 1883, at the age of 13, he had married Kasturbai Makhji, before seating for appearing matriculation examination. Mohandas and Kasturba had four children, all sons: Harilal, born in 1888; Manilal, born in 1892; Ramdas, born in 1897; and Devdas, born in 1900. But Goswami, the Patriot, remained unmarried throughout of his life keeping the desire in mind to serve the men of country who were in the distressed state of life.

Unlike Mukherjee, the president of India, the unknown **Patriot** was neither a naughty boy nor he had a mother with a commanding character as said by the president himself in the teachers' day celebration except the rituals of Hindu Pujas in Hindu house. Yet his self-desire, a desire of reading books, which he had earned by his own effort by getting the opportunity of working as a care taker of a library, where he could come in contact of many books, the reading of many of those books had widen his knowledge of thinking and the philosophy of sacrifice for others, and subsequently the call of national leaders had led him to the fight against the British, no matter if that had been non-violence, or disobeying of British law or what-not. As such he was a spirit of self-sacrifice dedicating the whole life for the service of others. At his youth he was a spirit of forceful volunteer to fulfil the desire of national leaders, whoever he was Netaji, or Gandhi, or any other, but again at his older age he was a spirit of a General in Command without uniform, to guide the left out Hindus of East Pakistan, who were passing their night and days in uncertainty, how to live alive, in the field of open air in open street, getting attacked any time on rioting in the shadow of dark, and burning of houses in the dark of night. It was he who stood like a pillar for the rightful demand of the tea-garden labourers and the downtrodden people for their means to survive.

At the end of his life, he had failed to find reasons in the greatness of Indian leaders, particularly with Gandhi, whose ideals had made him a lifelong volunteer of an Ashram, inspired him to sacrifice the life for the service of others. How he could believe that the 16 August 1946, the Direct Action Day, the day of killing, the non-stop killing without any resistant, was not a pre-planned conspiracy not only between Jinnah and Suhrawardy but also with silent approval of Gandhi because without an indirect approval of Gandhi such a massacre could not accomplished. Had it not, why did Gandhi not convince Jinnah by the bond of friendship as is visible in every public picture where Gandhi is embracing Jinnah as if they are the most intimate friend. It is not necessary to speak in every case to express the fact. A picture speaks itself. If the meaning of the picture was just the reverse, the meaning was not a bond of friendship, rather a display of inner rivalry, then Gandhi, the leader of more than 80% Indians, why had not risen the voice of protest, whatever way, think the best, but to stop the menace of threat or rioting.

But practically Gandhi did nothing, rather surrender to Jinnah with an excuse to the countrymen that partition had stopped the process of killing of Hindus by rioting. His lieutenant Petal and Nehru had sort out the modalities to complete the process of division. Nehru became the PM of India and space for Father of the Nation kept vacant.

The life of Patriot in Rangalkur Ashram: Rangalkur is the name of a village at the foot of a hill, a little away from the Kulawra Railway Junction of the district of Sylhet of Assam of undivided India, at present in Bangladesh. It became well-known for the existence of a Vidya Ashram, a centre of social work based on learning with labour and hence the name Vidya-Ashram, a centre testifying the history of the bygone days of last half century.

[Here is a picture of Gandhi with a poor villager dress with his favourite befooling machine Charkha but failed to display for the copyright restriction.]

The history goes back to 1921, the very known two brilliant students of the University of Dacca, Direndra Dasgupta and Purnendu Kishore Sengupta, had created the Vidya-Ashram at the Bank of River Padma. The Vidya-Ashram was established based on the ideals of Swami Vivekanda and Mahatma Gandhi. But the thunder of flooded water of Padma had washed away the Vidya-Ashram totally. In the year 1925, they had shifted the Ashram to Rangalkur. The then zaminder Binod Behari Dhar Chowdhury had donated more than 50 acre of land to Ashram. It was the volunteers of Ashram by dint of their labour and determination, they had converted the hilly jungles full of snake into a beautiful land of garden full of fruits and flower, daily vegetables, cows for milk, and centre of making clothes by Charkha, centre for manufacturing soap, oil, a learning centre of school, night school, and centre for free medicines.

1929, the Ashram performed its annual function, the Ashram was a voluntary centre of hundred boys at that time distributed into twenty voluntary working groups out of which ten groups remain engaged in the city in the distribution of self-made KHADDAR clothes to the public with a nominal prize. Since that time to bring discipline in the functioning of the Ashram, the working committee decided to keep the accounts of the Ashram, its performance and the aim of future works in public in every annual function. In the same year, the volunteers of Ashram had done a wonderful service in saving lives of a large number flood affected people. Besides the volunteers, there were thousands of floating volunteers working in the Ashram. In this short span of time the centre has managed to function with 1,200 Charkha machines for making clothes. It became a place of attraction for many young men to come to Ashram and work as volunteers. It became a resting place for political leaders to work and utilise the young volunteers for the service of the nation.

The unknown Patriot (Nikunja Bihari Goswami), passing the days at Srimangal knowing something of outer world through the library work under the grace of Behari Babu, who had brought for him the opportunity of library works at his tender age. After losing his mother at the age 13, he was under the shadow of father along with two other little brothers. But his burning desire to work for the country, had tempted him to leave the house at the age 17, in the dark of a night. After a long journey by walking, he had travelled by train without ticket with empty pocket and then a little distance with horse cart, and finally he reached the Ashram. But in Ashram he was blessed with the blessings of love of a saint-like personality of a person like Prunendu SenGupta. There was a destructive flood in 1929, in the district of Sylhet and Cachar, disrupting the communication system flooding the railway line running in between Karimganj-Kulawra and submerging the dwelling houses of large area. As a boy of Scout Nikunja Bihari Goswami came along with Md Ali Chowdhury, SDO of Maulavi-Bazar subdivision to help in the relief works. Here he came across with Prunendu SenGupta, two times elected member of the government of Assam and East Pakistan, who created the Kulawra Ashram. His dedicated life in the service of society attracted his mind and that service of attraction led him to take the decision to leave the house and go to Ashram to do a service to the society.

In this Vidya-Ashram, after taking training, many volunteers went to different places in different centres to work in the well fare servicing centre situated into the remote areas of villages. At that time, at the outset twenty-two centres were opened up in the district of Sylhet, Cahar, Dacca, and Chittagong like places. The service to the society does not remain limited to males only; it was also extended to women folks. Sarala Bala Devi and Jabeda Khatun Chowdhury of Sylhet district took the initiative to open centres for social welfare works. Other organisations such as Ram Krishna

Mission Servicing Centre also took the initiative for social works in different places.

In 1927, to control the anti-government activity, the Simon commission came to India. During that period, the woman leader Sarojini Naido came to Sunamganj to preside over a meeting, the gathering of young boys and girls, students, the workers was so much excited that it was impossible for the in-charge vice president Brojendra Narayan Chowdhury to control the gathering. The British Lord Cunningham came with a circular that to protest against the government, henceforth would be considered illegal and violator would be kept in jail for unlimited period. Protest against this draconian law started everywhere. In Sylhet, the Zaminder Brojendra Narayan Chowdhury of Pailgong and Basta Kumar Das of Sylhet took the responsibility of the protest movement. At that time Gandhi's non-cooperation movement just started. 7 May 1930, a group of forty volunteers under the leadership of Dhirendra Nath Das joined the non-cooperation movement breaking the 144 imposed by the government force. Under the command of the superintendent of police MrBomant and Jack of Assam Riffles killed all the volunteers by pushing the sharp knife of the Riffles to their breast.

In 1930, the Ashram decided to work for the people in consonance with the independent movement of the country. The British government brought much restriction over the Ashram as soon as the Ashram Working Committee announced its cooperation with independent movement of India. Many committee members were arrested, collection of money restricted as illegal, many such torture henceforth run over the Ashram. Apart from the Ashram works, he remain attached with the service of lower sections of the society, who are known as 'Namasudras' in a village area of Hakaluki-Hawor since 1935 to 1940. Later on, the servicing centres were extended from Beani-Bazar to Sri-mangle. Suspecting his activity anti-government, the British government kept Sri-Goswami in jail for more than six months. He was in the Ashram for a long time, afterwards he came to Sylhet and involved himself in the publication of news and press works apart from society works.

Gandhi returned from London without any positive result and he started the non-cooperation again. It was year 1932, the gravity of the movement was very much in Calcutta no doubt, but in this eastern region of India particularly in the district of Sylhet, it was in no way less than any regions of India. Thousands of volunteers and leaders get imprisoned. There was no space in the prison cell. Temporary prison cells were made by the British government to keep the mass in jail to give punishment. Brojendra Narayan Chowdhury, Bastana Kumar Das, Dharani Ranjan Paul, Khrud Chandra Deb, and many other men of importance imprisoned.

Among women workers leaders like Prvabati Dhar, Hiraprava Chowdhury, Sarala Bala Devi, and many others were imprisoned, and among young leaders like Aminur Rashid Chowdhury, Rathindra Nath Sen, Bomkash Das, and names of others are worth mentioning.

The movement did not remain limited to the district only, it spread to each and every sub-division. In MaulaviBazar sub-division, Dhrerendra Nath Dasgupta, Prunendu Kishore Sengupta, Abala Kanta Guha did not remain silent. They joined the non-cooperation movement with large number of volunteers to disrupt the functioning of the government. In Habiganj sub-division, Sibendra Chandra Biswas, Gopesh Biswas, and Suresh Biswas along with many others get imprisoned. In Karinganj sub-division, Suresh Chandra Deb, Suniti Bala Das, Sumath Nath Das, and many others came out in the street along with large mass of volunteers to dysfunction government, and in Sunamganj sub-division, Jatindra

Nath Bhadra, Chandra Biswas Das, and Lala Saradindu Dey devoted their strength and energy for the success of non-cooperation movement.

Vanu Bill Incident: It was a small place under Kamalganj Thana under Sylhet district, but the gravity of the incident was not small because issue of eviction has superseded all measure of human civilisation that touched the sentiment of British, the British who claim to be the most powerful and most civilised once, that compelled the British parliament to send member of parliament Miss Wilam Kinson and Krishna Menon to visit the spot of incident. The Manipuri peasants were under the obligation of paying taxes to the Zaminder of Pretim-Pasha. There was a long time dispute between the peasants and Zaminder with the Right of Demand. The peasants seek the help of district congress to settle the matter. Zaminder having being most powerful by the British policy of administration was not ready to settle the issue by giving the rights to the peasants. Undertaking the leadership the congress leader Prunendu Sengupta and Manipuri leaders Baikanta Sharma demanded the peasant's right by building a movement of non-cooperation through non-violence. The British government took a drastic step in favour of Zaminder to demolish the houses of peasants miles after miles with the help of elephants. The movement took a serious turn, thousands of people came in front to protest and get imprisoned. The news spread to Calcutta and then to London and finally to British parliament. The matter was settled through an agreement. The peasants' *right* was established at that time in the district of Sylhet.

Calcutta was in the West Bengal, but Sylhet was in East Bengal what was equally volatile and more volatile than Dacca, the prime city of East Bengal because it was the district through which the whole of Easter India was linked with the main land of India. In view of communication point of view this was a very important district and the government always keep sufficient force to keep it under control. It was 1933, a young revolutionary of the district Sylhet Ashit Bhattacherjee was hanged and the other associates' Biraj Madhev Dey, Gouranga Saha, and Guprendra Roy all were sent to Andaman for life long imprisonment because they were found to be guilty in a case of postal robbery of Itakhula. The whole district was immersed in the cloud of shock. The young blood of youths was in a dilemma, whether to go for violence or non-violence against British government.

In 1937, Congress President Pandit Jawaharlal Nehru came to Sylhet; it had brought enlightenment among the labourers of tea gardens. He had established a labour organisation centring Rangalkur Ashram and its leadership was entrusted with Prunendu Kishore Dasgupta. In the later course of time, it became the largest labour organisation in East Bengal and later East Pakistan. The total member was more than forty thousand. Congress worker Bastanta Das, who became the labour minister in East Pakistan Ministry after the formation of Pakistan, formulated a labour law for tea workers by dint of which the status of life of tea-garden labourers had been improved considerably.

In 1937, the Ashram Committee decided to invite the president of congress committee Netaji Subhash Chandra Bose as chief guest to their annual function. The president of the Ashram Dhrendra Nath Dasgupta was a close friend of Netaji, who called him Dhrenda; as such the invitation was accepted cordially. Dr Prafulla Chandra Ghosh, who became the chief minister of West Bengal later on, came here to become the President of the function. There were many other well-known persons such as Dr Nripendra Nath Bose, Labanya Lata Chanda, and many others were present in the meeting. The nearest rail station of Rangalkur was Kulawra. At that time the minimum facility of lighting a station by electricity has not reached to the station, but even then the station was illuminated by other sources of light. The news of Netaji's arrival has brought an enlighten brightness in the hearts of everyone. The people of Rangalkur, Kulawra, and the adjacent villages flock together in the Kulawra station to have a glimpse of their favourite leader Netaji.

It was rainy season; even then people nearing ten thousand accumulated to greet Netaji, well coming Netaji with laud welcoming voice standing on the road side when his car passes through the tea garden of Gajipur to reach to Rangalkur Ashram. It was beyond description to describe the poor condition of Ashram, except the two tin-roofed houses, all were made of other shelters roofed with Dry-Grass (Chan). Nearing one thousand people were accommodated in the Ashram on that night and entertained with food and shelter. It was raining and raining, there was little light but after reaching Ashram Netaji adjusted himself with all odds as if he was one of the volunteers of Ashram. The meeting was held even in the dark of night and cloudy weather till deed of night, which was a historic record of this Ashram.

The war declared in 1939, what was going on in full swing, Burma was attacked by Japan, and the British soldiers were retreating from Burma towards India, thousands and thousands of people are moving towards

India to the Eastern part of India crossing thousands of miles on foot. The Japanese attack was suspecting over Calcutta, the reports of stray incidents of bombing was also coming, as such people are preferring to go to interior places, crossing village to village avoiding big cities like Silchar or Calcutta out of fear of war. Nikanju Bihar Goswami organised relief centres in different areas and different places. Goswami organised few hundred volunteers to give day and night services. Everyday service for five hundred to a thousand people was arranged in a disciplined way of system. Supply of medicine, milk to babies and small children, Khichuree (mixed Dal-Rice), dal, rice, and dry food such as Chira, etc., to hungriest, were supplied free of cost. Hindus and Muslims all together helped the relief works due to the appeal of Goswami. A good number of women volunteers also worked in different relief centres of Kulawra. Goswami remained constant busy in relief works for more than six months. People were charmed on seeing the wonderful service of Goswami.

Chalibandar-Nirmala: Student home came into existence in the month of January 1961 due to the donation of a residential house by the sons of Umesh Chandra and Nirmala Bala Devi making Nikunja Behari Goswami as the trustee. However, the student home is named in the name of their parents. The beginning was started only with four students and that too without charging anything of fees. However, with the increase of space the number of students very soon increases to twenty-five with a very nominal charge of Rupees thirty per month.

At the beginning few professors were also accommodated along with students, however, their presence had brought a good academic atmosphere of learning whereby students were benefited very much. The names of few of them who were remembered are Anil Mitra, Susendra Paul, Biswanath Dey, Kalachand Roy, and Bimal Dey. However, by virtue of their talent, Anil Mitra and Bimal Dey have been subsequently promoted to the post of principal to propagate the stream of education. They were not only active in the field of academic progress but also at the same time they kept themselves in the service of society in the need of eventuality. They were all suffered under Pak army in 1971. The day 30 April 1971 was a painful memorable day to them as Kalachand Roy and his wife Manju Roy, their colleague was brutally killed by the Pakistan army on that day. Professor Roy was on his way to join Rangpur College as head of the Depart of Chemistry with his family. They left behind a girl of three and half years old and a son of one and half years old, however Professor of Mathematics of Rangpur College Reyaz uddin and his wife took the responsibility of these two young tads showing the example of loves of humanity in front of slaughter of Pak army.

It was 25 March 1971, Pakistani army torture began throughout East Pakistan to curtail the movement started by Bangobhandu Maujibor Rahaman. It was the Hindu Bengalis, who were the primary target. Finding no other alternative all the Hindu population irrespective of old-young, man-woman, boys or girls was compelled to leave the country to save lives. The Chali-banderStudent Home was attacked; each and every material of the student home was taken away. All the inmates fled away. The Patriot Goswami had taken shelter in a secret house. But depth of army searching increased so much that it was impossible to remain hiding. In one dead of night, Goswami had taken the journey on foot, a distance of 35 miles, to cross over to Karimganj, the border town of Assam of India.

16 December 1971, Bangladesh came into being, by January 1972, Patriot Goswami returned to Bangladesh. His Chali-bander Student Home and Gita Press have been totally destroyed. House structure destroyed, nothing of materials left behind. Out of nothing Patriot Goswami started the house construction himself to find a place of

shelter. The nation faced a humanitarian tragedy. How to solve the immense human problem, where thousands and thousands of men, women, children, father, mother, women who lost their husbands in the fight against Pak army, while the new government is just formed and yet to formulate its function. Patriot Goswami along with few other social workers met together in the house of well-known social worker Krishna Kumar Palchoudhury and formulated the work proposal to give shelter to many of them in few houses.

Chatra-Bas and Massima: In 1961, Suhashini Das, very popularly known as **Massima** was an invitee in the day of inauguration of the Chali-banderStudent Home named as **Umesh Chandra and Nirmala Chatra-Bas** and later on she became the all-time protector of the Chatra-Bas and not only that the big building on the northern side which was constructed later on was completely constructed under the care of Sri Pramatha Das of Panchha-Khanda and Suhashini Das of Sylhet both in finance as well as in construction work. In 1962, Vinoba Bhave, a follower of Gandhi came to the Chatra-Bas, and made a programme to visit the different districts of East Pakistan on foot to carry out his 'land gift movement' to acquire land out of gift donated by rich landowner, which was arranged systematically to give to the landless persons or peasants, the social worker Sri Prnendu SenGupta, Goswami, and Massima all together went out for a long sixteen days'journey in different districts, in districts of Dinajpur, Rangpur, village to village, carrying out meetings after meetings to fulfil the task of the mission. It was a work, a dedicated works for the service of the poor at the cost of physical onslaught and nothing else gave them an immense pleasure of satisfaction.

War between India andPakistan started 6 July 1965, Massima was in charge of Rangalkul Ashram, but here in student home, the living life of Umesh Chandra - Chatra-Bas, Sri Goswami, the social worker, a true worker of the nation, was arrested by the Pak army and taken him to jail and tortured him inhumanly out of hatred because he was renown as a Hindu social worker. It was spread in the air that Goswami is an Indian spy, who is supplying secret information of East Pakistan to the Indian government. Goswami became the target of everyday torture. After ten days, many more reliable Hindu people began to arrive in the jail. Gupi Krishna Chowdhury, Bimalendu Das (Sadhu Babu), Bimalankshu SenGupta (PachuBabu) of Sylhet, Banamali Ghosh of MauliviBazar, Ajit Chowdhury of SriMangal, Mana Muhan Chowdhury of Sunamganj, Pramatha Das of

PanchhaKhand, and many others were arrested and brought to jail. The war was ended after seven days, but the arrested peoples were kept in jail for more than six months. After the release from jail, Goswami engaged more in press work in the publication of paper news and the Chatra-Bas was left with SuhasiniDas (Massima).

The service of social work was to help the poor Hindus, who were displacing here and there for the torture of Pak army as well as for communal tension and to restore an atmosphere of peace through the preaching of religion in order to bring a climate of peace and stability. In 1969, Goswami along with forty Hindu religious people under the leadership of old revolutionary leader Trailakya Nath Chakraborty meet with the Governor-General Munam Khan of East Pakistan and put forward the various problem of the Hindu people of Pakistan, the right of enemy property, the destruction of Hindu temples, etc., but the result was nothing but a negative hope and despair.

Massima devoted her full energy in **Umesh Chandra Charta-Bas**, born in the month of August, the month on which India wins freedom 14 August 1947, where SuhasiniDas (Massima) has to work for the down trodden people, the year of her birth was 1915. She born in a village, a village which has a Thana, a post office and a medical service centre, the village has no school for girls, no road, and no means of communication centre except boat. The village girls never think of education as the guardians are also not interested to send the girl to school by boat to a long distance to Sylhet. If anybody wishes to learn something she has to walk 22 miles to reach to Sylhet, the district town. When she was 6 years old, two socially devoted persons, Sri Hriday Chowdhury and Bipin Chowdhury, came forward to establish a girl school in the village. Initially Mrs Sushila Devi, wife of Bipin Chowdhury became the teacher and requested the guardians by going door to door to send their girls to the school. Massima got the opportunity to go to school. She used to go to school on foot during dry season but on winter season, she used to go by boat where a boatman used to pick up the student from each house. This was how Suhasini Das had started her journey of life. She passed about fifty years of her life along with Nikunja Bihari Goswami in the activity of social works for the service of the countrymen.

To say a little of her life, it should be said that she was married at the age of 14, because early marriage was the norms of the day. She was now living in Jamtala area of the district town Sylhet where her husband was the owner of Kuti-ChandPress, the second largest press of Sylhet district. Although Sylhet was a district town but the town has no electricity, no communication vehicle such as Rishkaw or Motor cars except horse-car. At that time she heard of meetings going on in town area where people are asking for independence. This tempted her to learn more as her school education was stopped after marriage. One opportunity came to her as soon as she got familiar with an educated lady Sarju by name, who used to go house to house to coach the students. She began to learn English and Bengali both from Sarju. Slowly she learns how to read newspaper or other literature and that enlighten her knowledge to know about the country, the people, and what is about independence or independence movement.

In 1938, she had the opportunity to visit Calcutta with her husband where she had seen Victoria Memorial, Temple of Pareshnath, College Street, Belor Moth, and Nabadeep. The beautiful city of Calcutta what was built by British has changed her outlook and had brought a new hope of building a new zone of beauty in Eastern India centring Sylhet. This region has everything what the regions of Calcutta have not. It has plenty of agricultural land, land for tea garden, plenty of fresh water for any good use, it has hills, river, and even sea not far away. The development of the region will bring a place of heaven on Earth. She kept her imaginary thought under the shadow of her mind. At Calcutta one day at that time she could see a procession on the street carrying a dead body of a famous leader who was Jatindra Mohan Sengupta, where thousands and thousands of young boys and girls have participated and petals of flower are spreading over the dead body to show their last respect. She was astonished on seeing the respect of ordinary people for a leader. In disguise of her mind, it had created a desire in her inner mind-set to work for the society in her later life.

Very soon from the paper news, she came to know that the movement for independence had started in Bengal in different cities and towns, the people are in the streets of Calcutta, who were against the government works, the movement was civil disobedience movement, its impact has also reached to Sylhet district. The news was Ashit Bhattacherjee of Sylhet hanged for anti-government activity. It news had brought a climate of sorrow in every house when the people left to eat anything. The souls of Sylhet who were working for the independence of India rested in Brojendra Narayan Chowdhury, Basanta Das, Prudendu Kishore SenGupta, and Abalakanta Gupta at the first row followed by Satis Roy, Nikaunja Bihari

Goswami, Biresh Mitra, Surjya Moni Deb, and many others.

In 1939, Suhasini Das (Massima) became mother blessed by a daughter Nilema. She was growing under the shadow of her father Kumud Chandra Das. But a sudden storm of dark cloud came and makes her father sick, sick with fever, dangerous fever. Local doctors failed to cure him, Suhasini Das took him to Calcutta for further treatment but every attempt succeeded without any positive result and finally he had to succumb to take the last breath. Suhasini Das became widow at the age of 20.

Days of sorrow as if never tend to end, a new beginning starts with the memory of sorrowful days. Now she came across with the news of Mahila Samallen at Sarada Hall under the presidency of Ashalata Sen. However on the third day with the patronage of Madhuri Das of Jamtala both of them went to the women gathering. On hearing the speeches of Ashalata Sen, Saralabala Deb, Jabeda Khatun Chowdhury, and Naresh Nandini, she realised that there is lot of work left in life to do before passing the every moment in the sea of sorrow. The very feature what had stricken her very much was that after finishing their speech everybody sat together to make thread with BOX-CHARKHA. It created a new life in her mind. She immediately decided to start the work of thread making the arrangement at her home immediately. Accordingly the next day she made the arrangement to bring Box-Charkha from Bandore Bazaar. She got her initial training from Naresh Nandini. Thus a new life henceforth had started in her life. Very soon her house became a big thread making centre where number of Bengali and Manipuri girls used to come in groups with Charkha, to make thread. As it earns the reputation of a learning centre, she also has to go to other interior regions to give training. Thus her leisure life was transformed into a very busy learning engagement.

What was the under-lining meaning of Charkha—what had been understood by the different philosophers that are stated as such

(i) The spinning wheel enables us to identify ourselves with cores. The millionaires can imagine that money can bring for them anything in the world, but in reality it is not so. At any moment, the summon of death might have come and snuff them out forever. Losing one's life does not take a long time. One has to learn how to efface self or how to forget the vanity of ego voluntarily and learn the art of sacrifice in order to find God. The spinning wheel rules out exclusiveness. It stands for all-inclusiveness. It stands for all including the poorest. It therefore requires for everybody to be humble and to cast away pride completely.

(ii) Revival of the cottage industry, the only cottage industry that will remove the growing poverty. When one industry would brighten with glory and wealth, then all the other industries would follow the path of progress. The spinning of wheel is the foundation to build a network of economy to establish a stable and beautiful village and as such a beautiful life, when all other activities would revolve like wheel centred round.

(iii)The message of the spinning wheel is much wider than its circumference. Its message is one of simplicity, service of mankind, living so as not to hurt others, creating an indissoluble bond between the rich and the poor, capital and labour, the prince and the peasant, that enlarges the message of unity to all.

Political life of SuhasiniDas was not with politics but with the service of people, although the 1942 'Do or Die' Movement brought almost all men and women to the street and maximum volunteers to jail, and passed few days or few months in jail under the clash of food and shelter but the real tragedy started in her life after

1946, when the whole movement turned towards Hindu-Muslim clash of hatred. Her service of providing shelter to the homeless, food to hungry, help to the victims of flood, or storms and help to the very poor guardian-less child or old, shelter-less women were in search, how to provide food and shelter and where to provide.

India was divided and Pakistan was formed on 14 August 1947, population transfer continued in large-scale normal life was shattered, Bengali as a nation of religion became the question of the day and Bengali as a nation of Bengalis submerged although it get surfaced again after a lapse of about twenty-three years later when it emerges as a nation of Bangladesh in 1971. SuhasiniDas took the Kustarba-Gram-Sava Training and join Rangarkul Ashram in 1950 permanently. At the beginning her regular work was to go to houses of tea-garden labours and advise them how to keep the health hygienic, and how to keep them in touch with education. Thus Suhasini Das became a near and dear one to all the tea-garden labours and the people of nearby areas. Prunendu Kishore SenGupta was the president of the Ashram and Nikunja Bihari Goswami was in charge of the Ashram.

In 1954 onwards political activity of Prunendu SenGupta and Goswami was increased because SenGupta was elected from Kulawra constituency as a congress candidate and Goswami became very much busy with the press and paper 'JanaSakhti' and indirectly the responsibility of the Ashram as well as Chatra-Bas rested with SuhasiniDas.

[Suhasini Das is in the picture]

The critical period of Ashram 1955 to 1971: Prunendu Kishore SenGupta, NikunjaBihari Goswami, Durgesh Deb all congress man pass their time along with tea-garden labours, in their working centre where SuhasiniDas also accompany them time to time but that had created a bad atmosphere. The Muslim league workers did not like it because if it continues, Congress might have increased its vote bank which would go against the interest of the country. The Muslim league raised its voice against the link between Congress and tea-garden Labour union. Finding opportunity Pakistan government immediately bands the labour union. It also affected Rangarkul Ashram; the Pakistan government ceased the Fund of the union, Mike, and the car. It was a period of scarcity; SuhasiniDas was passing her days in anxiety. She started making of thread, and oil production in the Ashram itself, she even asked the tea-garden labours to bring their children in Rangalkur Ashram School. Somehow she maintained expenditure of the Ashram with much more difficulty. In 1958, the AirMarshell Auab Khan imposed military rule in East Pakistan because of political ground. Congress was declared illegal, Labour Union broken, and working centre was closed under lock. Fund, Mike, and car of the union, etc., were confiscated. Life under military rule became exhausted. It became impossible to continue with the servicing activity of the Ashram and not to think of any kind of political activity. Prunendu Babu preferred to stay at a distance and similarly Goswami remain at Sylhet with his JanaSakthi.

In 1965, there was a sea-storm in the coastal region of Chittagong, there was loss of life and property of many people and many families. SuhasiniDas went there along with her force of volunteers. NikujaBihari Goswami also went there, besides many other voluntary organisations who were working there to help the affected families. SuhasiniDas brought a group of boys severely affected to the Rangalkur Ashram; many of the boys are now established and had made their space in the society.

The war of 1965 war between India and Pakistan came to an end by agreeing to a peace agreement in between Indian Prime Minister LalBhadur Shastri and military ruler Ayub Khan at Tashkent under the initiative of Russia. The war continued for seven days, but many properties of Hindus were confiscated by the military rulers and declared them as enemy property which had not been solved for years together and not even today. In Sylhet district itself more than 70,000 Hindu families were affected by the act. This was not only the destruction of Bengali Hindus but the destruction of Bengalis and the nation of Bengal.

7 March 1971, Mujibor Bahaman declared independence for East Pakistan in front of lakhs and lakhs of the people of East Pakistan at Dacca. On the one hand fight for liberation started from 25 March 1971 and on the other hand fight for killing of innocent students, youths, intellectuals, and political leaders with specific target to Hindus continued and girls were kidnapped and taken to dark places. Everywhere people of Hindus or Muslims all leaving the country and moving towards India to save life. SuhasiniDas was passing her days and nights at Rankalkur Ashram in anxiety along with twelve parentless children, one very poor woman, and two maids. News coming that Benod Chowdhury, Hajir Mea of Rangalkur, Aminur Rasid Chowdhury, a man of immense of Sylhet were arrested and they were being tortured inhumanly, nearby Joy-Chandi village was burnt where fourteen people were shot dead by Pak army, all relative of Jamtala left for India, NikunjaBihari Goswami fled to India, Prunendu Kishore SenGupta preferred to hide in remote area for safety. One day at dead of night Pak army came to Ashram, and asked,'Open the door, we will search the house.' Keeping courage in heart SuhasiniDas replied search cannot be done at two o'clock night let it be done in the morning. Under such a strain of danger, she passed her days in the Ashram at that time.

16 December 1971, Pakistan army chief Lieutenant General A. A. K.Niazi surrendered to Indian army chief Lieutenant General Jagit Singh Aurora, joint commander of India and Bangladesh forces and the new nation Bangladesh came into existence. The feeling of hatred between Hindus and Muslim has reduced to the lowest point as the liberation of Bangladesh become possible because of India and the survival of more than 90 lakhs displaced people were possible because of providing them sheltered and food mostly by the voluntary service of the Hindu people and specifically by the Bengali Hindus because of the kith and kin of the language of mother tongue. In the prevailing suitable atmosphere Mrs Sulekha Roychoudhury, who is no more, who was the daughter of the sister of SuhasiniDas, who was like others had taken shelter in the streets of refugee camp of Tripura of India in 1971, due to Pak army onslaught but married with another street boy at that time, who is no other than the author of the book, expressed her desire to visit Rangkul Ashram and accordingly the arrangement was made. It was a memorable visit where it is known that the room where both the persons passed the night was the room where Netaji passed his stormy night in 1938. What a coincident, a moment of joy and satisfaction. She passed a part of her life in Rangkar

Ashram serving as an active volunteer before coming to India.

In 1973, NikunjaBihari Goswami and SuhasiniDas both were facilitated by Indian Prime Minister Indira Gandhi at Delhi. President V.V.Giri told them to send the names of all heroes who sacrificed their lives in Indian independence to fight against the British. Names of four hundred heroes were listed, but before completion of the work, Mujibur Rahman was assassinated. However, under volatile situation, Massima kept her activity confine in Ashram and Chtra-Bas keeping her vigilance in both places. Again on 17 November 1978, Prunendu Kishore SenGupta, the creator of the Ashram left the world forever. On the same day one hour before his death, a meeting was held with all the members of the Ashram including with large number of well-wishers, Prunendu Kishore SenGupta handed over the full responsibility over SuhasiniDas and makes her the permanent president.

SuhasiniDas could not pass a regular family life like others although she had a daughter, but after marriage she is staying in London, as such to fulfil the wish of her daughter she had undertaken a journey to England on 12 July 1982, via Moscow accompanied with Goswami. She reached to Plymouth of England, a city very near to sea. It is a country where people of all nations prefer to visit as such it gives the visitor opportunity to see people of many nations with diverse fashion and dress. In the period of three months' time, they visited the burial place of Raja Rammohan Roy at Bristol and British museum. In Birmingham, they attended a Hindu festival, the birthday celebration of Hindu god Krishna. Besides they visited many houses of Indians. In an occasion they were felicitated by the students of Indian origin giving money for grant for the service of poor in Bangladesh. Taking the memory of their journey they returned to the Ashram and confine their activity in Rangalkur and Chitra-Bas as the political atmosphere is changing very rapidly with the change of government. Very often during the performance of occasion like Pujas she used to visit school.

[A picture of Suhasini Das was here along with students, teachers, well-wishers, friends, and relatives in the event of Saraswati Puja in a school at Sylhet. Due to copyright restriction, the picture could not be shown here.]

[A pictorial memory of Suhasini Das.]

ISLAM in Indian subcontinent: Religion has done a vital role in the performance of daily works, social activity, in the process of study, or religious study, in the nature of employment, and political attachment by dint of which the Indian political leaders have divided the country based on religion, as such the study of religion in isolation may not be an unwanted topic in content of the book as discussed here. It presented here as a synopsis of the major religion of the Indian subcontinent, that is outlined here for the facts of history.

Today, two of the most populous Muslim countries in the world are Pakistan and India occupying the Indian subcontinent. Islam has had an incredible and lasting impact on the region in all aspects of life. However, even though centuries of Muslim rule by different empires and dynasties, Hinduism and other religions remain as important aspects of the subcontinent. The reasons for Muslim invasion into the subcontinent were justified by many factors. It is found a record of history that a ship filled with daughters of Muslim traders who were trading in Sri Lanka was attacked by pirates from Sindh (what is now Pakistan) who captured and enslaved the women. Seeking to liberate the women and punish the pirates, an expedition was sent out in 710, led by Muhammad bin Qasim, an Arab from the city of Ta'if.

Bin Qasim's military expedition into this distant and remote land was made successful due to the prevailing social issues in India. The caste system, which originated from Hindu belief, divided society into different social classes. Those on top led wealthy, comfortable lives, while those on the bottom (particularly untouchables) were seen as the scourge of society, similarly, the Buddhists, who were also oppressed by the Hindu princes throughout the country. With the entrance of Muslim armies, which carried with them the promise of an equal society, many Buddhists and lower caste-Hindus welcomed the Muslim armies. Buddhists as well as the lower castes, accepted Islam as Islam offered them an escape from the oppressive social system they were accustomed to. With the conquest of Sindh, Muhammad bin Qasim showed that Islamic law's protection of religious minorities was not just for Christians and Jews but also for Buddhists and Hindus.

[7]

The Linking Unit: The **Patriot**, Nikunja Behari Goswami, a silent worker, who had sacrificed his life keeping the ideals of Gandhi in his mind. He was a Hindu, who was born as a Brahmin, but he was equally concerns with the sufferings of the Muslim people.

To know the mind-set of the Muslim people, it is also necessary to know a little bit of Islam and its growth as such a chapter is linked here as 'Islam and Its Growth'.

Let us look at Islam and its growth. The Islamic state expanded very rapidly after the death of Muhammad due to two basic principles: (1) conversion of unbelievers to Islam; (2) conversion of the Islamic community's opponents by military conquests. Expansion of the Islamic state was an understandable development, since Muhammad himself had successfully established the new faith through conversion and conquest of those who stood against him. Immediately after the Prophet's death in 632, Abu-Bakr, as the first caliph, continued the effort to abolish paganism among the Arab tribes. The language Arabia became the unifying force of unity in political consolidation as it was the language of Quran.

In the economic front the merchant elite of Arabia succeeded in consolidating their power throughout the Arabian Peninsula and began to launch some exploratory offensives towards northern Syria. The conversion to Islam was boosted by missionary activities with those of Sufis. Their activity was to mix with the local populace to propagate the religious teachings. These teachings also bring an attachment with economy as many Muslims were in trade business in different regions. Conversion to Islam makes them a reliable trade pattern, a trade worker, and so on. The trade expansion increases the expansion of the Ottoman empire, thereby that resulted in Islam's spread outwards from Mecca making in roads towards both the Atlantic and Pacific Oceans and the creation of the Muslim world.

Expansion of Islam was exploded under the first four caliphs. During the reigns of the first four caliphs (632–661), Islam spread rapidly. The expansion of Islam by wars became possible because of devotion of the people to Islam and faithful to the concept of jihad. Muslims are obliged to extend the faith to unbelievers and to defend Islam from attack. There was a difference in the concept of jihad and 'holy war', but underneath of them, the idea was in the path of expansion of Islam. The Islamic cause was also aided by political upheavals occurring outside of Arabia. The Muslim triumphs in the Near East can be partly accounted for by the long series of wars in the Persian empires. In 636, Arab armies conquered Syria. Syria had a Christian majority within its modern borders until the Mongol invasions of the thirteenth century.

The Muslims conquest of Persia helps them to win Iraq and, within ten years after Muhammad's death, subdued the whole of Persia. The first complete translation of the Quran into Persian occurred during the reign of

Samanids in the ninth century. According to historians, through the zealous missionary work of Samanid rulers, as many as 30,000 tents of Turks came to profess Islam and later under the Ghaznavids higher than 55,000 under the Hanafis school of thought worked in Persia. The volunteers of Ghaznavids later invaded the Indian subcontinent in the eleventh century.

In 640 the greater part of Egypt was converted to Islam with little resistance. By the end of the reigns of the first four caliphs, Islam had vastly increased its territory in the Near East and Africa. The new conquests of Islam were governed with remarkable efficiency like authority typical of military organisation. Unbelievers in the conquered territories became increasingly interested in the new religion and accepted Islam in great numbers. In addition to the obvious power of the religious message of Islam, the imposition of a personal tax on all non-Muslims encouraged many to become Muslims. Islam was and remains one the most effective religions in removing barriers of race and nationality. The new religion converted and embraced peoples of many colours and cultures. The feature of equality encouraged the expansion of the religion.

Through the business of trade very easily Muslim cultures were brought in the Indian subcontinent, in the places like Malaysia, Indonesia, and China. It is estimated as of January 2011, there were 1.62 billion Muslims, in the world making Islam the second largest religion in the world. The religion which came last only in the sixth century has risen almost to the top. The expansion policy no doubt a well calibrated strategy that had superseded all other religious thinkers of the world.

Arab explored with new spirit under the Umayyad. The first three caliphs of Islam were chosen in consultation with the elders and leaders of the Islamic community, and a pattern was established for selecting the caliph from the Karaysh tribe of Mecca. The fourth caliph, Ali, who was the son-in-law of Muhammad, was devoted to Islam and believed that leadership of Islam concerning the Islamic community should remain in the family of the prophet. The followers of Ali were later called Shiites ('party of Ali'). Ali and his followers were opposed first by Muslims under the leadership of Muhammad's widow Aisha, daughter of Abu Bakr, and also later by the forces of Muawiyah, the governor of Syria, who was a relative of the third caliph.

In 661 Muawiyah proclaimed himself caliph, made Damascus his capital, and founded the Umayyad dynasty, which lasted until 750. Thus the caliphate became in fact, although never in law, a hereditary office, not, as previously, a position filled by election. Umayyad military campaigns of conquest for the most part were highly successful. The Umayyad navy held Cyprus, Rhodes, and number of Aegean islands. But the mighty force of Greek for the first time checked the Muslim advance. However, the spread of Islam Westward across North Africa remained in full swing as the Umayyad armies kept their victory of success non-stop.

The next logical expansion for Islam was across the Strait of Gibraltar into the kingdom of Spain. The governor of Muslim North Africa sent his general, Tarik, and an army across the strait into Spain. In 711, seven years later the kingdom came under Muslim domain. The Muslims advanced across the south-western France, but they had established their influence in a territory, a little of north, but halted by a greater force to their inroad into Europe. Meanwhile the Muslims had turned their expansion towards East and move forward to Central Asia. By the turn of the eighth century, they had expanded their influence as far as to the land of Turkestan and the Indus valley. The first large-scale Arab campaign in the Indus valley occurred when the general Muhammad bin Qasim invaded Sind in 711.

In Bengal, Arab merchants found their entry through the port of Chittagong. This has helped the Sufi missionaries to start their invasion of conversion and also settled in the region as early as the eighth century. Spectacular Eid ul-Fitr procession by the Muslims in the Mughal empire was found to be seen in Bengal. During the time of Ikhtiyar Uddin Bakhiyar Khilji's control of the Bengal, the convert was awarded with bracelets of gold.

The powerful Umayyad dynasty became the ruling class of Arab world with Arab military aristocracy. They became the most privileged class greatly out numbered by non-Arabic converts to Islam. They were Arab but not by birth as such there exists a difference of class between them. The resentment of class difference has brought down the Umayyad.

Let us look at the expansion of Islam afterAD 750. It had started the creation of Shia and Sunny. A large numbers of non-Arabic Muslims of Arab world is known as the Shia. The Shia group of Muslims continued to regard Ali and his descendants as the rightful rulers of the Islamic community, and believed that in every age a messiah-like leader would appear and that he must be obeyed. The majority, called Sunni because they were the 'orthodox' perpetrators of Muhammad's Sunna, or tradition, upheld the principle that the caliph owed his position to the consent of the Islamic community. The numerical superiority of the Sunni Muslims has continued to guide the Muslim community in the present world. The process of Muslim expansion had continued as it is controlled by different efficient groups. Since the 1960s, many Muslims have migrated to Western Europe. As a result, Muslim population in Europe has steadily risen.

[8]

The Linking Unit: The **Patriot**, Nikunja Bihari Goswami, a silent worker, who had sacrificed his life keeping the ideals of Gandhi in his mind. He was a Hindu, who was born as a Brahmin, but he was equally concerns with the Muslims as well as the Christians, as such a chapter concerning the **Christianity and its expansion** is enclosed here.

Christianity is expanded due to its magnanimity. It is a favourite view of historians that Jesus was born at a time when the world wanted him very much. The world conditions and the actual process of Christianity were in conformity with the evolutionary laws as regarded in the light of modern interpretation. The fact of the evolution was that the original Christianity is most intimately connected with Judaism, which is nothing but the parent religion of Christianity. The known world, however, at the time of Jesus was largely under Roman dominion. This was a belief that Jesus was born in the land of earth to save mankind. The Roman empire was then comparatively at peace under the blessings of Jesus, and it was the firm belief of St Paul that the Christianity was brought to Roman empire by Jesus to maintain peace throughout the empire. Christianity spread initially from Jerusalem throughout East, into the places such as Mesopotamia, Asia Minor, Jordan, and Egypt, and extending from Greece to Libya.

The Jews believe in the existence of one God. **All other nations had a variety of gods and** they were worshiped in different peculiar forms and methods. In most of the pagan religions there were elements of truth and beauty, but they lacked in ethical principles and in moral application to life. In the doctrines of Buddhism there found to be the existence of spirit and devotion for the purpose of the development of humanity but the intricate mythology, racial and other limitations of Buddhism forbade that, although it conquered the half of Asia, as such it never thought that it should ever become a universal faith.

Christian theology is expressed through the teachings of Christian churches existed world over. The professions of faith of state that Jesus suffered, died, buried, and were resurrected from the dead, in order to grant eternal life to those who believe in him and trust in him for the remission of their sins. Among Christian beliefs, the death and resurrection of Jesus are two core events on which much of Christian doctrine and theology is based. According to the New Testament Jesus was crucified, died a physical death, buried within a tomb, and rose from the dead three days later.

The history of the Catholic church begins with the teachings of Jesus Christ, in the Roman empire. Bishop of Rome is also known as Pope, who was once destined to resolve doctrinal and policy issues of Roman empire and later the bishop of Rome began to act as a court of appeals for problems that other bishops could not resolve.

The single God concept (monotheism) unlike Hinduism was nothing new to Romans either, though Christianity did initiate a change in philosophy where that God stood above both the emperor and Rome itself. The church not only established strict laws and religious doctrine but it wiped out heretic and divergent thoughts. The Catholic church virtually destroyed those other sects and Paganism along with the force of the doctrine of Christianity or force of violence unlike that of Hinduism but almost like that of later Muslim religion if not so severe in the action of implementation. This might be one of the reason for day by day the degradation of Hindu religion, Hinduism, and rising of Christian religion, Christianity to a little extent and the rising of Muslim religion, Islam very rapidly.

The impact of Christianity delighted the spirit of humanity. Jesus has given the mankind something for which the people prefer to celebrate his birth even two thousand years later. It is hoped that everyone would enjoy this account in the delightful spirit of Christmas. Even most of the non-Christians at least respect Jesus as a great moral teacher. Christianity is responsible for the way the society is organised and for the way the human beings died. The Christian contribution to the society is enormously extensive in every sphere so to say to laws, to economics, to politics, and also to art and cultures.

In the Greco-Roman world: (1) a woman was somewhere between a free man and a slave; (2) a woman has no value of life as women has low status in the society so as to throw out new female infants to die from exposure; (3) an unmarried woman has no value, and therefore it was illegal for a widow to go more than two years without remarrying. But Christianity was the first religion to raise voice against all inhuman torture.

Again Christianity was the first religion that implemented the law through church that no one should force widows to marry, and also allowed widows to maintain their husband's estate. They were supported financially and honoured within the community so that they were not under great pressure to remarry if they didn't want to. In all these ways Christian women were provided far greater security and equality than did women in the surrounding culture.

In India, widows were voluntarily or involuntarily burned on their husbands' funeral pyres. Christian missionaries were a major influence in stopping these century-old practices and ideas in cooperation with few Indian reformists. During the ruling period of Rome or Greece, infanticide was not only legal, it was applauded, it was commonly held in Rome that killing of one's own children could be an act of beauty. It was the Christian church by dint of their forceful argument succeeded to convince the people that resulted in the end to bring an end to infanticide. The modern pro-life movement is largely Christian that was being thought of right and justified from the very beginning of Christianity. Christian document were made dated from the late first century or early second century, that contained instructions against abortion. These were the welfare activity that is prevailing in the present generation what are nothing but an advance thought of the good of mankind.

In the earlier Christianity, there was the system of **slavery** in the society. But in the course of time, Christianity elevated the roles of those oppressed in society, by accepting women and slaves as full members and they are being allowed to participate equally in worship and allowed to get the benefit of property rights. Two-thirds of the members of the American abolition society built in 1835 were Christian ministers.

The ancient world was unknown with any organised charitable institution. It was in the days of Christianity, there was rise of innumerable charitable organisation. An important aspect of Christian ministry was his emphasis on helping the neediest and lowliest in society. Christianity has created culture's powerful emphasis on compassion, on helping the needy, and on alleviating distress even in distant places. If there is a huge famine or reports of genocide in Africa, most people in other cultures are unconcerned, the Christian society moves forwards for rescue works. However paradoxical it appears, people who believed most strongly in the next world did the most to improve the situation of people living in this world. Christianity has made the family life beautiful and ideal for the society. The Protestant Reformist has brought the education for the masses in Bible literacy.

Many of the world's languages were first set to writing by Christian missionaries in order for the people to read the Bible. In America, the first law to require education of the masses was also passed by the Puritans, the Reformist Christians. For the first two hundred years in America, children's reading texts emphasised biblical literacy. The emphasis on literacy was so intense in colonial America that in the early 1800s the illiteracy rate was only of 1 percent. Although America's constitutional government is not specifically Christian, but it could be argued that its roots are taken from **biblical doctrines**. In this regard here are just a few possible arguments in its favour.

The US Constitution was approved by the signature of 50 Orthodox Christians out of 55. The concept of building the constitution was to look to the good of mankind based on the biblical doctrine, what is written in Bible of Christianity in regards to the sinfulness of mankind. The idea that all men are created equal as enshrined in the Declaration of Independence is a biblical doctrine. Many other aspects of laws are based on equality such as the law of the judicial, legislative and executive branches of administration. Apart from that, nearly all the founders of modern science were Christians. These include men such as Keppler, Boyle, Pascal, Pasteur, Newton, et al.

It may be concluded by saying that if the West gives up Christianity, it will also endanger the **egalitarian values**, the values based on the principle that all people are equal and deserve equal rights and opportunities that Christianity brought into the world. The present day Christianity has turned towards scientific exploration. It has been a major influence on the mathematical sciences, particularly in the seventeenth and eighteenth centuries. There is a widespread belief that Christianity and science, particularly mathematical science, were on opposing sides but that was prove to be false for the fact that the people who like Copernicus, Kepler, Galileo, or Newton perhaps did as much as anybody to revolutionize the mathematical sciences in the sixteenth and seventeenth centuries, were all deeply religious Christians who in many ways saw their scientific work as a religious undertaking.

The Linking Unit: The **Patriot**, Nikunja Behari Goswami, a silent worker, who had sacrificed his life keeping the ideals of Gandhi in his mind. He was a Hindu, who was born as a Brahmin, and also died as a Hindu as he was cremated with the customs and traditions of Hindu religion. But his mind was in search of the division of mankind as Hindus and Muslims. His heart was in search of the life of the people of 'India, Pakistan, and Bangladesh' after being segregated by division. As such a chapter is here described to know the lifestyle of the people of all these regions.

5 The Present Condition of India, Pakistan, and Bangladesh

[1]

India, Pakistan, and Bangladesh before partition belong to one country India, but all three are sovereign independent country now having its own rule of law, yet the nature of the people, the culture of the people, and above all the language of the people in many cases remains to be the same. The country became different, the boarder area became different, the communication became restricted yet travelling by passport and visa is not stopped as such the information of good or bad, good economy or bad economy would continue sometime in an atmosphere of good friendship or sometimes in an atmosphere of bad friendship and will never ceased to zero as if the blood circulation of life continues till the last drop of blood. So it is necessary to write about the regions in order to describe the status of life of any region or the region of Bangladesh.

Let us talk of INDIA. India is an agricultural country and a multicultural country with diversity in language and customs. In the past few years particularly during congress rule India has gone through several ups and downs, but still India is standing amongst all the nations holding her head high up in the sphere of economy, agriculture, and IT sector. Let us throw some light on the specific sectors.

The economy of India is the seventh largest in the world by nominal GDP and the third largest by purchasing power parity (PPP). The country is grouped along with other industrialised country as one of the G-20 major economies, a member of BRICS and a developing economy with an average growth rate of approximately 7%. The significant growth rate is that India had super seeded the growth of the People's Republic of China by last quarter of 2014; as such India's economy became the world's fastest-growing major economy.

In the sphere of petroleum products and chemicals, both the sectors are the major contributor to India's industrial GDP, and its export have extended over 34% of its export earnings. The contribution of the world's largest refinery complex in Jamnagar is in no way less. Besides, the export and import of gold, precious metals, precious stones, gems, and jeweller accounts for the largest portion of India's global trade. The industry contributes about 7% of India's GDP

What is about industry? Presently India is witnessing an IT boom which mainly relies on outsourcing of jobs from the developed countries of the world, such as country like America or other countries of Europe. It also showed its progress in advance treatment in medical science resulting a steady rise in the hospital and healthcare industry, tempting the patient of other countries to come to India for better treatment with less expense. Simultaneously it has shown its progress in hotel industry, travel, and tourism and also in aviation industry due to few air companies. If private companies in USA can bring economic miracle, why should not private companies in India have been tested. Now it had shown positive results because many of private industries played a key role in the rising of economy.

Some of the private companies are the key players of India, which are reliance, TATA, Infosys, Bharati Airtel with active foreign participation of telecom giants such as Vodafone, pharmaceuticals such as Glaxo-Smith, ceramics such as Saint-Gobain, electronics such as Nokia, Apple, and Intel, etc. Share markets have recently seen several up and downs because of many factors, but the IT industry is also played a part due to the condition of recession.

By the time India has extended its export of IT services, BPO services, and software services. The worth of service of exports in 2013–14 has reaches to the extent of $167 billion. It is also the fastest-growing part of the economy.

Let us look at the industry in global front. India has emerged as the fastest growing major economy in the world as per the record of Central Statistics Organisation (CSO) and International Monetary Fund (IMF). According to the Economic Survey 2015–16, it is expected that the Indian economy will continue to grow more than 7 per cent in 2016–17. The improvement in India's economic fundamentals has accelerated in the year 2015 due to strong government's initiative in reforms, and RBI's control over inflation. India was ranked at the highest globally as per the global consumer confidence data.

According to IMF World Economic Outlook record of update of January 2016, Indian economy is expected to grow at 7–7.75 per cent during year 2016–17, despite the severe ups and down in the global market. The Economic Survey 2015–16 further had forecasted a growth more than 7per cent for the third successive year 2016–17 and might have start growing at 8per cent or more in next two years. The launching of Make in India campaign had increased foreign direct investment (FDI) in India by 29 per cent during October 2014–December 2015. The Nikkei/Market Manufacturing Purchasing Managers' Index (PMI) for February 2016 was reported at 51.1 that indicate an expansion in Indian manufacturing activity for a consecutive second month in series, as both domestic and foreign demand increased due to lower prices.

The steps taken by the government in recent times have shown positive results as India's gross domestic product (GDP) for 2015–16 is Rs 113.5 trillion (US$ 1.668 trillion), as against Rs 105.5 trillion (US$ 1.55 trillion) in 2014–15. The economic activities showed significant growth in 'financing, insurance, real estate, and business services' at 11.5 per cent and in other sector such as 'trade, hotels, transport, communication services' at 10.7 per cent. The different report released in September 2015, indicated India could grow at a potential of 8 per cent on average in the period of 2016 to 2020 powered by greater access to banking, electronic technology, and in urbanization of smart city incentive.

In the **recent economic scenario**, Telecom was the dominant sector, investments is increasing day by day in this sector. Total private equity (PE) investments in India for 2015 reached a record high of US$ 19.5 billion through 159 deals, according to the Money Tree India report. According to the World Bank, India's per capita income is expected to cross Rs 100,000 (US$ 1,505.4) in FY 2017 from Rs 93,231 (US$ 1,403.5) in FY 2016. Numerous foreign companies are setting up their facilities in India on account of various **government initiatives** like Make in India and Digital India. Mr Narendra Modi, prime minister of India, has launched the 'Make in India' initiative with an aim to boost the manufacturing sector of Indian economy.

SBI, UBI, SEBI are the major players in banking industry. Indian postal departments and railway departments are not lacking behind as they have made a significant steady progress. These two sectors have made India proud of. But depth of unemployment and contribution of services being remained unbalanced, it stands as a major worry for the government.

Prime Minister Narendra Modi launched the Start-up India initiative and initiated the Start-up Action Plan, which includes creation of a Start-up fund worth ofRs 10,000 crore (US$ 1.47 billion) apart from other incentives such as no tax on profits for first three years. Now all obstacles have been removed for the British telecom giant Vodafone, India's second largest telecom operator, who plans to invest over Rs 13,000 core (US$ 1.91 billion) in India, to upgrade and expand its network. Even facilities have been provided to China to invest in India in smart phone sector, where Chinese smart-phone handset maker, Vivo, has set up an assembly unit in India at Greater Noida which will initially manufacture 150,000 smart-phone units a month, to produce three smart-phone models, namely, Y11, Y21, and Y15S.

Hyderabad is set to become the mobile phone manufacturing hub in India and is expected to create 150,000–200,000 jobs, but the newly formed state Telangana did not remain behind. Government aims to double IT exports to Rs 1.2 trillion (US$ 17.61 billion) by 2019. General Motors plans to invest US$1 billion in India by 2020, Hyundai Heavy Industries (HHI) and Hindustan Shipyard Ltd have joined hands to build warships in India. In thetourism sector the government of India announced that all the major tourist spots like Sarnath, Bodhgaya, and Taj Mahal will have a Wi-Fi facility as part of digital India initiative. In the case of Varanasi, the ancient religious city of India, the government has started providing free Wi-Fi service at Varanasi Ghats.

[2]

Let us talk of present politics of India and Pakistan as well. Presently BJP is ruling at the centre with majority under an active and visionary man of personality (Modi), although lacking in majority in **Rajya Sabha**. Congress is in opposition with a humiliating number. The election result of 2014 has witnessed people confidence in Modi government and a total rejection to congress. The interest of younger generations have found to be more in politics as is evident for joining politics in large number although increase in population is not in downward trend or remain standstill. Pakistan still remains the centre of worry of foreign politics in the sphere of stability of India in economic front and reputation of India abroad for foreign investment.

There is initiative how to increase the purchasing power of an average Indian consumer, which is necessary to boost demand, and hence the spray of development, by giving incentive to the investors. Finance Minister Mr ArunJaitley stated that the government is looking at a number of reforms and resolution of pending tax disputes to attract investments. Government is under his utmost endeavour how to bring up

Digital India initiative, digital infrastructure, and the digital literacy in Indian set-up. Currently, the manufacturing sector in India contributes over 15 per cent of the GDP, but the government of India is thinking to take it up to 25 per cent of the GDP under the 'Make in India' initiative. Prime Minister Narendra Modi announced at the International Monetary Fund (IMF) conference on 'Advancing Asia: How He Had Given the Incentive –Investing for the Future' in New Delhi that the government will continue to bring in new reforms for transforming economy without resorting to undervaluing its exchange rate to boost trade. The government of India plans to build five new railway links with its neighbouring country including hilly regions of Nepal and Bhutan which will boost India's economy. At the same time it will promote growth, employment, and prosperity in the region.

The COMMON man still remains under the sections of suffered community. The last pay commission has recommended an increase of salaries for employees. On the other hand few steps have been taken for the increase of farmer's economic condition, in the way of providing facilities such as growth insensitive manure, watering, storage, and marketing to bring an incentive to increase the status of life. Rather the news of farmer suicide, student suicide due to immense pressure, petty politics, pollution, etc., still continues the important news of the day.

In the case of **Pakistan** on 14 August 1947, the dream of Pakistan **finally** became a reality. August 14 is an auspicious day for Pakistan, the day when the country gained its independence from British rule. But how many Pakistanis know how Independence Day came about? With the exception of students of history and political science, the majority know little of the efforts that went into making Pakistan. The reasons for the creation of Pakistan were crystal clear. As the nineteenth century ended, Muslims of India found themselves in a depressive state, as the Muslims began to notice that Hindus are occupying positions of strength over them. They sought to find a place where they could voice their grievances and seek rightful position. In response to this desire the All India Muslim League (ML) was formed in 1906, thus the voice of the Muslims were expressed through ML. The primary objective of ML was to gain the rights of the Indian Muslims. On 14 August 1947, the dream finally became a reality, although it took over a million to die in the transition period of the creation of the country.

Sixty-eight years later where does the country stand? The thinking of some Pakistanis is explained here. According to **a 51-year-old Pakistani**, the creation of Pakistan was not necessary. Initially, there was a feeling of nationhood and everybody took pride having being a Pakistani. In the beginning life was simple and there was much happiness as in the new country people looked after each other as brothers and sisters. That, however, changed over the years. People get suffered in all spheres.

According to his observation the government functioned well and the bureaucracy showed fair responsibility, and there was no corruption charge in the administration of the government. Things began to change in the '70s and became worse in the '80s. The country, instead of making progress, went down economically and politically. Despite these drawbacks, there was faith in the minds of the people that the country would return to the right path of progress. People were happy to see a democratic government in 1988, but it was nothing but a farce. It paved the way for the army to take over. General Musharraf came to power and succeeded in stabilising the economy and seemed to give good direction to the country. Further according to him democracy must rule, but for that good leaders are needed and he was in search of good leaders in Pakistan.

According to one such **Mohammad Hassan** what he had expressed as if he had given up all hope. According to him Quaid-e-Azam (Jinnah) was an able leader. He had the ability to take on to the British and the Indian congress and fight for Pakistan and he won Pakistan in the end but where is the happiness of the people. According to him, creation of Pakistan was nothing but the losing of a greater area of India.

According to his view had Liaquat Ali Khan would visit the USSR instead of going to the USA, Pakistan would not face current deplorable situation. It is USA who is responsible for the deplorable situation of Pakistan. Ayub Khan's tenure gave the country an economic stability, a growth of industries, agriculture, and trade, but why was East Pakistan treated badly to bring the greatest recession and destroy the country? According to him, Mr Bhutto's foreign policy was good, but his domestic and economic policies were bad and also very bad for East Pakistan. It was the belief of the public that Pakistan's involvement with Afghan war is the reason for the current insecurity problems of the country. Although Musharraf's rule brought Pakistan's stability to a certain extent, but subsequently introduction of

Mr Zardari had spoiled the country's economy due to inefficient administration.

Who was Musharraf, a military ruler, who was elevated to the four-star appointments by then Prime Minister Nawaz Sharif in October 1998? He was the mastermind of a Kargil infiltration that brought India and Pakistan to a full-fledged war in 1999. But again he staged a military coup allowing Musharraf to seize control of the government. He again placed Prime Minister Sharif under house arrest, but subsequently he brought a rapid change in the policy matters of domestic as well as in foreign affairs and brought stability in economy.

Who was Zardari, the son of a wealthy Sindhi tribal leader, born in Karachi in 1955, who married Mrs Bhutto, the daughter of the first elected prime minister of Pakistan, in 1987 and appointed an investment minister in his wife's administration in the year 1990? He was accused by other political party for taking personal commissions on government contracts. Pakistan's state anti-corruption body had put forwarded a charge against him, who had amassed a property empire worth of almost £1 billion, with a large house in France, luxury residents in Britain, Spain, and Florida. He also had bank accounts in Switzerland. As soon as his wife Mrs Bhutto was deposed in 1990, Mr Zardari again came in the limelight of corruption charges. His charges lead him to prison but again released in 1993, when Mrs Bhutto was back in power.

He returned to prison again when his wife lost power in 1996. All these charges were formally dropped as part of an amnesty granted by General Pervez Musharraf, the president, in the year 2007.

Following Mrs Bhutto's assassination in December 2007, Zardari was rested with the leadership of his wife's Pakistan People's Party (PPP). He became the president after a wave of sympathy for the cause of Mrs Bhutto's assassination. But Pakistan's National Accountability Bureau under a successful court verdict overturned the amnesty. Subsequently Nawaz Sharif came to power. This was the history of power politics of Pakistan. But people want peace and economic stability.

According to him, people are hoping for a better life and a better economy with Nawaz Sharif, but people are disappointment by his action of progress. Pakistan made promises. If it could follow right path, it could show tremendous progress but so far without looking any progress, people are getting dishearten.

To speak about economy, the **economy of Pakistan** is said to be the twenty-sixth largest in the world in terms of purchasing power parity (PPP), and forty-first largest in terms of nominal gross domestic product. Its GPD is 4.4. However for the time being Pakistan appears to be very poor because it is predominantly an agricultural country when it gained independence in 1947. Pakistan's average economic growth rate in the first five decades (1947–1997) has been increased to some extent and it became higher than the growth rate of the world economy. Its average annual GDP growth rates were 6.8% in the 1960s, 4.8% in the 1970s, and 6.5% in the 1980s. But in 1990 its average annual growth fell to 4.6% because of political as well as economic recession.

Decades of internal political disputes and low levels of foreign investment have led to slow growth and under development in Pakistan. The sector like agriculture that accounts the 1/5 of total output, textiles major sector of exports remained uncared and unaccounted, how the country can think for progress. The country's economy goes down, and under-employment remains high. Over the past few years, low growth and high inflation having in high food prices led the people to be the victim of poverty.

As a result of political and economic instability, the Pakistani rupee value depreciated. In the concern of governance to maintain stability and security in the country, government discarded the insensitive activity for the foreign investment in the country. Pakistan remains stuck in a low-income, low-growth trap, with growth averaging about 3.5% per year from 2008 to 2013. Other long-term challenges including investment in education and healthcare for the good of the nation remain hanging.

The other factor such as building of foreign exchange reserves did not happen by the profit of economy. It was only possible after costly borrowings against Euro. Besides, the foreign investment as especially from China, a Chinese pledge to invest USD 42 billion remains as a memorandum of understanding (MoU) and not foreign direct investment (FDI) commitment that requires a minimum of 10 percent investment. Falling oil prices provided a good opportunity, as it provides breathing space to the economy. To take maximum advantage of falling oil prices requires developing a strategy, a planning and determination to get the best result through better management. But Pakistan having being in turmoil because of domestic insurgency, the designing of any plan for future prosperity could not be undertaken at the present state of status of the country.

Pakistan's economy remains in the doldrums, as it is still faced with social unrest due to uncertain political and economic environment caused by old-fashioned economic growth strategy. Since independence the pace of growth has averaged above 4.00 percent making the country almost poor to poorest. It is because of high poverty rate, low literacy rate, poor infrastructure, and outdated agriculture technology; lack of industrialisation, poor healthcare system, the living standard goes down. A closer look at the present economic indicators, Pakistan's economy would be dangerously imbalanced.

[3]

Hindu-Muslim unity of India was disturbed after the division of India. After the formation of Pakistan in 1947, on the basis of religion the Hindu-Muslim unity is diminished to the lowest degree. That was mainly due to the political thinkers of the country, Jinnah, Gandhi, and many others. The division of a country on the basis of religion is found nowhere in the world till today. What we find in the world in other regions or countries where people are living together having being with difference in faith of religion such as Protestant and Catholic are living together in UK and in other regions of Europe. It was not one year or two, even thousands of years could have not been sufficient to remove the pain of hatred that was being installed in the minds of Hindus and Muslims by the division of the country on the basis of religion. Gandhi became great internationally, for the independence of India by non-violence, but the people of India know how the independence came to India, by the division of the country, by the killing of millions of people of the region and displacing millions. The poster generation would never excuse the leaders who did it. It never certifies the farsightedness of the Indian leaders. It had created an everyday clash of conflict between the people of the two countries. The clash of hatred has been reflected in everyday affairs in the clash of boarder, in consecutive four wars, and several terrorist attacks time and again. Each country realises that the result of such clash of hatred was nothing but the loss of few lives and property. Now Gandhi was honoured in every country, everywhere as a man of saint who brought Indian independence.

But many in India think differently. According to them, Gandhi was the man to sow the seeds of Hindu-Muslim hatred, although Gandhi never wanted the division of the country. His desire was a mass protest against the British through non-violence. But the situation turned it to violence and leads to state of a point of no return. The solution came through the division of the country. Thus

Gandhi, however big he was, he could not get the honour and respect of all those victimized people. According to them Gandhi was the man of instrument to the cause of killing of millions, and millions to be uprooted from their ancestral home and hearth. However, Gandhi had realised his mistake, the mistake to carry out independence movement with 'non-violence'. But it was too late to do anything better other than surrender, otherwise, another Mugal empire would likely to be emerged.

Relations between India and Pakistan have been turned from bad to worse due to a number of historical and political events. The events related with the occupation of the power of chair culminated by the violent partition of British India in 1947. The good relation of Hindu-Muslim before partition has been turned into bad to worse after partition because the partition was done based on religion. Thus partition was the cause of hatred. The clash of hatred did not remain confine to the partition of India alone, but it extended to other regions. Such as the creation of Kashmir conflict and the numerous military conflicts fought between the two nations. Consequently, even though the two South Asian nations share linguistic, cultural, geographic, and economic links, their relationship has been vitiated by hostility and suspicion.

Soon after the independence, India and Pakistan established diplomatic relations under the obligation of the norms of international law but the violent action of partition and numerous territorial claims had over shadowed their relationship. Since after independence, the two countries have fought three major wars, and one undeclared war. The Kashmir conflict is the main centre-point of all of these conflicts in addition to the Indo-Pakistan War of 1971. But again there have been numerous attempts to improve the relationship— notably, the Shimla Summit, the Agra Summit, and the Lahore Summit. Since the early 1980s, relations between the two nations deteriorated further particularly after (1) the Siachen conflict, (2) Kashmir insurgency (1989), (3) India-Pakistan nuclear tests (1998), and (4) Kargil war (1999).

Certain confidence, building measures were taken to de-escalating tensions, such as the 2003 ceasefire agreement and the Delhi-Lahore bus service. However, these efforts have been polluted by periodic terrorist attacks. Such as (1) the Indian parliament attack (2001),(2) the Samjhauta Express bombing (2007),(3) the Mumbai attacks (2008), and (4) the recent Pathan Coat attack. The result was the cancellation of the on going India-Pakistan peace talks.

Narendra Modi's efforts of peace misfired. In November 2015, the Indian Prime Minister Narendra Modi, who had brought an excitement of new hope of new India and a development not only of India but to the world, a vibrant world for the mankind by his foreign tour to Western, Eastern, and Middle East, thought to finish the obstacles of development at the doorstep of neighbouring Pakistan. He not only invited Pakistani Prime Minister Nawaz Sharif at his inaugural oath taking ceremony but talked and agreed to the resumption of bilateral talks. Meetings were held between the foreign secretaries and the national security advisers of both nations. Prime Minister Modi made a brief, unscheduled visit to Pakistan while en route to India, becoming the first Indian prime minister to visit Pakistan since 2004. Despite those efforts, relations between the countries have remained frigidly cold under the inner burning of communal hatred that was created at the birth and subsequent events of Kashmir as well as of East Pakistan leading to victory of war to Bangladesh. The country being remained in economic stagnation, the frustration of distress gets reflected in the repeated acts of cross-border terrorism. It was not the desire of the people of Pakistan to kill innocent people by the act of terrorism, but it is the outburst of communal hatred that was being installed in the minds of the Muslim of India, now in Pakistan at the outset by the movement of non-violence.

Gandhi solved the leadership problem by the division of the country; Jinnah became the premier of Pakistan and Nehru the PM of India. About half a million Muslims and Hindus were killed in communal riots following the partition of British India. Millions of Muslims living in India near the territory of present Pakistan and Hindus and Sikhs living in Pakistan emigrated under compulsion of threat and violence on the verge of religion. Both countries accused each other of not providing adequate security to the minorities emigrating through their respecting territory.

It was a Hindu majority state **Junagardh** consisting of more than 80% Hindus, whiles its ruler Nawab Mahabat Khanwas a Muslim. Mahabat Khan acceded to Pakistan on 15 August 1947. Pakistan confirmed the acceptance of the accession on 15 September 1947. India did not accept the accession as legitimate because, the state is surrounded by Indian territory on three sides as such on the point of views of India, Junagadh was not contiguous to Pakistan, and that the Hindu majority of Junagadh wanted to be a part of India. The Pakistani point of view was that since Junagadh had a ruler and governing body it is his prerogative to join any country either Pakistan or India as it desires so. Junagardh remained in India with people's support of 98% votes.

Kashmir conflict: Kashmir was a Muslim-majority princely state, ruled by a Hindu king, Maharaja Hari Singh. Mr Singh, the ruler of the state, preferred to remain independent and did not want to join either the union of India or the Pakistan. He preferred to remain as an independent state. The allegation was that the Hindu Maharajah of Kashmir attempted to change the predominantly Muslim demographics of his state by engaging in an ethnic cleansing of Muslims from the Jammu section of his state, as his state forces massacred thousands of Muslims in Jammu and expelled thousands in an effort to shift the population ratio in favour of Hindus. This precipitated a revolt by the Muslims in the Poonch district of Jammu and Kashmir against the Hindu Maharajah. Backed by Pakistani paramilitary forces, Tribal's forces invaded Kashmir in October 1947. Had it been true, the population of Kashmir by the lapse of sixty-five years would have been a total of Hindu majority. Moreover there would not have been an exodus of Kashmiri Pandits from Kashmir to other places of India.

But the same was not repeated by Indian forces in East Pakistan to enter East Pakistan in the month of January and February of 1950 to maintain law and order when millions of Hindus were killed, tortured, and forced to evict from their ancestral homes. The fact of the matter is true or not, that could be proved by the records where Hindu population in East Pakistan had been reduced from 47% to less than 12%.

The Pak forces advanced fast and captured Baramulla on 25 October. Kashmir's weak and ill-equipped security forces were not match to fight against Pakistani forces. Finding no other way, the Maharaja of Kashmir turned to India and requested India for troops to safeguard Kashmir. Indian Prime Minister Nehru was ready to send the troops. But the acting Governor-General of India, Lord Mountbatten, did not agree to that unless the Maharaja acceded to India. Hence, considering the emergent situation Maharaja signed the instrument of accession to the union of India on 26 October 1947 that was the beginning of the conflict of Kashmir.

Pakistani had created a war-like situation by sending most of the Hindu Bengalis from East Pakistan to

India. In 1949, India recorded close to 1 million Hindu refugees, who flooded into West Bengal and other states from East Pakistan (now Bangladesh), owing to communal violence under state patronage. Instead of war, Prime Minister Nehru and Sardar Patel invited Liaquat Ali Khan for talks in Delhi. A pact of agreement (April 1950) was signed which totally goes in favour of Pakistan. All Muslims returned to West Bengal but not a single Hindu went back to East Bengal, because unlike India that was declared an Islamic state. Is it a justice done to the Hindu Bengalis of West Bengal? The Hindu youngsters of Bengal fought for independence of India, made the British administration standstill by civil disobedience movement, bravely went to gallows; never get afraid of going to the cellular jails of Andaman, what for? Is it for vanishing from Bengal after being struggling hard for survival?

Since birth the present generation is hearing in India, particularly in Bengal, Islam, Hinduism, and Hindu-Muslim, who is friend or who is foe? Is there any other country in the world where religion gets the top priority directly or indirectly for the question of stability and future prospect? Who is responsible for that? Who is the leader, who has guided people to the present status of existence? Indian subcontinent is a beautiful region full of natural resources. There was a time when science was not developed; people were in search of natural wealth for survival. The people of all the seaside European countries deprived of natural resources went out towards east of Asia in the search of trade to survive. It was the reason why it is seen in the record of history that started from the UK, Spain, Portugal, France, or Greece, people of all these countries search out towards Southeast Asia including India. But it was a pity to see that the Indian leaders overlooking the great wealth of the region, discarding the great potential of the source of development engage themselves in the narrow outlook of power politics. The worst and the greatest disaster was done by bringing religion in the power politics to achieve their respective goal of destination throwing the common people to fight to the last for religion forgetting the sources of bread and butter and the worst allowing the people of the region particularly of Bengal to die under repeated famine. This was the history of our country and the history of activity of the achievement of our leader and leadership. The intelligent people of the West went away developing their economy with the new skill of science throwing the people of India in the hips of dust of matter and material.

The Indo-Pakistani War of 1965 started following Pakistan's design to infiltrate forces into Jammu and Kashmir. The five-week war caused thousands of casualties on both sides. It ended in a United Nations (UN) mandated ceasefire and the subsequent issuance of the Tashkent Declaration.

War of 1971 has liberated Bangladesh. Pakistan has two wings, in the East, it is East Pakistan and in the West, it is West Pakistan. East Pakistan was occupied mostly by Bengali people, while West Pakistan was occupied mostly by the Punjabis and also by others speaking mostly Urdu. In December 1971, following a political crisis in East Pakistan, the situation soon went out of control in East Pakistan mostly because of language issue and economic disparity. India intervened in favour of the rebelling Bengali populace. Soon there was a bloody war, resulting in an independence of East Pakistan which get separated and became Bangladesh.

In the War of 1998–1999, Pakistan's adventure in occupying the high peaks in Kargil of Kashmir misfired. Pakistan army intruded across the line of control and occupied the very high peaks in Kargil sector in Kashmir. The Indian army regained some of the posts that Pakistan has occupied being backed by the Indian air force. Pakistan later withdrew from the remaining portion under international pressure.

Pakistan caught red-handed for bombing the Indian embassy in Kabul in 2008. Indian embassy was attacked in Kabul by a suicide bomber. 7 July 2008 at 8:30 AM local time, Afghanistan, US intelligence officials reported from the record that Pakistan's ISI intelligence agency had planned the attack. Pakistan denied initially. But immediately United States President George W. Bush confronted Pakistani Prime Minister Yusuf Raza Gilani with evidence and warned him that in the case of another such attack he would have to take 'serious action'.

Pakistani terrorists created a bad precedent by the attack of Indian parliament. The attack on the Indian parliament was by far the most dramatic attack carried out allegedly by Pakistani terrorists. India blamed Pakistan and at one stage that both nations brought to the brink of a nuclear confrontation in 2001–02. However, international afford brought back peace. What was the reason for doing such a heinous crime? The reason is crystal clear, the hatred, the hatred of Hindu-Muslim originated at the division of the country. Gandhi's non-violence movement was the incentive for the outburst of violence out of hatred. Apart from this, the most notable incident was the hijacking of Indian Airlines Flight IC 814 en route New Delhi from Kathmandu, Nepal. The plane was hijacked on 24 December 1999, one hour after take-off and the plan was taken to Amritsar airport first and then to Lahore, Dubai, then finally landed in Kandahar, Afghanistan.

Under intense media pressure, New Delhi complied with the hijackers' demand and freed Maulana Masood Azhar from its captivity in return for the freedom of the Indian passengers on the flight. This man later became the leader of Jaish-e-Mohammed, an organisation which has carried out several terrorist activities against Indian security forces in Kashmir. On 22 December 2000, a group of terrorists belonging to the Lashkar-e-Toiba stormed the famous Red Fort in New Delhi. The 2008 Mumbai attack was carried out by ten Pakistani terrorists, who killed over 173 and wounded 308. The sole surviving gunman Ajmal Kasab who was arrested during the attacks was found to be a Pakistani national. This fact was acknowledged by Pakistani authorities. At the creation of Pakistan, Gandhi's policy of non-violence encouraged the Muslims to create onslaught of violence. Similarly after the formation of Pakistan, India's policy of no-counter attack encouraged Pakistan or Pakistani terrorists to carry out series of attacks one after another to hackle and humiliate India in all front. The greatest skilled fighter Hitler captured France in no time and attacked United Kingdom by dropping bombs here and there, but the Allied Forces counter-acted non-stop; the result was the defeat and death of Hitler. Friendship is established with the attachment of love and attraction of strength and not with only of love and sacrifice of strength as that is being exhibited by Gandhi in the creation of Pakistan.

It is good to see India is responding to the natural calamities occurred in Pakistan in exchange of Pakistan's response to Gujarat earthquake in India. In response to the 2001 Gujarat earthquake, Pakistani President Pervez Mushrraf as gesture of goodwill sent a plane loaded with relief supplies to India from Islamabad to Ahmadabad. That carried two hundred tents and more than two thousand blankets. Furthermore, the president called Indian PM to express his 'sympathy' over the loss from the earthquake. In response to the 2005 Kashmir earthquake, India sent 25 tonnes of relief material to Pakistan including food, blankets, and medicine. Large Indian companies such as Infosys have offered aid up to $226,000. On 12 October, a cargo plane went with seven truck loads of army medicines, fifteen thousand blankets and fifty tents. On 14 October, India dispatched the second consignment of relief material to Pakistan, by train through the Wagah Border. Similarly India must give reply to Pakistan in response to Pakistani terrorist attack on India. The natural law of stability justifies, action must be preceded with counter action to bring the peace of natural stability.

[3]

Let us look at Bangladesh. The partition of British India and the emergence of India and Pakistan in 1947 severely disrupted the economic system. The united government of Pakistan expanded the cultivated area and irrigation facilities, in such a low incentive that improvement did not keep pace with the population increase, as a result population in general became poor to poorer between 1947 and 1971. The strategy of development based on industrialisation by the plan of five-year terms went to West Pakistan. The lack of natural resources in East Pakistan makes it heavily dependent on imports and created a balance of payments problem. Thus neither a substantial industrialisation program nor an adequate agrarian expansion, happened in East Pakistan making the economy down to down and reducing life of ordinary people to the state of famine. The people began to fight for independent country. Bangladesh came into being on 16 December 1971 as a sovereign independent country after the surrender of Pak army to the joint force of Indian army and Mukti Bahini of Bangladesh.

Sheikh Hasina was re-elected prime minister in January 2014 in an election marred by an opposition boycott. She tried hard to revive economic condition and stability in the country in spite of anti-government demonstrations and a transport blockade. Garment manufacturing accounts for over 90 percent of export earnings. The April 2013 collapse of the Rana Plaza garment factory brought a disaster in the industry, which killed over a thousand people. It had brought a bad international reputation for the industry. It violated the normal working conditions of labour and safety standards. It had brought a change in the labour laws and amended the system for obtaining necessary permits for industry. Business start-up became simpler, with required capital, along with safety norms. Despite all efforts, Bangladesh remains one of the world's poorest nations.

Bangladesh has been wracked by political protests over the past two years. Industry suffered initially due to opposition violence that killed over 120, the government jailed over 7,000 opposition members. For the last two months, the daily strikes and protests have continued, keeping the country at the point of violence. Hashina did not allow slowing down the activity of the industry.

The industry begins to show growth. The Hasina government wanted to stop the violence at the very root. As such in 2014, a tribunal was set up to investigate the human rights violations committed during the 1971 war for independence. She never dared to carry out death sentences against Islamist leaders without waiting for opportune time, which is very rare in the world of politics.

The **economy of Bangladesh** is the thirty-second largest in the world by purchasing power parity and is classified among eleven emerging market economies in the world. Bangladesh has shown tremendous growth in the economic sector. According to IMF, Bangladesh's economy is the second fastest growing major economy of 2016 under Hasina administration. It GDP (the Gross Domestic Product) is at the rate of 6.7%. Dhaka became the wealthiest Bangladeshi division and its contribution in GDP is of US$231 billion in a year. And the Chittagong Division serves as the largest export hub of the country.

Growth is expected to inch up to 7.1% by the end of FY2016, underpinned by stronger garment exports and also by rising private consumption as government employees find their wage increased. It was a gradual increase, from FY2014 to FY2015, the growth index increases from 6.1 to 6.6 % and up to 6.7% in FY2016, despite a short period of political protest at midyear that disrupted transportation and services in 2014, although growth in agriculture moderated to a lower grade to 3.3% from 4.4% because of harvests debacle.

Politics of Bangladesh was guided by Mujibur Rahaman for the period of 1971 to 1975 in particular. He was the founder father of Bangladesh, 7 March 1971, he announced civil disobedience in East Pakistan, 26 March 1971, Pak military of West Pakistan started operation, and Mujibur Rahaman was arrested and taken to West Pakistan and kept under military custody. Bangladesh liberation movement started, the movement continued for nine months, killing, torture, and eviction continued and finally on 16 December 1971, the declaration of independence of Bangladesh came into being.

Mujib helped Bangladesh to enter into the United Nations and the non-aligned movement. He travelled to the United States, the United Kingdom, and other European nations to obtain humanitarian and developmental assistance for the nation. He signed a treaty of friendship with India, which pledged extensive economic and humanitarian assistance and began training Bangladesh's security forces and government personnel. Mujib forged a close friendship with Indira

Gandhi. The report of seventy thousand people dead shocked Mujib and started political unrest giving rise to increasing violence. In response, to increasing violence on 25 January 1975 Mujib declared a state of emergency. On 15 August 1975, a group of junior army officers invaded the presidential residence with tanks and killed Mujib, his family and all of personal staff. His daughters Sheikh Hasina escaped as she was outside of the country.

The ruling period of Ziaur Rahman (1975–1981) started after the killing of Mujibor Rahaman. Mujib's death plunged the nation into many years of political turmoil. The coup leaders were soon overthrown and a series of counter-coups and political assassinations paralysed the country. However, the order of administration was largely restored after a coup in 1977 under the control of the army chief Ziaur Rahman. Declaring himself president in 1978, Ziaur Rahman thought wisely to bring restoration in administration and stability of normalcy. He signed the Indemnity Ordinance, giving immunity from prosecution to the men who plotted Mujib's assassination and the plan of overthrowing Mujib's government. He carried out a national election in 1978 and won the election with 76% vote.

Ziaur Rahman enacted several administrative measures, some to discipline the army, some to solidify his power and some to win the support of far-righted groups including Islamic political parties. However, he was silent to say anything against Awami League leaders.

He re-introduced multi-party politics, he allowed Sheikh Hasina, the exiled daughter of Sheikh Mujibur Rahman, to return to Bangladesh in 1981. He also allowed earlier banned Jamaat-e-Islam, leaders to do politics under different party name. But he was highly criticised for that as Jamaat-e-Islamic party collaborated with the Pakistani army and unsuccessfully working in preventing Bangladesh's independence and thereby the party had committed war crimes. Gloam Azam, the exiled chief of the Jamaat-e-Islamic, was allowed to come back and visit his ill mother to Bangladesh in July 1978 with a Pakistani passport on a visitor's visa.

He also appointed some war criminals in ministry. He welcomed the other anti-liberation political entities like Muslim League and other Islamic parties. He gave foreign appointments to several men accused of murdering Sheikh. Zia gave jobs of ambassadors to many of Sheikh Mujib's assassins such as Major Dalim, Major Rasid, and other majors to African and Middle Eastern nations. Zia was criticised for ruthless treatment of his army opposition. Although he enjoyed overall popularity and public confidence, Zia's rehabilitation of some of the most controversial men in Bangladesh aroused fierce opposition from the supporters of the Awami League and veterans of Mukti Bahini. Amidst speculation and fears of unrest, Zia went on touring to Chittagong on 29 May 1981, where he was assassinated by the dissident elements of the military.

The ruling period of Ershad (1982–1987) started after the assassination of Ziaur Rahman. Ershad maintained loyalty to the new president Abdus Sattar, who had led the Bangladesh Nationalist Party (BNP) to victory in elections in 1982. Army Chief of Staff Lieutenant General Hussain Muhammad Ershad assumed power in a bloodless coup on 24 March 1982. Ershad became president on 11 December 1983. He granted important rights to tenants for the first time in the history of Bangladesh. Ershad played a key role during the SAARC Summit in 1985, which was the first summit held in Dhaka uniting all member states of South-east Asian states. He brought the leaders of India Rajiv Gandhi and Ziaul Hague of Pakistan together.

To bring popularity, Ershad approved amendments to the constitution of Bangladesh which declared Islam is the state religion, abandoning state secularism. He held the 'first democratic elections for village councils' in 1985. Ershad and his supporters founded a political party, Jatiyo Party, by name in order to restoring civilian rule. In 1986 he was nominated as the president by the Jatiyo Party. However the election was boycotted by the Bangladesh National Party, led by Zia's widow Khaleda Zia, which accused Ershad's government of trying to legitimise the military autocracy. The Awami League of Sheik Hasina, daughter of Sheikh Mujibir, also participated in the process of election. The Jatiyo Party led by Ershad, won the elections.

The two general elections were widely opposed by the opposition parties. BNP boycotted the election in 1986. There were reports of violence, human rights abuse, and inefficient administration during Ershad's tenure. There was unrest in the country. However, the government gained legitimacy and reputation of fame by the participation of the other major opposition party, Awami League, and Jamaat-e-Islam, the largest Islamist party of the nation. The government tried its level best with the coordination of all other parties to subsidise the unrest of the country.

The two terms of Khaleda Zia was noticeable for the period 1991–1996 and 2001–2006. Begum Khaleda Zia became the head of the BNP, who organised a coalition of political parties opposed to Ershad's regime. In elections held in 1991, Begum Khaleda Zia led the BNP to victory and became prime minister. In the next round of general elections of 1996, the Awami League came to power. The Awami Leaque, with other opposition parties, demanded that the next general elections to be held under a neutral caretaker government and that provision for caretaker governments to manage elections must be incorporated in the constitution. The ruling BNP refused to act on these demands.

Opposition parties launched an unprecedented campaign, calling strikes for weeks after weeks. The government accused them of destroying the economy while the opposition countered that BNP could solve this problem by acceding to their demands. Finding the government's adamant attitude, the Hasina Party contemplated to take a drastic step. In late 1995, the MPs of the Awami League and other parties resigned from the parliament. Parliament completed its term and a general election was held on 15 February 1996. The election was boycotted by all major parties. The new parliament, composed mostly of BNP members, amended the constitution to create provisions for a care taker government (CTG). The parliament hastily introduced the Care taker Government by passing the thirteenth amendment to the constitution. The parliament was dissolved to pave the way for parliamentary elections within ninety days. The parliamentary elections were held under a neutral caretaker government headed by retired chief Justice Muhammad Habibur Rahman. In the 12 June 1996 elections, BNP lost to Sheikh Hasina's Awami League. Winning 116 seats, the BNP emerged as the largest opposition party in the country's parliamentary history.

However, her party again came to power in 2001. Her government's term going to end in 2006, the scheduled January 2007 elections could not be held in time due to political violence and in-fighting. The opposition party bringing different kinds of charges against the government, demanded immediate resignation of the government. Due to political unrest, the government could not hold the election in time. The delayed election resulted in the possibility of a military takeover. On 11 January 2007, Army Chief General Moeen U Ahmed, along with a group of military officers, intervened to stage a bloodless coup and impose a state of emergency.

It is surprising to notice that at present in Bangladesh politics two ladies are holding the countries administration either as BNP or Awami League Party. After independence in 1947, Pakistan government one after another military ruler exploiting the Easter Part of Pakistan, i.e., East Pakistan without carrying out any large-scale profitable industry, any academic institute of advanced technology or any modern technology for agricultural growth of production. The people remain in strain of hard labour and remain alive by the gift of nature of almighty. The fish of water and the paddy of land are giving them the energy to survive. Both the leaders of the party, one is the widow Begum Khaleda Zia, the wife of Ziaur Rahman, and the other is the daughter of Mujibur Rahman, Bangabandhu of Bangladesh, did not remain in the closed door as the protector of house, as the general custom of Bengal woman. The call of thousands of poor, thousands of exploited people, exploited students, innumerable downtrodden in the verge of dyeing brought them in open city, brought them in front of public to tell them don't be disheartened, we the people of Bangladesh would create a new country, a new Bangladesh. As such it is fight between the two parties for the betterment of the people to give them better opportunity, better food, better communication, and better education and better status of life.

[4]

BNP (Bangladesh Nationalist Party) party was founded on 1 September 1978 by former Bangladeshi President

Ziaur Rahman. Begum Khaleda Zia came into the picture of Bangladesh politics after the assassination of Ziaur Rahaman. The assassination of her husband, the party president Ziaur Rahman, in the Chittagong Circuit House by a small group of military officials on 30 May 1981 had brought the greatest shock at her life. Although crowds of hundreds and thousands of people started protesting in major cities like Dhaka and Chittagong, and the funeral of Ziaur Rahman turned into one of the largest one with the participation of millions of people in Dhaka, her agony kept her in isolation for a while. But almighty has given her the strength and energy to proceed with the ideals of her husband to serve the people.

The party also holds the record of being the largest opposition in the history of parliamentary elections of the country with 116 seats in the seventh national election of 1996. The party is the symbol of Bengal nationalism as such the party floated the ideology of Bangladeshi nationalism as its core concept. BNP and students wing was the driving force in the 1990 uprising against the autocratic Ershad rule. The rightful protest of BNP supported by the public compelled the Ershad government to come down and thereby the party restored democracy in Bangladesh. Begum Khaleda

Zia was serving as the party's chairperson since 1983. She was elected as the first woman prime minister of Bangladesh and second in any Muslim country of the world in 1991.

II

The 'Awami League' Party of Bangladesh was initially started with the name as 'All Pakistan Awami Muslim League' founded in Dhaka, the capital of the then Pakistani province of East Bengal, in 1949 by Bengali nationalist Maulana Abdul Hamid Khan Bhashani, and later supported by Huseyn Shaheed who was asked to become the prime minister of Pakistan. The party later changed the party name as 'Awami League'. The party fought for independence against the military ruler of West Pakistan. The party under the leadership of Sheikh Mujibur Rahman, the founding father of Bangladesh, had achieved independence after a loss of few millions of countrymen. The party began to function since 1973, but very soon in 1975, the party was overthrown by the assassination of Sheikh Mujibur Rahman. It was an inhuman barbaric assassination as all the member of the family young, old or kids were massacred, but by the grace of almighty (Allah), the fortunate daughter Hassina survived as she was at that time of assassination was not in the country. After assassination the country was in turmoil, the lives of people are surviving only by the gifts of nature. After a span of military rule democracy was restored in 1990, when the Awami League emerged as one of the principal players of Bangladeshi politics. The young students were not remain in behind. The student wing of the party came in front with a new name as 'Bangladesh Chhatra Leaque'.

The ruling period of Sheikh Hasina (third term) might be extended as 1996–2001, and again in the period of 2009–2014, and after 2014 she is continuing for the third term. In December 2008, the caretaker government organised general elections where the Awami League and its Grand Alliance (with thirteen smaller parties) took a two-thirds majority of seats in the parliament. Sheikh Hasina became prime minister, and her party formed government in 2009. Sheikh Hasina is the present prime minister of Bangladesh. She is holding the office since January 2009. She previously served as prime minister from 1996 to 2001. She is the eldest of five children of Shekh Mujibur Rahman, the founding father and first president of Bangladesh, and widow of the nuclear scientist M.A.Wazed Miah. Hasina's political career has spanned more than four decades during which she has been both prime minister as well as opposition leader. She returned as prime minister after a landslide victory for the Awami League–led Grand Alliance in 20008, when the party took two-thirds of the seats in parliament. In January 2014 she became the prime minister for the third time after winning the 2014 parliamentary election, which was boycotted by the BNP-led alliance. She remained rigid to hold the election as scheduled. Hasina is considered one of the most powerful women in the world, ranking forty-seventh on Forbes' list of the 100 most powerful women in the world in 2014.

On 11 December 2008, Hasina formally announced her party's election manifesto during a news conference and vowed to build a 'Digital Bangladesh' by 2021. Her Party Awami League and its Grand Alliance (a total of fourteen parties) won the general election held on 29 December 2008 with a two-thirds majority. But Khaleda Zia, leader of BNP-led coalition (4-Party Alliance), rejected the results of the election by questioning the chief election commissioner for the new concept of 'stage-managing the parliamentary election'. Finally Hasina was sworn into office as the prime minister for the second time on 6 January 2009.

After being prime minister, Hasina honoured the terms of agreement and accordingly the party chief Hussain

Muhammad Ershad was made president. Hasina became the prime minister for the third time after winning the general election in January 2014, which was boycotted by the main opposition BNP led alliance. The election has been called 'an electoral farce'. But Husina got the public support.

[4]

The Linking Unit: The **Patriot**, Nikunja Behari Goswami, a silent worker, who had sacrificed his life keeping the ideals of Gandhi in his mind. He was a Hindu, who was born as a Brahmin, and also died as a Hindu as he was cremated with the customs and traditions of Hindu religion. But his mind was exhausted in the search of bringing a united spirit of development in the regions, a criterion was thought of as practised in other countries. Here in nut shell the idea is outlined to give a piece of satisfaction in the mind of the unknown Silent Patriot in absentia and expressed as **'Political Power vs. Scientific Power'**.

Political Power vs. Scientific Power is explained as follows. What is political power – **Power** is nothing but the ability to influence or control the behaviour of people. The use of power in politics need not involve force or the threat of force. Political power depends upon a political party that depends upon its activity in performing the social activity. A political party is assigned with a specific name. The rise of a political party depends upon the image of the party specifically upon the image of the party chief and the performance of the public works.

What is scientific power–The scientific power of a nation lies in its contributions in the field of science and technology. Manufacture of new materials will flood the country with the technique of industry bringing new useable products in the market. New technology will lead the country in the discovery of new products. The economic status of the nation will be lifted up by the export of these to outside. The knowledge of science would enhance in the production of many machines and tools, utilised for the purpose of communication, and for production of new materials to create new chemicals and what-not.

What is natural economic powerhouse? The most important is the availability of minerals. China has the world's largest population with plenty of natural resources. It is the world's largest producer of gold, rice, wheat, rare earth metals, industrial metals, and coal. Although oil is one of few major commodities where China is abundant but even then China has respectable rubbing shoulders with Iran since long. Water is another gift of nature. Some of the world's largest rivers—the Yangtze, Huang He, Brahmaputra, Indus, Mekong, Pearl, and Amur origin existed there, giving China the opportunity of creating the source of world's biggest potential for hydropower and centre of bountiful water. This is an enormous lucky opportunity of nature to become a centre of luxury for a country located around the Tropic of Cancer, while most areas in this latitude are surrounded with nothing but deserts.

What is artificial economic powerhouse? Britain led the industrial revolution and dominated the European and world economy during the nineteenth century? It was the major innovator in machinery such as steam engines (for pumps, factories, railway locomotives, and steamships), textile equipment, and tool-making. It invented the railway system and built much of the equipment used by other nations. As well it was a leader in international and domestic banking, entrepreneurship, and trade. It has established a global British empire. By dint of his broadness of mind and huge potentials of administrative capacity it had made the British empire of its own by opening 'free trade,' with no tariffs or quotas or restrictions. It created the Royal Navy and trained the same with utmost efficiency. The powerful Royal

Navy protected its global holdings, while its unique legal system provided the best of tools in administration for resolving disputes inexpensively within a very short span of time.

The rising of British empire was the exposure of efficient management. By the time of 1870 and 1900, economic output per head of population in Britain and Ireland rose by 500 per cent, generating a significant rise in living standards. However, from the end of nineteenth century onwards Britain experienced a gradual economic decline as other nations such as the United States and Germany began to rise up in science and technology. In 1870, Britain's output per head was the second highest in the world after Australia. But our political leaders of that time instead of learning the art of science remained busy in the performance of religious activity to develop the conscious of mind in the search of creator and creation. But much later after 1945, Japan learnt the art of science in the land of Britain, and very soon became one of the Asian prides of nation by becoming a country of an economic giant of the world.

The people of Britain might be of white skin, where Indians are not, but the Britain has given the Indians a lot, the education, the language English, by dint of which the whole region is integrated, a bond of travel communication being established, besides the establishment of contacting communication link through English. In the field of administration and trade Bengal was a fortunate state to get the highest benefit. It was not only the building of one of the finest city of Calcutta adjusting the three villages, but also of creating the industrial belt starting from Howrah to Asansol and improving the Calcutta seaport and communicating it with the West and African countries via Suez Canal. Had the Bengalis cherish with British, they could rule the British empire by virtue of their dedication to work and the strength of population compare to British.

Why Western country like Britain, France, Portugal, and Spain did come to India and South-east Asia? It might be noticed that the historical record reveals that it is the political power that tempted all the Western countries to go to the South-east Asian countries to do trade and bring the benefit to the country in the darkness of science. It was in this period science was unknown and manufacture of scientific product was not known to the people. During the 1500s and 1600s the Europeans were successful to move long distance with ships. They always think for their country how to bring economic prosperity. As they were surrounded by the sea of nature, the natural God has not given them much of natural minerals that compel them always to make in their way out to other continent in search of wealth. Many of Europeans countries in their endeavour had reached to India and South-east Asia for trade and they have spread out there as such that they were in full control of the international trade of Asia. Thus they were successful in diverting the profits made out of trade from Asia to Europe. As a result, the many countries of Europe became stronger while Asian empires and kingdoms of Asia became weaker.

By the 1800s the Europeans were in a position to establish their authority over Asia, particularly in the territory of the Indian subcontinent and South-east Asia. Portugal, Spain, the Netherlands, Great Britain, France, and the United States had established their colonies in South-east Asia. The Portuguese had the least impact on South-east Asia, as they captured Malacca in 1511, and they hold it until the Dutch seized it in 1641. Otherwise, they acquired only a small piece of area on the island of Timor, South-east of Bali.

On the part of Spain, the adjacent country of Portuguese ruled the Philippines from its conquest of Cebu in 1565 and Manila in 1571 until its defeat in the Spanish-American War in 1898. Dutch colonialism of Netherland falls into Dutch East India Company that lasted from

1605 to 1799 and in 1825, after the Napoleonic Wars it began to bring the Indonesian archipelago under its administrative authority. This process was completed during the 1930s. At the end of the Second World War, the Dutch had hoped to retain its colony, but the Indonesians opposed the return of the Dutch, setting up a republic in 1945. In 1949, after four years of fighting, the Indonesians gained their independence with the assistance of the United Nations, which served as a mediator between the Indonesians and the Dutch.

The country of Great Britain, a country of importance to India, as it had made its colony in India after the battle of Palassey, is to count a lot, to remind the ruling of India, the long battle of independence struggle of India, and lastly the partition of India based on British proposal of bifurcation of India. The British conquered Burma, fighting three Anglo-Burmese Wars in 1824–26, 1852, and 1885–86. Unlike other colonies which maintained their ethnic identity, Burma became a province of British India, making Burma under the administration of two sets of rulers, the British as well as the Indians. In 1935 the British decided to separate Burma from India because of independence turmoil in India, and Calcutta in particular, making the agreement effective since 1937.

But at last Burma was able to negotiate its independence from Great Britain in 1948.

The other areas were also ruled by the British, such as Singapore (founded by Raffles in 1819), and Malacca (Melaka, acquired in 1824), as the Straits Settlements. The Straits Settlements were used as a base for British expansion into the Malay Peninsula between 1874 and 1914.

The lives of Indians were busy with almighty as God has given them minerals, hill, planes, rivers, and what-not. Indians did not require moving out to other places in search of food and foodstuff. It appears that the source of development in the absence of science was trade. The Indians never tried to learn the art of trade. The most of the common people used to spend their time in prayer, worship, and a little in agriculture. However the product of agriculture was not in abundance because of lacking in the art of 'Grow More Food' due to which very often the outbreak of famine had taken away lots of lives of poor Indians.

The country of France is equally important which is bigger than United Kingdom and the most vibrant country in the Europe. But France is also like other Western countries in search of doing trade with South-east countries and India as well and also in their effort to establish colonies in the moment of opportunity. As the country is less rich with natural product and the Asia is rich with natural product, their aim was to establish trade, establish colony and transfer the wealth as much as possible to the country of their own.

Thus France moved into Vietnam in 1858, capturing Saigon in 1859. Using the south, the then called Cochin China, as a base the French moved out towards west and north completing the conquest of Indo-china by 1907 including Laos and Cambodia. The French also wanted to retain their colony after the Second World War, but the Vietnamese rejected French rule. However, the Vietnamese defeating the French got their independence at the Geneva Conference in 1954.

The United States did not remain behind to establish trade in South-east Asia as the US moved into the Philippines as a result of the peace settlement with Spain in 1898. However later on, the Filipinos were granted a Commonwealth (internal autonomy) government in 1935 and independence in 1946.

Economic revolution after Science found to be seen in the twentieth century after the discovery of science and utilisation of science in the manufactures of hundreds and thousands of useable materials that had changed the world scenario. All Western countries slowly went away from the South-east Asia regions, but scientifically they manufactured the scientific products and marketed the products in Asia, the trend of economy changes its track. It was no longer now a trade and colony but it had changed its trend in the process of manufacturing goods and transformation of goods to the countries in demand. Thus economy rested with the West first as a means of trade before the discovery of science and now again the economy rested with the West after the discovery of science and manufacturing of goods.

But in India, the Indian leaders were not in any way concerns with the economy of the country, as such poverty, famine, and food crisis was very much prevalent in the country. There was division between rich and poor, clash between religious people, only because of the demand of more food. The demand leads to party. The British ruler utilised their brain to sustain the division among the people and as such separate system of living, with separate custom has emerged and thereby segregated the people of the same country. The power hungry people utilised the religion to reach to their goal of power.

[5]

The Linking Unit: The **Patriot**, Nikunja Behari Goswami, a silent worker, who had sacrificed his life keeping the ideals of Gandhi in his mind. He was a Hindu, who was born as a Brahmin, and also died as a Hindu as he was cremated with the customs and traditions of Hindu religion. Although he had travelled to Delhi to receive the award from the Indian Prime Minister Indira Gandhi, and visited other places of North and South India, besides United Kingdom for the cause of personal visit, but most of the time he remained in the district of Sylhet besides his occasional visit to Dacca, Chittagong, and other places of East Bengal or East Pakistan or Bangladesh, which had acquired the different names in his life time. As he has spent the major part of his life in Sylhet, with a dream in mind to make it a place of history remained incomplete, a description of the place is outlined here under the heading **Importance of Place** to note the place how important it was.

Let us talk of Importance of Place. Everybody knows the place of importance of London, Washington in the West, and Calcutta in the East during British India but nobody knows SYLHET, a place of importance in Bengal once, and because of its importance in terms of its geographical position, importance in terms of hills, planes, rivers, and vast cultivable land, a land of importance of its position existing below sea level, and because of the existence of different categories of people intellectual, skilled workers, hardworking people specialised in growing tea like products in the slop of hills, and paddy in the vast land of planes and again trained people to live over water by the easy movement over the surface of water, performing trade and business with the wealth of silent water what had drawn the attention of the administration time to time to make it a part of making its fortune to become a part of Assam during British period being ceased from Bengal, but after independence its fortune again changes to become a part of East Bengal cum East Pakistan and after liberation of Bangladesh it became a part of Bangladesh. Let us know why and how all these places become the places of importance.

LONDON is a place of civilisation. It has a history dating back over two thousand years. During that time period, it has grown to become one of the most significant financial and cultural capitals of planet Earth. The City of London was once a tiny part of the wider metropolis of the present Greater London. It is the capital and most populous city of England and the

United Kingdom, standing on the River Thames in the south-eastern part of the island of Great Britain. It was founded by the Romans, who named it Londinium. London's ancient core, the City of London, largely retains its 1.12 square mile (2.9 km^2), and in 2011 London had a resident population of 7,375, making it the smallest city in England. However, one should not have forgotten that the place has experienced plaque, devastating fire, civil war, aerial bombardment, terrorist attacks, and widespread rioting.

It is astonishing to hear that the city of London, the centre of civilisation was suffered with **Plague**. How it had happened? It happened due to biting of flea, which lasted from 1665 to 1666. But it did not completely die down because the new outbreak occurred with other forms of Plague, which is usually transmitted through the bite of an infected rat flea and it continued until 1750 causing the death of a hundred thousand people, almost a quarter of London's population.

The city was affected by fire which is known as **the Great Fire of London**. It was a major conflagration that swept through the central parts of the English city of London, from Sunday, 2 September, to Wednesday, 5 September 1666. The fire gutted the medieval city of London, the old Roman city wall, but the Palace of Whitehall was saved. It consumed 13,200 houses, 87 parish churches, St Paul's Cathedral, and most of the buildings of the city authorities. It is estimated to have destroyed the homes of 70,000 of the city's 80,000 inhabitants.

It was a city of English **Civil War** (1642–1651). The war was in between the supporters of the parliament of England, who are called **Roundhead** and the supporters of the King Charles I of England, who are called **Cavaliers** or Royalists. The Cavaliers claim rule by absolute monarchy while the Roundhead party claim the right of parliament to be supreme to control over executive administration. Most of Roundheads appear to have sought a constitutional monarchy in place of the absolute monarchy as sought by Charles I. There was series of armed conflicts and political machinations between parliamentarians and royalists. The first war was in between 1642–1646, and the second war was in between 1648–1649, among the supporters of King Charles I against the supporters of the Long Parliament, while the third (1649–51) saw fighting between supporters of King Charles II and supporters of the Long Parliament. The war ended with the parliamentarian victory at the Battle of Worcester on 3 September 1651.

The overall outcome of the war was threefold, the trial and the execution of Charles I, the exile of his son, Charles II; and the replacement of English monarchy with the Commonwealth of England. However, at the end of the English Civil War the system of monarchy was abolished completely and the system of **Commonwealth of England** was established.

Lightning War (World War II) was a spectacular war for London to remember. The strategic bombing of the United Kingdom was started by Nazi Germany during the period of Second World War. It was the time period of 7 September 1940 and 21 May 1941, sixteen British cities suffered aerial raids with at least 100 long tonnes (tonne, the unit of measurement) of high explosives. In a period of 267 days, London was attacked seventy-one times, Birmingham, Liverpool, and Plymouth eight times, Bristol six, Glasgow five, Southampton four, Portsmouth and Hull three, and a minimum of one large raid on eight other cities.

This was as a result of a rapid escalation of war starting on 24 August 1940. It was the retaliatory attack of Hitler as the UK Prime Minister Winston Churchill attack Berlin with its RAF (Royal Air Force), the aerial warfare force of UK. By robust repeated attack of Hitler over the country of Winston Churchill in revenge more than one million London houses were destroyed or damaged and more than forty thousand civilians were killed, almost half of them in London ports and industrial centres outside of London were also attacked. The main Atlantic sea port of Liverpool was bombed, causing nearly four thousand deaths. The North Sea port of Hull, a convenient and easily found target was subjected to 86 raids with a rough estimate of 1,200 civilians killed and 95 percent of its housing stock destroyed or damaged. Other ports were also bombed, and also the industrial cities like Birmingham, Belfast, Coventry, Glasgow, Manchester, and Sheffield.

But the bombing failed to demoralise the British into surrender or significantly failed to damage the war economy. The eight months of bombing never seriously hampered British production and the war industries continued to operate and expand. By May 1941 the threat of an invasion of Britain had gone away as Hitler's attention had turned towards the East. On 22 June 1941, Adolf Hitler launched his armies eastward in a massive invasion of the Soviet Union along with three great army groups with over three million German soldiers, 150 divisions, and three thousand tanks smashed across the frontier into Soviet territory. Thus Britain was saved from the threat of surrender. Now London is a place of humanity, visitors without fear and anxiety travel and flooded the London Airport Heathrow every year, a beauty of a small place of the universe.

The capital WASHINGTON is the memory of George Washington, the founding Father of USA. Washington, D.C., is formally belonging to District of Columbia and commonly referred to as 'Washington', 'the District', or simply 'D.C.'is the capital of the United States. The capital district was created by the signing of an act on16 July 1790, that being located along the Potomac River on the country's East Coast. The US Constitution provided for a federal district under the exclusive jurisdiction of the congress and the district is therefore not a part of any US state.

However the states of Maryland and Virginia each donated land to form the federal district, making settlements with Georgetown and Alexandria. The federal district is named in honour of George Washington, one of the United States' Founding Fathers and the leader of the American Continental Army who won the Revolutionary War, the city of Washington was founded in 1791 to serve as the new national capital.

Washington had an estimated population of 672,228 as of July 2015. Commuters from the surrounding Maryland

and Virginia suburbs shifted to the city and thereby the city's population gets increased by more than one million during the working days. The **history of Washington** is tied to do its role as the capital of the United States being originally inhabited by an Algonquian-speaking people, who are the most populous and widespread North American native's language groups.

The **Burning of Washington** in 1814 was an attack during the war period between British forces and those of the United States of America. On 24 August 1814, after defeating the Americans at the Battle of Bladensburg, a British force led by Major General Robert Ross occupied Washington, and set fire to many public buildings, including the White House and the Capitol, as well as other facilities of the US government.

The attack was in part of retaliation for the American destruction of Port Dover in Upper Canada. It marks the only time in US history that Washington, D.C., had been occupied by a foreign force. However, within less than a day Americans in a hurricane attack killed the British troops and regain control of the city.

CALCUTTA CITY is a pride to India, but it was the product of British India. There were three large villages along the east bank of the river Ganges. These three villages were brought together by the British from the local landlords and shaped it to a modern city of Calcutta. At the outset the British landed here as the Mughal emperor granted East India Company freedom of trade in return for a yearly payment of 3,000 rupees. The capital of Bengal was Murshidabad, around 60 miles north of Calcutta. In 1756, Siraj-ud-daullah, Nawab of Bengal, attacked the city and captured the Fort of Calcutta, as the Nawab did not like the British to increase its influence in Bengal. But looking to the future prospect, the Fort was recaptured in 1757 by Robert Clive when the British defeated Siraj-ud-daullah on the battle field of Plassey.

In 1772, Calcutta became the capital of British India, and the first Governor-General Warren Hastings moved all important offices from Murshidabad to Calcutta. Till 1912, Calcutta was the capital of India, when the British moved the capital city to Delhi. In 1947, when India gained freedom and the country got partitioned between India and Pakistan, Calcutta was included in the Indian part of Bengal, West Bengal. Calcutta became the capital city of the state of West Bengal.

Kolkata (Calcutta) grew rapidly in the nineteenth century to become the second city of the British empire. This was accompanied by the development of a culture that fused European philosophies with Indian tradition. Raja Ram Mohan Roy was a visionary to turn the Bengal to a Western progressive mind-set by the abolition of prejudices like Sati-Dhao. The city is also noted for its revolutionary history, ranging from the Indian struggle for independence to the leftist <u>Naxalite</u> and tradeunion movements. Besides labelling Calcutta as the 'Cultural Capital of India', 'The City of Processions', 'The City of Palaces', and the 'City of Joy', the city has also been glorified by the birth of few prominent people such as Shri Ramakrishna Paramhamsa, Swami Vivekananda, Rabindranath Tagore, Kazi Nazrul Islam, Subhas Chandra Bose, and Mother Teresa of Rome.

The dream of Job Charnock was to make Calcutta a Dream City. The dream of making Calcutta to a modern city was the thinking of a British merchant Job Charnock in long back of 1686, as the place of Calcutta on the bank of River Hooghly would make it an ideal settlement, and as such by 1698 the villages of Sutanuti, Gobindapur, and Kalikata had been formally signed over to the British East India Company. The British thereupon created a miniature version of London-on-Hooghly, with stately buildings, wide boulevards, English churches, and grand formal gardens.

The grand illusion vanished abruptly at Calcutta's frayed edges where Indians servicing the Raj lived in cramped, overcrowded the place with slums and bastes. The most notable hiccup in the city's meteoric rise came in 1756, when Siraj-ud-Daula, the Nawab of nearby Murshidabad, recaptured the city. Dozens of members of the colonial aristocracy were imprisoned in a cramped room beneath Fort William. By morning, around forty of them were dead from suffocation. The British press exaggerated numbers, drumming up moral outrage back home, the legend of the 'Black Hole of Calcutta' was born.

The following year, Clive of England arrived in India and retook Calcutta for Britain and made peace with the Nawab, promptly sided with the French and later soundly defeated Nawab at the Battle of Plassey (now Palashi). The late nineteenth century Bengali Renaissance movement saw a great cultural reawakening among the elite and middle-class residents of Calcutta. This was further integrated with a bond of unity by the massively unpopular 1905 division of Bengal. Although the division of Bengal could not be sustained because of the attachment of Bengal unity being galvanized by the patriotic song of Bengal, anyway it sowed the seeds of the Indian Independence movement with the under current feelings of two Bengal. The clever British allowed the Bengal to get reunited in 1911, but promptly transferred their colonial capital to less trouble area of Delhi. Initially there was loss of political power but had little effect on Calcutta's economic status. But afterwards the affect was realised slowly and after partition, the impact of devastation was very much devastating.

Around four million Hindu refugees from East Bengal arrived; choking Calcutta's already overpopulated bastes. For a period, people were dying of hunger in the streets, creating Calcutta's abiding image of abject poverty. Making of makeshift bamboo huts beside the rail lines on the tracks was the common picture of the day where children were playing on the tracks and their parents cook and clean in the makeshift bamboo huts. No sooner had these refugees been absorbed than a second vast wave arrived during the 1971 following India-Pakistan War. Thus a place changes its appearance with the change of time.

6 A Spectacular PLACE–SYLHET

[1]

It was the most favourite and dear place of the **Patriot** (Nikunja Bihari Goswami) as he could see its enormous inside potential while the British ruler had seen only its importance as centre of communication to the whole of Easter India making the administration compelled to snatch the district from Bengal to Assam in 1874. The British idea was to enter Assam through the present Meghalaya; the central link is to reach Shillong of Meghalaya from Sylhet via Tamabil, the climate of Shillong being the best choice for the British people. It is the centre Sylhet, to the north, Assam, Arunachal and Bhutan, to the East Mizoram, Manipur, and Nagaland and further East Myanmar.

But after partition of India, Sylhet was separated from all the Indian states as it is now a part of Bangladesh. But he (Silent Patriot) was not disheartened, even during the bad time of communal tension, in the advent of lakhs of people proceeding towards India leaving their ancestral home, he advised many of them to his capacity not to leave the birthplace, he himself never thought to leave Sylhet, he outright rejected the proposal of Indira Gandhi in 1971 in the occasion of award ceremony to stay in India at the choice of your place. He believes in good time and bedtime. His belief was that bad time has gone and good time is in front.

New Modi government and the Bangladesh present government have undertaken lots of programme to improve the relation of the two countries; it would not only bring development in the region but also would help to enhance the status of life of the common people of this region. He was hopeful in his life time that a day will come when all the regions will be integrated in communication in road, rail, and air, in the spectra of development in setting industries, in the exploration of new technology and above all in the exchange of culture and amusement as it is now prevailing among the different countries of Europe in the form union of nations. Almost all the countries of Europe are more or less happy, economically strong and maintaining a high status of life.

In the case of the spread of religion, what is seen, when Sufi is finding its centre at Delhi, Bengal, Hyderabad,

Dhaka, the place Sylhet was included as a place of importance to spread Sufism. Sylhet is a prominent Islamic spiritual centre and home to numerous Sufi shrines. Sylhet has a reputation as the **spiritual capital** of Bangladesh and also recognised as the Holy Land of Bangladesh. It hosts the fourteenth century mausoleums of Shah Jalal and Shah Paran. It is also the ancestral home of sixteenth century Krishna Chaitanya (Mahapravu Sri Chaitanya) in what is now rested in the name of Golapganj Upazilla of the district.

Sylhet is a major city that lies on the banks of Surma River in north-east of present Bangladesh. As of the 2011 census, the city has a population of 479,837. It is surrounded by tea estates, sub-tropical hills, rainforests, and river valleys; it is a tourist attraction centre. The city has one of the highest literacy rates in the country. Many people of Sylhet live abroad, particularly in London of the UK. The people by nature prefer exploration, to move distance places and search for available opportunities, that nature made them visitors and settlers in different places of the world. Today they are found to be present not only in UK in abundance, but also in the different states of USA, Malaysia, Singapore, Myanmar, Indonesia, and Sri Lanka besides the Arab world.

The Sylhet municipality was constituted during the British Raj in 1867. It was a part of the Bengal presidency and Assam Province. It became a part of East Bengal again after the Partition of British India in 1947. Now Sylhet district is sub-divided into four districts (Zilah), Habiganj, Moulivibazar, Sunamganj, and Sylhet. It is again divided into thirty-five Upazila.

Sylhet became a focal point for Bengali revolutionaries during the Bangladesh Liberation War in 1971, because it was the home town of General M. A. G. Osmani, the commander-in-chief of Bangladesh Forces. The Sylhet division produces most of Bangladesh's tea yield, fertilizer, and natural gas. It is also known for its cane, citrus, timber, and agar wood. Sylhet is often visited by the Bangladeshi diasporas, particularly from the United Kingdom to its Osmani International Airport of Sylhet.

The dream of Silent Patriot of making London on the bank of Surma River sounds absurd but nothing is impossible. The city of London, standing on the bank of Thames, smaller in size in compare to River Surma, having an area of 1.12 sq.miles with population strength of 7,375, suffered with plague for years together, devastated by Great Fire of 1666, succumbed with 80,000 inhabitants, destroyed with Civil War for a long period (1642–1651), and finally burnt to ashes by the bombing of the Nazi government of Hitler reducing all the major cities like Birmingham, Liverpool, Plymouth, Bristol, Glasgow, Southampton, Portsmouth, and Hull to the ground had risen again to rebuilt London, again to make a centre of attraction for the tourists of the world to see the magnificent Westminster Abbey and the Buckingham Palace. Similar to the creation of city of London on the bank of River Thames, the city of SYLHET, on the bank of River Surma having with larger square miles and larger population is also possible to be emerged as it was once dreamt of by **Patriot** Nikunja Bihari Goswami.

His dream was to think of an airport like Heathrow, although by the time Osmania International Airport is built up of mini structure. It is a place connected by River Surma, connected by sea, Bay of Bengal by crossing a little distance to Port of Chittagong and also connected by road and rail. The sub-divided four districts, Habiganj, Moulivibazar, Sunamganj, and Sylhet, are the best and appropriate places to remodel and endure to design to restructure like that of the place of Manchester, Birmingham, and London in serial upto South, Southampton of extreme south, Plymouth of extreme South-west, and Glasgow in the North, besides the other places of Liverpool, Bristol, Portsmouth, and Hull to bring the *dream* land to a reality.

It is also connected to the Port of Chittagong by the national road and by Bangladesh Railway track. The Bangladesh-India border in Tamabil is located to the north of the city, an important gateway to the north-east of India. Sylhet is also home to the Shahijalal University of Science and Technology, the expansion and improvement of the university might lead to the formation of Oxford and Cambridge. The imagination of *dream* city of Sylhet might have brought a kind of satisfaction in the departed soul of Silent Patriot Nikunja Bihari Goswami.

The beauty of Sylhet lies with its four sub-division, now districts (Zillah), Habiganj, Moulivibazar, Sunamganj, and Sylhet, again with its divided Upazilas spreading its extension towards villages, in the language of Kabi Guru Rabindranath Tagore 'GRAM-BANGLA'. Each village has its wonderful characteristics; one such village is called Derai. Let us have an idea of the village, how it survives, how it gives a service to the people in the day to day life, how it brings inspiration in the progress of life, in sports, in community service without a pinch of thought of religion, and above all in the act of entertainment is a wonder to know, but the greatest tragedy lies when we see today, all such kinds of activity had vanished from Derai, the beauty of GRAM-BANGLA no longer exists only due to power politics of the few politicians of the nation.

There was only one man who came from North India to Sylhet who was no other than Gandhi with a Fakir dress, who had enlightened the people, particularly the Hindu people with a so-called God's spirit of 'non-violence'. His idea was to corner the British administration and compel the British to surrender to Indians. He lives in Delhi, Calcutta, Bombay, or London of big cities and always encountered with elite sections of the cities, how he could understand the simple mind-set of village people. As the local Muslim leaders did not like the spirit of non-violence, they asked the common Muslims not to join non-violence movement.

The God's spirit of 'non-violence' had created a kind of mis-understanding among the common people which had spread to every corner of villages and destroyed the beauty of GRAM-BANGLA where the people were living as one entity of one family. The Hindu-Muslim mis-understanding spoiled the unity of one family of one village. This was not only in one village but in every village of Bengal particularly in East Bengal, where the people, all community of all religion, or non-religion no matter who were living together, helping each other in distress and in the event of any danger, and again enjoying together in the spirit of laugh and laughter. But who had destroyed the beauty of GRAM-BANGLA?

The more one will speak for the little village Derai, the more painful he would be. The existence of Derai, the development of Derai, the amusement of Derai all rested mainly with one family, the family knows by a name called CHOWDHURY Bari (Chowdhury House or Chowdhury Villa). It has a long history why it was so called. The depth of the history of this family goes beyond seven generation. It started with Jiban Deb, DeepChand, Suprup Roy, Sudarshan Roy followed by Sukhamoy Roy and Rasamoy Roy. It was a small script of land area, a very low land area connected by a river called Kalni Nadi, remains almost under water during rainy season. The Chowdhury House consisting of greater land area, comparatively a little high land area, was a centre of getting together, a centre of meeting place and a place of amusement. But the importance as well as the activity of the house was increased a step further due the administrative policy of the British government. In order to collect government revenue, Lord Cornwallis came with a new formula and extended it to the extreme corner of Bengal. Since 1793, a permanent class of landlords or Zamindar was created for the collection of revenue. Since then the family house was transformed into CHOWDHURY House.

The activity of CHOWDHURY House brings a tale of pain and pleasure. The pleasure was that all village people of Derai, as well as the people of other nearby places such as Chandipur (a Muslim-dominated place), Chandpur (a Hindu-dominated place), Dhal, Koldum used to come to this house on a regular basis to exchange their views, happiness, and sorrow as if it is the place to put up any complaint and again it is the place where complain would definitely be solved. In the course of time, the place Derai has improved a step further. At that time education was a remote thinking for the village people. But the CHOWDHURY House has enlightened their family members by education by sending their family member to distant Calcutta of West Bengal for learning the beauty of language English, the art of administration or the rule of law, where the British had not only transformed the three villages of that area to create the beautiful city Calcutta to make it the capital of British empire but also created a college in the name of Presidency College for giving education to the Indian people through the language of English. The CHOWDHURY House thought for the education of the village people.

The Chowdhury House offered a part of their land for the creation of a school, today what is now dazzling as Derai High English School. The idea was developed on seeing the learning on Panchakhanda, another place in the Gram-Bangla of Sylhet 8 miles away from the district town Karimganj. Rasamoy Chowdhury of Chowdhury family, the first BA of this region gave a dedicated service to this school till his death. Here is small picture of Derai house made in a course of journey still existed bearing the symbol of the house and testifying the old memory in imparting the inspiration in the field of education, sports, and amusement.

[A picture of CHOWDHURY House, a recreation centre of GRAM-BANGLA, Derai.]

It was spectacular to remember the art of amusement. During that period of time, there was no electricity, no cinema or any tools of cinema. But there were few village people who had been born here with inborn quality of the scene of art and the spectra of vision. What they did, they made big screen by plain cloth and designed the same with different colour, and finally by placing the coloured screen at the back of theatre room they could produce the wonder, by the display of light in an atmosphere of dark. It gets turned into a scene of sea, which is in no way less than the scene of present day cinema. Like that they could produce any scene as they wish to bring the art of cinema even in the period of dark days when nothing was known to them. It was here, the centre of such activity, how one could forget, there lays the beauty as well as affinity of Gram-Bangla.

The house brings pleasure when one remembers the past and the attachment of the house with the incidents of the past. Adjacent to the CHOWDHURY house there was a vast open land although it goes underwater during rainy seasons, which is used by the village boys for sports especially for football, a very popular game for the region and thereby Derai has produced national football players. But the memorable think was that for any competition or big play sometimes with town players of nearby Sunamganj, all the players on their return would visit the CHOWDHURY House and enjoy the mango fruits as they know the house is full of mango trees. They would not rest only in the outer house; they would go inside and enjoy any other fruits on their own as if they are the members of the house. What a splendid pleasure one can enjoy is beyond description.

Derai has developed by the time as a centre of culture. The performance of pleasure through the songs of Hason Raja was the source of inspiration for the area. The performance of theatrical function was a regular feature of the place. The CHOWDHURY House was the centre of all activity and the nearby school was the place of centre for display. People of all category of all religion without age group, without distinction of boys and girls, male or female flock together to enjoy the display of theatre. It was a small village, it has a small market, people of nearby places use to come to the market to enjoy, someone by sailing of something again the some others by buying of something. As the roads were not good enough, people prefer to come by boat, of course, in the rainy season it must be with boat as all the roads remain underwater.

It was a kind of amusement as well as enjoyment. The life of these common village people were not luxurious as they were always in economic scarcity, but their mind was always luxurious as they enjoy in the process of boating in the journey and enjoy by talking with people in free mind in the gathering of market without bothering who is Hindu or who is Muslim, here they feel as if they are here one, people of one village, people of one market. They are a friend in need and they are a friend all the time.

The dedicated teacher of CHOWDHURY House had a greater plan in his mind. It was not only his service as a teacher to teach all the boys and girls of the village but also made the village a beauty of BANGO-GRAM in the language of poet Rabindranath Tagore. He had a plan to educate his children in different sectors of technology and utilise them in building the village Derai, but by the time the political leader particularly Gandhi by his own strategy had designed a plan in secret in collaboration with another non-Bengali leader Jinnah to divide India and divide Bengal on the basis of religion. Everything was done in a moment of emotion; the clever Jinnah for the fulfilment of Pakistan for Punjabis utilised the spirit of Bengal leaders and Bengalis under the cover of Arab and Islam and started the movement of rioting in Calcutta of Bengal instead of Punjab to get Pakistan.

It was too late for Bengali Muslims to realise that a Bengali is a Bengali; he could never be an Arabian or a Punjabi under the cover of Islam. The realisation came after a gap of twenty-three years by dint of which Bangladesh came into being. But in the meantime much water has flown over the river Ganga. The West Pakistani Punjabi rulers utilised the simple-minded Muslim Bengalis to root out the Hindus from their ancestral home of East Bengal in the name of Islam due to which their percentage has fallen down from 47% to less than 12%. Bengali Muslims could not realise how much damage they have done to Bengal or Bangladesh. Had the Hindus and Muslims been together, like the black and white of USA, the fate of Bengal would have been different, it might not be a superpower but at least a powerful, respectable democratic country where the Hindus would give their full support and energy in building the nation as it would be a nation of Bengalis and not of Hindus or Muslims.

Bangladesh has come into existence. But by the time Bengali Hindus of Bangladesh has almost finished, and this is a huge loss to Bangladesh. How the Bengali Hindu force of Bangladesh was perished it had now transformed into a record of history. These people fought for independence of India, but the fruits of independence were enjoyed by the people Northern India. The Hindu people of East Pakistan came here in India as refugee due to the torture of Pakistan army, but the Nehru government sent them far away to Dandakaurnya and also had taken them to a place of inhabitable hilly regions of Madhya Pradesh. Most of the refugee died and finally few of them had return on their own to Calcutta. Why Nehru had done it. It was because he never wanted that out of these people another Netaji should come out to endanger his throne. The dedicated teacher of CHOWDHURY House is no more but his children are there.

His ambition was partly fulfilled as he could educate his children but he could not utilise his children in the beautification of Derai. Today his children are out of Derai because of political situation. The political situation has compelled them to stay away, to stay away from their ancestral home, a home of seven generation. Who has made them **vagabond**; today they were living in different places of the world. They were not only in Calcutta, Mumbai, or Banaras of India, but also in abroad in Canada and USA. Their dream was to make Derai a city of Venice as its similarity was very much with the city of Canal, or the city of Bridges or Venice. The transportation of Derai and Venice is nothing but boat, a common feature for both the places. That was why it was a dream in the minds of the sons of the dedicated teacher that Derai would be a new Venice. Venice is one of the capital cities of Italy. It is located in the north-east of Italy consisting of small islands in the Venetian Lagoon. No doubt it is a city of Canal but again the canals are connected by bridges and so it is also called a city of Bridges. If the river Kalni of Derai is connected by bridges at different places, it would be in no way less than Venice.

The population of Venice was not large enough nearing 250,000. Its beauty has attracted the tourists and thereby its population gets increased. The beauty has made it a famous place for sweethearts, lovers, artists, and poets. If Derai transformed into a Dream Land, a city of canal, it could attract tourist through its water root that could be developed at ease and could made a wonder of the globe. If the beauty of Venice could made it a magical city, why did it not Derai to be a city of BANGO-GRAM. London is a place of UK surrounded by sea, a place of beauty, similar to that Derai is a place of Sylhet surrounded by river and water everywhere, why did it not a centre of beauty. God has given the natural beauty; it is the people of the place have to utilise the beauty of nature to make it a beauty of heaven. One day if the *dream* comes true, the sole of Silent Patriot Goswami would get the greatest satisfaction even remaining in heaven which he could not get in his life time in Earth.

Derai is just the one example of GRAM-BANGLA, what was destroyed by our leaders for political power is full of sorrow and pain. There are many such places where the people were living since generation to generation under the bondage of love and brotherhood, were destroyed by our political leaders for their gain of profit at the cost of sufferings and destruction of the common people. There was oneness in the display of culture, oneness in the taste of enjoyment, oneness in the physical appearance, why not the people of Indian subcontinent, the people of India, Pakistan, and Bangladesh could live together. It was not become possible because of power politics, politics with the power of chair. Gandhi was the glory of all as he had single-handedly compelled the mighty British to hand over the administration though he worked silently under the cover of a *saint*. But he had broken the heart of the ordinary people of GRAM-BANGLA. Who were the victims out of the power politics of political leaders, who were nothing but the common people, and the common citizens? The destruction of Gram-Bangla is an irreparable loss to Bengal as well as to Bangladesh.

The Linking Unit: The **Patriot**, Nikunja Behari Goswami, a silent worker, had sacrificed his life keeping the ideals of Gandhi in his mind. He was a Hindu, who was born as a Brahmin, and also died as a Hindu and cremated under Hindu customs. Many of his friends, relatives, and country men have left him. One of his known people of same place having qualified in Dacca University have gone to India after partition and engaged himself in social work like him in the building of an educational institute at Shillong. A little of his activity is entitle here to bring a kind of satisfaction to the heart of Silent Patriot in absentia.

7 Revolution of Science and Its Effect

[1]

That person was no other than **Veteran Sudhin Dutta**, who migrated to Shillong of Assam from Sylhet after partition of India and devoted his strength, energy in the service of the society. There was much similarity between them in the thinking of their service. The Silent Patriot involved himself direct in the service of the society while Veteran Dutta thought to serve the society indirectly. He was a scholar highly educated as such he devoted himself to do his best from academic point of view. He began to construct a college at Shillong. Accordingly Shillong College began to function, a college that faces enormous problem at the beginning in management, construction, and finance, but in the long run by dint of his enormous activity and determination every pieces of the act of problem has been materialised and stabilised to a beautiful pattern to make the college as one of the beautiful Institute in the construction of building, in academic activity of teaching and maintaining a huge collection of books in a library keeping neat and clean making the library as if an art of beauty of museum in the beautiful place of Shillong of Meghalaya.

The purpose of the institute was to bring people of different sector in the college in the form of academic discussion, seminar and enlighten the young generation to provide their service to build a better living region in this Eastern part of Indian subcontinent apart from imparting education. In this respect, the college authority invited once a professor of science on 12 March 2016 to talk on the contribution of science to the Indian society. Accordingly professor delivered his lecture on science, where he had outlined how science could change the spectra of the region if our political thinkers could think of it deeply instead of power politics bringing religion to divide the people.

[Professor Roy Choudhury delivering an academic lecture in front of students and teachers and other people of a different stream in Shillong College.]

As the discussion was related with **science and society**, it was noted here for everybody concerns, no matter the person belong to India, Bangladesh, or Pakistan or any place of anywhere. Shillong was once a place of thick jungle, but the British had made it a place of beauty as they were favourable to live in cold climate. They landed here travelling through Sylhet the only land-linking road connecting Sylhet to Shillong to get entry into Assam, where the adjacent states extended to Burma. As at that time the only communication language English of British administration was unknown to most of the people except only to few people of Sylhet. Thus these English knowing people of Sylhet became very near and dear one of British people. They set up their administrative unit here with the help of these people to extend British administration in Assam. Thereby a lot of English knowing people of Sylhet migrated to Shillong to take over the administration of Assam in British period. It was one of the reasons why today also quite a good number of people of Sylhet is presently living in the city centre of Shillong.

The substance of his talk was nothing but the matter and material of the world and their use for the benefit of mankind. It is the nature of every common citizen to see the good of the existing matter and to acquire the status of power of the matter. Similarly it is necessary to look into the method of skill and how to utilise the skill of intelligence to seat in the power of chair in the name of service to the society. But the power what is remained hidden in the material world if discovered and come in light, that exceeded all human powers, such as the power of atom bomb, the power of computer science, power of medicine, or the power of rocket. In India human intelligence is used to the best of its capacity to acquire the seat of power, if that intelligent is used in the case of matter to discover the hidden power existed in the matter, the situation might have been different. People would not be divided with the issue of religion. The world would have been different. Even today we know a little of the material world, we know the devastating power of atom bomb, due to one element of uranium of material world, not to speak of the other ninety-two elements of the material world, what had been harnessed by the Japanese people for the benefit of the mankind and thereby the discovery of nuclear reactor has come into being and Japan had made its fortune even after being converted to ashes by atom bomb.

Professor talked about carbon and carbon compounds and its use in medical science, without going into depth, he had given an idea how a compound is made of, examined and how the actual structure and shape of the compound is determined by the help of machine of spectroscope, because it is the carbon compound that will react with body structure of carbon compound as if a fight is going on between two resellers, the defeat of one reseller will only come out with the joy of victory for the other, as if it is the joy of curability. Thus the germs being infected in the body that have destroyed the carbon pattern of human body are rectified by the carbon content of the medicine carrying out a reseller fight in killing the germs inside of human body. Thus there is always a joy of victory behind some kind of destruction. Joy of victory lies in harnessing atomic energy behind the destruction occurred out of atom bomb, similarly the joy of victory lies in the discovery of medicines of carbon content utilised in the destruction or killing of germs.

If the material world of uranium is talk about, the atom of uranium consists of more than one type of atom which is called the isotopes of uranium atoms. The isotopes uranium -235 and another atom of plutonium -239 were selected by the atomic scientists because they readily undergo fission that means break down easily giving off energy. Fission occurs when a neutron strikes the nucleus of isotope, splitting the nucleus into fragments and releasing a tremendous amount of energy, what is the atomic nature of this matter. The fission process becomes self-sustaining as neutrons produced by the splitting of atom strike nearby nuclei and produce more fission. This is known as a chain reaction and that is what causes an atomic explosion. The atom bomb was made based on this principle. The dropping of two atom bombs on 6 August 1945 at Hiroshima and 9 August 1945 at Nagasaki compelled the king of Japan to surround as it had caused the death of few lakhs of Japanese army. Thus here also there is a victory of joy behind the destruction of lakhs and lakhs of human lives. It was because behind the destruction of human lives there remains the source of harnessing huge energy.

Now who has discovered the tremendous hidden power of the material world? It is the human brain. After the destruction of Japan into ashes by the **atom bomb** in 1945, the Japanese politician thought to learn the skill of harnessing material power, instead of knowing the skill of human power in power politics. In the world war, the United Kingdom was the worst affected country due to the repeated bombing attack of the Nazi government of Hitler over all the important city centres of the United Kingdom. As such scientific research was going on there very fast, lot of products out of materials world was manufactured, and thereby the country had stabilised its economic power.

Thus Japan after getting destroyed by atom bomb surrendered in exchange of learning science in the land of **United Kingdom**. Within a time period of fifteen years, Japan came forward with the discovery of nuclear reactor. The atomic energy of atom bomb that destroyed lakhs and lakhs of people to ashes is now stored in nuclear reactor and get transformed into electric energy.

It opened up the Japan's electronic technology in all available sectors making the country an economic giant in the world. The conversion of heat energy into electrical energy is not difficult to understand. The energy released in the fission process generates heat. A common method of harnessing the thermal energy is to boil water to produce pressurized steam which will then drive a steam turbine that turns an alternator and generates electricity. Thus Japan proved to the world that material power is in no way less inferior to human power.

Now let us talk about material science of computer as it became one of the most important learning subject matter of the present world. The material product is Silicon and the smallest particle electron of its atom in contact with electronic circuit has produced the wonderful machine of computer partly collaborated and contributed by the Indians too in the research conducted by the IBM company of USA for a long period of more than thirty years, resulting with the publication of PC in the market on 12 August 1981. After the dropping of atom bomb by USA over Japan and showing the magnitude of devastation the world was stunned. Japan went in search of hidden power of material science, but in India, Indian leaders were in a joyous mood to get independence and chair of power as the atom bomb terminated world war and British was no longer a force, although crying for famine was very high in Bengal.

The record of Gandhi's activity tells the secret of politics. Gandhi projected himself a saint by wiring the dresses of a Fakir, living in poor house of Dalit, eating vegetables and doing occasional fasting, as if he was for poor Indians working as a saint, but he was busy with political thinking behind the scene on his own way. Finding his non-violence movement against the British has created hatred in between Hindus and Muslims instead of huge mass protest, he went on secret collision with Jinnah in Jinnah's house at Bombay to stop the violence originated out of hatred. Finding no other alternative, it was decided finally to divide the country with specific demarcated area. Jinnah was happy with Pakistan and Nehru became the first prime minister of India. It appeared in public that Gandhi embracing Jinnah as if a family dispute had been settled.

Had he not been in power politics and he would have gone for the search of material power, he could bring an economic prosperity first in India like that of Japan. After knowing the hidden power of uranium -235 and plutonium-239 isotope, the leaders of other country were trying their best to know the hidden power of other atoms of the material world. The thinkers of Europe, USA, and UK tremendously started the research activity to know the power of the other elements of the material world. USA being not affected at all by the debacle of atom bombs in the war, the people being remained in a state of happiness, they refuse to take the strain of undergoing research activity to be undertaken by different companies in the land of USA.

Finding no research workers at USA, the companies of USA had undertaken the different project to carryout research activity with Indian students in India. In this respect IIT Kanpur was established in India in 1956. Seeing the progress of America, RUSSIA did not remain behind. Russia also came forward in establishing IIT Kharagpur in West Bengal of India. During that period, a power struggle between the two superpowers was going on in India in order to utilise the Indian students in the search of computer knowledge. American teachers and Russian teachers encircled India to harness Indian brain to find out the hidden power of the material world. After a certain interval of time IIT graduates came out with success, but the tragedy was that all graduates were accommodated abroad. Government of India never thinks of technology or economy. It continued for long twenty-five years, of course even now it is in process, the IIT graduate goes to USA as usual but now only the number is not 100%.

It is only recently few Indian companies have come up, Infosys company, a computer company working on information technology, outsourcing, since 1981, under the command of N. R. Narayan Murthy, making Bangalore the head-quarter, TCS company, a computer company working on information technology, consulting, business solution, since 1981, keeping head-quarter at Mumbai, under the command of J. R. D. Tata, and Wipro, another Indian company under the command of Premji is working on keeping the head-quarter at Bangalore.

It is good to hear that now Modi is saying 'the creation of smart city', similarly, Bangladesh Prime Minister Sheik Hussina is saying 'Bangladesh will be digital by 1921'. These are encouraging news for the people of the regions. Whatever way anybody can think but nobody can go against the natural phenomenon of the universe. If we look to the contribution of great scientists, we could see a clear picture. Newton said every action has a reaction, Galileo said,'Earth moved around the Sun.' If the sunlight is in one side, the darkness will be in the other side. A new building cannot be made without the destruction of the old one. God has sent every human being as a soldier to earth fitted with strength and energy to cultivate and glorify the life of universe utilising the strength of the body and human brain energy, but not **wasting the strength and energy** as a gift of sacrifice or as a virtue of tolerance in the form of non-violence.

[2]

Gandhi's theory of 'non-violence' to bring peace without utilising strength and energy is against the nature and also against the ethics of almighty. He contemplated the theory to apply in the case of independence movement of India was against the natural phenomenon. The world event justifies the fact, in USA Lincoln had brought a *peace* of unity after the destruction being occurred in Civil War, in France *peace* of democracy was established after French revolution, and after the killing of king, in China a *peace* of economic progress was sustained by Mao-Se-Tag after carrying out a massacre under a cultural revolution. Thus the natural phenomenon is that to get something one has to sacrifice some other thing. Thus Gandhi's movement of non-violence movement was against the natural phenomenon that was why the *unity* of India was destroyed. However it was a difficult task, almost next to impossible to bring the different units of India together and also to bring the people of different religious faith together as he had stricken hard to the sentiment of religion under the cover of a Hindu *saint*.

Had he been worked as a real politician instead of a religious politician, and had not carried out a religious movement like non-violence based on ethics of 'tolerance' of Hinduism, he could have done well to the society of Hindus and Muslims equally and succeeded to keep the unity of the nation. Gandhi might be a pious man but his political thinking was not good for the mankind. By the movement of 'non-violence', he had done the greatest harm to India and Indian people and also the mankind. The natural ethics of humanity is to utilise the strength and energy given by God for the betterment of mankind. If the strength and energy is not utilised and wasted as 'sacrifice' or as a gift of 'tolerance', it would be a misuse or an activity against the wishes of almighty or against the phenomenon of nature. As such it would violate the natural phenomenon. Any work against nature cannot bring fruitful result already proved by the scientists of the world. Thus it could be said that although Gandhi was honest, faithful, and above all *saint* like nature, but he had done a natural crime against the nature by carrying out 'non-violence' movement in India, as the movement is against the ethics of almighty as well as against the natural phenomenon.

[2]

The Linking Unit: The **Patriot**, Nikunja Behari Goswami, a silent worker, who had sacrificed his life in the service of the mankind. He was a born Hindu Brahmin, who died as a Hindu and cremated under Hindu customs. He thinks for his country as well as for mankind. As the progress and prosperity of a nation cannot be upgraded without the cooperation of the neighbour country, he prefers a good relation with all neighbouring country. With the spirit of his desire, a little description of each and every neighbour country if not possible at least a few of them is enlisted here.

Let us talk of neighbouring country Nepal. It is a nation as a part of the highest mountain Himalayas and resting at the foothills of Himalayas. It is lying in between two big countries China and India as such its history and culture is partly influenced by the two countries as well. Although it's national and most spoken language is Nepali, but due to the arrival of outside settlers in groups through the ages, it has transformed into a multi-religious, multi-cultural, and multi-lingual country.

The **bilateral relations** between the People's Republic of Bangladesh and the Federal Democratize Republic of Nepal have been progressive since the foundation of Bangladesh in 1971. The two nations are separated by the 'Siliguri Corridor'—a small stretch of territory of the Indian state of West Bengal that lies between southern Nepal and northern Bangladesh. As both the nations are members of the South Asian Association for Regional Cooperation (SAARC), the understanding between both the countries is good and progressive for economic prosperity.

Nepal did not take part in on the Indo-Pakistani War of 1971, but the then Kingdom of Nepal became one of the first nations to recognise Bangladesh, a free independent sovereign country, on16 January 1972. Pakistan in retaliation had broken off its established relation with Nepal. With Bangladesh, Nepal saw an opportunity to obtain access to port facilities in the Bay of Bengal to bolster foreign trade—something it had sought when Bangladesh was a part of Pakistan, to limited success. The relation between the two nations had improved a step further when the 1975 military coup in Bangladesh brought to power a government that distanced the country from India. It was because both nations were in the same path to counter the influence of their largest neighbour India. In April 1976, both nations signed bilateral agreements to develop trade, transit, and civil aviation. The transit agreement exempted all traffic-in-transit from duties and other charges. The relation improved further a six points of entry and exit for Nepalese traffic were set up. In 1986, Bangladesh demanded the participation of Nepal in talks with India over the distribution of water from the Ganges River. Bangladesh's exports to Nepal were increased by few millions by exporting mainly the pharmaceuticals, garments, plastics, handicrafts, and other goods. On the other hand Nepal exported $53 million worth of goods, which are largely agricultural product such as pulses, lentils, rice, and wheat.

Bhutan: The Kingdom of Bhutan is a small landlocked country in South-east Asia, situated at the eastern end of the Himalayas. It is bordered to the north by China and bordered to the south, east, and west by India. To the west, it is separated from Nepal by the Indian state of Sikim, farther south it is separated from Bangladesh by the Indian states of Assam and West Bengal. Bhutan is glorious by its largest city Thimphu, the capital.

Bhutan existed as a patchwork of minor warring groups under Lama (Guru) until the early seventeenth century. During that time, a group of people under a military leader Ngawang Namgyal cultivated a distinct Bhutanese identity, which is different from religious persecution in Tibet, and unified the area, which is known today as Bhutan. British came to India in the eighteenth century, but Bhutan came under the British empire only in the twentieth century. In 2006, based on a global survey, Business Week rated Bhutan the happiest country in Asia and the eighth happiest in the world. In 2016, the World Happiness Report published by the United Nations ranks Bhutan as the eighty-fourth happiest country.

In 2008, Bhutan made the transition from absolute to constitutional monarchy and held its first general election. Bhutan became a member of the United Nations since 1971. Bhutan is also a member of the SAARC. The Kingdom of Bhutan was the first country to recognise Bangladesh's independence since then there being existed a strong bond of relations between the two countries. In recent years, the two countries have committed to a strategic development partnership, encompassing hydro-power, free trade, and transport. They are common members of SAARC having their resident embassies in Bhutan.

It is a historic record for Bangladesh where the King of Bhutan sent a telegram to the acting president of the provisional government of Bangladesh on the morning of 6 December 1971, where Bhutan became the first state in the world to recognise the new country. It was later followed in the day by India. It becomes a historic record, a memorable record of history for Bangladesh. The government of Bhutan conveyed to the government of Bangladesh by saying that the people of Bhutan convey their great pleasure in recognising Bangladesh as a sovereign independent country. It was also said that the government of Bhutan as well as the people of Butan are confident with full faith that the great and heroic struggle of the people of Bangladesh to achieve freedom from foreign domination will be crowned with success in the coming future. Further, the government and the people pray for the safety of the great leader Sheikh Mujibur Rahman and hope that God will deliver him safely from the present peril so that he can lead the country and the people in the great task of national reconstruction and progress.

Bhutan and Bangladesh signed a bilateral trade agreement in 1980, granting each other the most preferential status for development of trade. However the agreement was renewed during the official visit of Bangladesh Prime Minister Sheikh Hasina Wajed to Thimphu in 2009. In 2014, the visit of Bhutanese Prime Minister Tshering Tobgay to Dhaka, Bangladesh, granted duty-free access to ninety products. Bhutan has a potential to generate more than 50,000 MW of hydroelectricity as such the two countries have come together under negotiations to jointly develop hydropower in the region. The 2014 SAARC Framework Agreement also supported the electric grid integration project to pave the way for energy trading in the region.

Besides energy, Bhutan is very much keen to use Bangladeshi seaports at Chittagong, for the transhipment of cargo. A sub-regional transit network between Bangladesh, India, Nepal, and Bhutan is under active consideration by SAARC and is being supported by the Asian Development Bank. To this effect the four countries have signed an agreement for the easy movement of cargo, and also the passenger and personal vehicle movement between them. Bhutan and Bangladesh have actively cooperated in the field of flood control in the aftermath of severe floods in Bangladesh in 1988; in return Bangladesh also extended support to Bhutan following the 2009 earthquake.

The Linking Unit: The Patriot, Nikunja Behari Goswami, a silent worker, who had sacrificed his life keeping the ideals of Gandhi in his mind. He was a Hindu, who was born as a Brahmin, and his forefathers were once the custodians of the Hindu religion, but today why the religion has reduced to a religion of destitute and poor? Let us discuss here the public opinion with regards to Gandhi as the Silent Patriot sacrificed his life for the ideals of Gandhi.

Q. Why Mahatma Gandhi wasn't officially announced as 'Father of the Nation' of India? Politics of India is guided by few people who are cunning and power-monger. Well Gandhi cannot be called officially the **Father** of the Nation as it is against the constitution, but still he had been declared by Nehru as the **Father** of the Nation. Why? It is true he passed a poor life, he thought for down trodden, dressed as Fakir and posture as saint. But his inner intention was nothing but politics. He was successful to project himself a leader of common people, but why he did the drama of Fakir and saint?

If it is analysed, it is possible to discover his secret desire behind his saintly covered life. It had been proved several times that he had a strong weakness towards Nehru family. There were reasons of course. He went to England, he came across with a different lifestyle there, he had realised he was not at par with others in England. By the grace of god, he succeeded to get a law degree. The same degree was acquired by Jinnah, Liaquat Ali khan, C. R.Das, and many others. Their proficiency was unparalleled and so they preferred to practice in the region of Inner Temple for some time. Gandhi had realised he was lacking in certain respect. So after degree he preferred to return without lingering in London, he tried first to practice at Bombay, but very soon he had also realised that he could not stay in Bombay any longer as he has no client. Opportunity came he went to South Africa, he was not happy there too very much with his sons, as they were not very obedient to him. Anyway he came back to India in 1912. He faced the same problem, no client. He took the shelter under Motilal Lal Nehru. He was satisfied with the works under the great lawyer Motilal Nehru.

To fulfil his inner desire, he was thinking to start something like Satyagraha as he did at South Africa, but Motilal and many other lawyers did not support him. But he remembered in South Africa when he was thrown out of the bus, people showed sympathy to him; when he was thrown out of white restaurant, people showed sympathy to him. He thought people's sympathy is the greatest political force. In India, majority of the people are Hindus, who are very much religious-minded. So before starting the movement, a religious movement of 'non-violence', was contemplated. He changed the dress as Fakir to win over the poor and downtrodden and converted himself into a saint to win over the religious sentiment of Hindus. His ambition was accumulation of large gathering against the protest of British administration that would bring results. He thought he could be known to public through Nehru family. Since then he began to favour Nehru, how to make him the congress president, he saved Nehru's daughter Indira for not to get a khan title after her marriage, and later he favoured Nehru to become the PM of India directly bypassing the congress candidate Sarder Petal.

It was quite natural for Nehru to declare Gandhi as the **Father of the Nation** and also the independence by 'non-violence' to increase Gandhi's glory and undermine Netaji although British PM Attlee said British had to leave due to massacre of British force by Azad Hind Fauj of Netaji. Well Netaji addressed Gandhi as the father, thereby he had shown his greatness of mind because it was Gandhi who is responsible to compel him to leave the country, and Gandhi refused to accept him as congress president even after winning the election against his candidate SitaRam Pattovia. Here lies the mind-set of great greatness or less greatness of a great leader.

He was a Fakir and posture as a saint, not to work as a monk or for the poor, if so he should first work in coordination with the government to save the lives of millions who were dying in the famine in Bengal. But he started the movement against British to capture power for Nehru. His goal was to acquire the chair of power at Delhi at whatever cost. When Jinnah became very much aggressive, Suharwardy became determined to do massacre on 16 August 1946, Gandhi did not come forward to talk either with Jinnah or with Suharwardy to come to an amicable solution. It is the nature of Gandhi not to talk with a man who is blind under the emotion of violence. It would be a fruitless talk. It was also true Jinnah and Gandhi both are brother-brother, friend-friend, embracing one another as the Indians do but not in the atmosphere of violence. The fortune did not support everyone every time. The success of non-violence emerges as violence at the back of the movement in Calcutta. The Hindu-Muslim rioting disheartened Gandhi, even though the solution came through the division of the country, but he was restless. He used single handedly his weapon of **fasting** to stop further loss of life. Finally he succumbed to assassination.

Thus Gandhi behaves like a saint of Hindu religion and a man of **'tolerance'** in the movement of non-violence and a man of **fasting**, as the weapon of movement was to mesmerise the common people, although he had failed to make fool Tilak of Maharashtra, C. R. Das of Bengal, the young Netaji, and Rival Jinnah.

Now let us come to the achievement, instead of United India, a divided India was resulted in utter disappointment. But the satisfaction was that the Delhi was rested for Nehru and Jinnah was also happy by getting Pakistan. But again it cannot be denied that an atmosphere of hatred for ever get established between the two countries. Thus after 65 years of independence a state of insecurity prevails in India where in every election a Hindu-Muslim chaos continues, while in Pakistan such kind of chaos could not be seen except military intervention. Pakistan became a centre absolutely for Muslims for Muslim religious faith but India cannot be said a force absolutely for Hindus for Hindu religious faith. Who is benefitted by the division of India? Pakistan is benefitted from Islamic point of view but India is benefitted from secular Democratic point of view.

Now Gandhi is the Father of the nation. This news was spread in 1947 not only in every state of India, but also to the whole world. At that time a good relation with China was established at the outset by the first PM Nehru of India based on the principle of non-violence of Gandhi. At that time because of this principle an atmosphere was prevailed in the country where we heard Hindu-china Bhai-Bhai. But China taking the advantage of friendly atmosphere attacked India in 1962 to capture the Indian territory. India was going to lose its sovereignty. Since that time, India government under compulsion had to rethink the Gandhian policy of non-violence for the nation. The present generation is now rethinking 'non-violence' that has cost India to divide under the guidance of Gandhi, a greatest loss has been done to the nation.

When Subhash ChandraBose had left India with a mission to liberate India from foreign rule and he was in Germany, from there he had addressed the nation India and referred Mahatma Gandhi as the epithetical Father of Nation. This term was first used by a great leader with a great mission showing respect and to align all Indians for the revered cause. It was the call by Subhash Chandra Bose that had resulted in making Gandhi as Father of Nation who was looking as a simple and saint-like person. It was not sycophancy but a torrent of respect to a deserved one. It should not be the reason which had made him Father of Nation. It was not with any such official provision. A lot of freedom fighters had popular designations. We had 'cha-cha' Nehru, 'netaji' Subhas Bose, 'deshbandhu' Chittaranjan Das, 'gurudeb' Rabindranath Tagore, 'deshpran' Sasmal, and many more.

Again why is Mahatma Gandhi not officially the 'Father of the Nation'? It was because the Indian constitution doesn't allow such titles. The article 18 of Indian constitution stated clearly that no title, not being a military or academic distinction, shall be conferred by the state, no person holding any office or trust under the state shall, without the consent of the president accept any present, emolument, or office of any kind from or under any foreign state right to freedom. That was why Mahatma Gandhi officially should not be called the 'Father of the Nation'?

Hence, **Father of the Nation** was a title, people of India had bestowed upon him out of sheer love and respect and that was due to the imposition of Nehru. He was an aged person and father like figure that is why he was fondly called **Bapu**. He was most loveable to Hindus no doubt but why not to Muslims. He would have been a successful leader had he win the heart of Muslims. There lies his failure. It was because the general people do not want to separate Muslims, but the leadership failed to keep the Muslims together with the Hindus.

Like every notable individual, Gandhi too had a fair share of controversies in his life with regards to some of his decisions, some debatable ideologies, extending partiality and favouritism to some particular leaders, unfair treatment to the likes of Netaji and Sardar Patel, special affinity to the Nehru family, division of India after an understanding with Jinnah of Muslim League, etc. That was said that, there is no way to deny what a gigantic figure he had been in the context of India's socio-political movements and freedom struggle. His idea of non-violence has earned him international respect and recognition because he could mesmerise or befooled the Hindus of India by 'non-violence'. It became possible as Gandhi very tactfully utilised the ethics of Hinduism of 'tolerance' in the form of non-violence. But Muslims were not satisfied with 'non-violence' the kind of religious movement. Gandhi however big but why he had not given importance to the sentiment of Muslims was best known to him. Apparently we find it was the reason why at Calcutta that atmosphere of hatred gets encouraged and that finally led to violence and rioting. Even in the history of India, there is one man Gandhi who is the leader of India to get independence. To many people in the West, India and Gandhi are synonymous. It's rather unfortunate and a matter of shame that the Nehru family had been making a mockery of his surname by using it for their own political and financial gains and to rule over India for the past sixty years. It's only because of this surname that they've been able to have so much influence on India and Indians. But that doesn't undermine the fact that if there's one individual that deserved to be called the **Father of the Nation**, it was *him*.

Q. Why was Mahatma Gandhi not the prime minister of India? Politics of India is guided by few people who are cunning as well as intelligent. Gandhi was a simple, faithful religious intelligent person but not cunning. It was his ability that made him a man of international imminence for the cause of guidance of independence movement but he was criticised for the division of the country. He had done harm to the beautiful country of India by division, no doubt, but there was no alternative at that moment of time to save the nation from civil war. It was necessary also to think who should be the right person for the post of PM of the country in absence of British administration. He was working under Motilal Nehru, and he could know each and every member of the family very closely as such it was his choice Jawaharlal Nehru might be the right person. There were many unknown factors worked in the division of the country.

He started the 'non-violence' movement, a religious movement in order to bring the majority Hindu people to the street to protest against the British first. Without the involvement of large number of people no movement could be successful. It was his belief; the thrust of large Hindu people would compel the Muslims to join the movement. In order to convenience the Hindus he turned a Fakir as well as a saint. But the situation turned other way beyond control. The ultimate solution was nothing but division, a setback in the vision of Gandhi. The outburst of present generation is that Gandhi was the person to destroy the brotherhood of Hindu-Muslim. Many people had raised the question why did Gandhi humiliate the Hindu religion by bringing it to politics in the form of 'non-violence' befooling the Hindus.

Many people take different view against Gandhi. According to them in the desperation of preserving the glory of non-violence he was determined to help Pakistan, where Gandhi said, 'When my work is done here in India, I shall go to Pakistan to stop killing there.' It would make no sense to make such a person the head of a country when he thinks to go elsewhere to save the people. It did not justify his greatness. The question is if you feel for Pakistan so much how you could allow Pakistan to be a separate country. That did not support the leadership capacity. Gandhi had distorted from his principle. His principle was United India how he could deviate from it. He would be remembered for ever if he could die for the protection of the principle of United India. People followed everything what he said. If they didn't, he would simply threaten to fast till death. According to them, a man of such kind of attitude should not be fit enough for the chair of PM. Apart from that, there was a difference of ideology. Nehru was a socialist. Patel was a capitalist. Gandhi was neither a communist or a socialist or a capitalist. A country needs a man with a vision. Gandhi was a man without any fix vision. God has given him enough fortune to become an international icon, but he should not be the PM of India.

In the question of pragmatism, Patel, VP Menon, and Nehru did not use Gandhism to unify India. They used force, unrelenting, unflinching force. Gandhi understood everything. He realised the fact that sometimes one would have to abandon his ideology to get things done. **Let others do their job.** Great leaders understand that other people's contribution is just as important as theirs. For example, even though Benjamin Franklin led the American revolution, he had no desire to become the first US president. He let George Washington, John Adams, and Thomas Jefferson to do that job. At the end, we may never know why he did not become the first prime minister. But evidence points to the few reasons.

A multitude of factors contribute to their actions. The first factor might be his age. Any newly independent country requires at least some amount of continuity in leadership. Otherwise the power tussle that could unfold after the leader's demise might spell disaster for the country's unity. Let us look at the case of Pakistan in

1950s. The heads changed several times in the small period of time leading to loss of focus on any progressive activity in the state. This was possibly one of the reasons why Gandhi left away from PM.

There was a change of **mission on the part of Gandhi**, who had undertaken to look after the more challenging task, the mission of changing the social norms in India to eradicate practices like untouchability, etc. He felt this was equally (if not more) important for the future of our nation. His ultimate goal was to make every one realise and conquer his/her inner ego and establish a truly equal society rather than enforcing one by law directly. Sadly, he could not make much of a progress before his departure. The principle of 'ideology' kept him away from the post of PM. Above all he feels Gandhi's belief in Satyagraha (or to put more aptly: people power through non-violent protests) as the ultimate power that no office can bestow. He was successful to control or stop rioting because of his kind nature for the destitute which was liked by the people. If he were the PM, he could not have achieved this without force.

Also the fact is that he believed in the possibility that office of political power could corrupt or atleast taint even idealists. So he preferred to stay away from any official post. It was because holding any official post one is supposed to refrain from any self-possessed ideologies and acts in a neutral manner and takes forward even those who don't subscribe to your views. Gandhi seldom had any accommodation for people who deserted his ideology of Satyagraha. So probably for that here remained away from the post of PM. whatever the case, there would have been no way in which Gandhi could have become PM? However, suffering was there in his mind because he failed to keep India united.

Q. Do you think Mahatma Gandhi could have avoided the partition of India? Why or why not?
According to many, it was clear from his activity that Mahatma Gandhi was more interested for the glory of non-violence rather than the unity of India. He was more interested for the power of chair of Delhi, and less for the unity of India. Why? It was because, he knows, if Nehru is in the chair, he would be benefited. A leader is known by his action and not by his speech or writings in books. If Gandhi was a faithful leader without any prejudices, he should work for independence of India with the satisfaction of all Indians. A leader should have that capacity to convince all. A leader should see the future, if you failed to see the future; how can you be a leader in true sense for the betterment of the citizen? Is it the better future of India that India-Pakistan is fighting

directly or indirectly since sixty-five years even after partition?

The question again arises, where is your foresighted vision, why did you give the opportunity for the Muslims to think separately? Jinnah was in congress, once he represented congress probably in 1914 in the political mission to London. Why did he left congress. One should not forget 1937, Lucknow session of congress, not a single Muslim was taken in the ministry. Not to speak of Bengal, Nehru, congress president, did not agree to form ministry with Fazlul Haq, the KPP party, not a party of aristocrat. He had been pushed to ML to join Suhwardy, who later finding no alternative join hands with Jinnah to carry out DIRECT ACTION Day to get Pakistan.

Let us look at the leaders of other country, F. D. Roosevelt, three-time American president, who by the policy of American Liberalism brought together white ethnics, black Americans, and rural Southerners together. They raised no objection to live together and work united. Did Gandhi similarly create Indian Liberalism to bring together, the Hindus, Muslims, or Dalits together? Why could the leader Gandhi not do the same? Why did he become a Hindu saint? Why did he not a neutral politician in his dress, behaviour, and speech?

A leader must have an aim. Well for Gandhi it was independence of United India. If so under no circumstances you should compromise with the unity of India. If required, the leader should have the courage to fight for it up to the last breath of his life. Did Gandhi have the mental strength to do that? Well, Jinnah asked for Pakistan, Gandhi had two options, to convince Jinnah under all circumstances keeping the unity of the nation at the top, if failed take the reverse action. Gandhi, a leader of 98% people, should not bow down to a leader of 2% people. To reach to the destination it is natural a leader has to pass through the events of success or failure as we find in the case Winston Churchill or in the case of Mao-Sa-Tsang and many others, but Gandhi succumbed to pressure easily that justified his weak nature and not a strong leader like character, which had brought the misery to the nation and the uncertain future to Indians.

Well, there might be civil war, if so what. War will come out with a true India. Gandhi has made the youths of India less energetic if not coward by the mantra of non-violence. According to many, Gandhi is responsible for the sufferings of the present generation. He is also responsible for the killing of millions and millions to root out from their ancestral home and hearths. Even then Indians observe Gandhi Joyanti to show respect. His movement of 'non-violence' was against the principle of nature. Water roll down from hills to sea, what is natural, similarly destruction is necessary to build a new building. Atom bomb brought destruction true, but it had opened up door for scientific exploration. Democracy brought in French after French revolution. 'Non-violence' was nothing but to restrict your strength and energy given by almighty to you to utilise to live in the universe as a better animal. As such 'non-violence' movement is against the dictum of God. Today Indians are the victims of partition. Is it not due to Gandhi's non-violence movement?

It was interesting to discuss the fact that Jinnah was initially a strong proponent of a united India. He didn't agree with Sir Syed Ahmad Khan's views that Muslims are culturally, linguistically, and politically very distinct to be represented by Hindu dominated INC. He joined INC (1885) and Muslim League that was formed in 1906. He helped to bring Muslim League and INC together on a common platform in the Lucknow Pact of 1916 and helped them to reach to an agreeable solution; 30%

electoral reservation for the Muslims. But his neutrality shifted gradually. Why? Who is responsible for that?

Grand advent of Gandhi in national politics with non-cooperation movement(which Jinnah didn't approve of) leading to Jinnah's diminishing voice in the party affairs, had risen the domination of Hindu leaders in INC. INC's disapproval of Muslims' relevance in national politics, which Jinnah took as an imminent danger to the relevance of the Muslim community at large in a 'Hindu' India. Increasing animosity between Hindus and Muslims, jingoistic fantasy of RSS clearly dictates terms to the minorities for peaceful co-existence with the majority as 'wholly subordinated to the Hindu nation, claiming nothing, deserving no privileges . . . not even citizen's rights' which were the facts.

The Indian National Congress's under estimation of Jinnah also played a HUGE role in the events that led to the inevitable. Jinnah's success was greatly assisted by the continued blunders of the congress leaders and Gandhi in particular. Nehru considered the Muslim League nothing more than a bunch of the elitists and had at times, mocked Jinnah of his political aspirations.

Despite league's fair performance in 1937's provincial elections (109/482 Muslim seats), INC ignored them and instead shook hands with Jamiat-e-Ulema-Hind in the UP. The provincial congress governments made no effort to understand and respect their Muslim populations' cultural and religious sensibilities. The Muslim League's claims that it alone could safeguard Muslim interests thus received a major boost. Significantly it was only after this period of congress rule that it took up the demand for a Pakistan state. Another curious fact is that Jinnah actually had never asked for a separate state (even the word 'Pakistan' had been coined by Rahmat Ali, a Cambridge undergraduate in 1933 when Jinnah had already returned back to England away from active politics), but a separate Muslim electorate within the dominion India under a clearly defined strict federal structure. That is what he demanded in the 1946 Cabinet Mission as well. Congress rejected that disdainfully.

Gandhi did all he could to have an independent united India. But he couldn't prevent the partition because he had become a 'back number', as he lamented, and could not convince even those closest to him, like Nehru and Patel, to agree to make Jinnah the prime minister. Is it the signal of the failure of the leadership of Gandhi or is it the display of love and sympathy for Nehru as well as Petal too. How can the vision of a leader get distorted by the symptom of failure or by the love or sympathy of a particular person? Is it the love of country or the future of the country is less important than the love and sympathy of an individual? Leaving everything Gandhi went to Calcutta which was raging with violence and oozing human blood all around. As a leader, he should know it before and accordingly he should be prepared for that. He neither felt it necessary before hand to talk to Muslim leader to stop violence nor did he prepare his volunteer force to stop the senseless act of violence. He was pressing for the share of the money for Pakistan. When the whole nation was celebrating independence, he was pacifying violent rowdies and mourning the deaths of his countrymen. Although he was a saint, he was a political leader but without firm determination and fix vision. His encouragement with 'non-violence' led to destruction. Who is a successful leader, who can see the future? Gandhi was lacking in farsightedness.

On this background there comes a book named *Indian Musalman* by W. Hunter. In summary, the extract reveals that the Britishers are here only and only for money (exploitation). They want to rule (and exploit) India forever. But as soon as the majority would understand this, they would go on fighting. In that case the minority would be the natural ally of the Bristers. The British should play the minority card against the majority, if so this would weaken the society internally and thus the weakness would engulf the entire movement.

So economically it is wiser to have Muslims as friends and use them. The oppression after 1857 had created a remarkable social and economical difference in the conditions of those two communities. Thus the British had clear objectives in their mind and were implementing divisive strategies since 1875–80. INC formed in 1885, but that never could visualise the British strategy. Afterwards Gandhi appeared with a chauvinistic motive to increase his importance without determined policy of unity and a vision of determined objective. The prime minister of India had made Gandhi an international hero by declaring 'Father of the Nation' and encouraging the image of Gandhi in the world, but the failure of Gandhi in the effort of keeping the country united cannot be hidden.

If India and Pakistan was not divided, the United India would have been a country of power to reckon with. Both India and Pakistan would have escaped the wrenching experience of Partition with its communal violence and pain of suffering in killing the fellow brothers and sisters and displacing them from their place of birth and from their ancestral place of living generation to generation. The suffering caused by the secession of Bangladesh could have been avoided. The dispute over Kashmir would not have occurred, and the act of terrorism would not have arisen. A three-tiered India would have had at least the same industrialisation that has occurred and the areas that are now Pakistan and Bangladesh would have profited from it. It would have been a vast 'free trade zone' with no equal in the world. It would have been a democratic republic, without military dictators.

There would seem to be no reason why Muslim voters could not have exercised their franchise, just as they do in present-day India. United India would be the world's largest country (1.4 billion people), the world's largest Muslim country (500 million), although that would be the world's poorest country (over 600 million hungry). In undivided India, religion might have dominated political debate, as it did in the '30s and '40s, and consensus on reform would be hard to build internally, but the progress of economic prosperity would have eliminate the religious bitterness in keeping the country together as is now existed in the United States, where the oppositely cultured black and white are living together because of strong economic bonding.

United India need not have been the world's poorest country. The resources, attention, and energy that have gone into the continued hostility since Partition could have been utilised into development. The foreign policy of India would not have been dominated by relations with Pakistan and Bangladesh keeping huge budget allocation for defence instead of development of the region. The spirit of game in sports would have been entirely different. The greater intensity and frequency of Hindu-Muslim riots would have vanished with the feelings of brotherhood and love for the country as it is now in USA. Arms industry would have lost fortune. The Indian army (Indian+Pakistan+Bangladesh) combined would have the **world's largest army** in terms of military personnel overtaking China or any other country. Currently, India is second to China.

The subsequent four Indo-Pak wars would not have happened. If the historian Charles de Gaulle who could write books and pamphlets advocating the union of the Welsh, Scots, Irish, and Bretons into one people, why not the people of India, Pakistan, and Bangladesh are not to be considered as one people as they live in the same air and weather, cherish with the same spirit of pleasure and think as same for a better future.

Why did a large number of Muslim in India decide to stay in India after Hindu-Muslim partition of India in 1947? Then why was Pakistan (East-West) created in the first place? This question is asked in good faith and out of curiosity to know about the mind-set of Muslims who settled in India despite Mohammed Ali Jinnah and his colleagues' accusation of discrimination against Mohammedans, which led to the Indian-Muslim partition of India. This questing was definitely pinching Jinnah very much, probably that might be the reason why did Jinnah in his dying bed said 'he did the greatest blunder in his life time by dividing India'. But it cannot be denied that the grievances of Muslims were not heard of and taken into consideration in proper time and place. Gandhi was great as he was successful to convince the congress and made himself very popular among the common masses but mostly it remains limited to Hindus only. The subsequent political events of Lucknow, Calcutta, Punjab, and Assam the Muslim population discarded Gandhi as their leader and turn their attention towards Jinnah. Muslims were scared of Gandhi because very often he was out spoken of the creation of Ram Rajya. The teachings of Gita might be great or good to Hindus but for the purpose of administration of the nation, a nation of the people of different religious faith, the religious uttering should have been avoided. Apart from that the very appearance of Gandhi, a political leader having the appearance of a Hindu saint is detrimental and not befitting to be a leader of a country of multi-racial community.

It was only the Muslims of Punjab went to West Pakistan and on the eastern side Muslims of Bengal went to East Pakistan. The Muslims of other states of India did not go to Pakistan in general. This shows that 'a separate state for the Muslims of India' as said by Jinnah was not the desire of the majority Muslims of India. The creation of Pakistan by the division of India was done very hurriedly. Of course the political situation of that time demanded a hurried solution. It was easy to say Gandhi was not responsible for the division of the country, Gandhi was always in favour of United India, but his activity right from the beginning was not for Indian independence for United India. What a leader is saying is not important, but what a leader is doing is important. The INC and Gandhi cannot escape the responsibility of ill-treatment to Muslims to get their rightful share in United India and made them enemy to Hindus. However now the situation is changed in India, whether the economic prosperity or religious prosperity would get the priority, the time in future would speak the truth.

8 The Blessings of the Departed Soul

[1]

The Silent Patriot, Nikunja Behari Goswami, is no more today, had he been alive he could have got a sigh of relief on seeing that his Dear Bengal (East Bengal) is no longer under the occupation of terrifying animal of Punjabi Pakistani and the present Prime Minister Ms Hasina, the daughter of Bango-Bhandu Mujibur Rahaman, the lone survivor has emerged as the source of fiery leader by the blessings of almighty for the survival of new Bengal liberated as BANGLADESH. Here in Bangladesh, under her guidance, a future is going to emerge where poverty would vanish; people would live under the climate of brotherhood, friendship and love of humanity. The political stability would bring happiness to the country, happiness to every house, and happiness to every family and people would learn to enjoy the life after learning the art of Bengal culture. The fire brand leader, the lone surviving leader, the daughter of Sheikh Mujibur Rahaman, the God gifted surviving leader, would vanish 'terrorism' from the soil of Bango-Bondhu once for all in any time, setting an example for the other countries as she did by hanging the killers of Bango-Bondu and made a record in the history of world, where his neighbour country, India, the greatest democratic country of the world failed to do that where many of the convicted criminals were passing their days in jails as the government dare to hang them.

However the good news is that Ms Hasuna is going stronger and stronger year after year earning the confidence of not only the people of Bangladesh, but even the people all around the world. Ms Hasina became prime minister in 1996 and remains in office till 2000, although her Awami League government had a thin majority in the parliament. She came to power after two decades that followed the bloody change over of 1975. Despite those limitations, her government took some remarkable steps to improve relation with India. Overall, it tried to reverse certain post-1975 political trends and to rejuvenate the pro-liberation spirit that was needed badly for a secular polity in a country and she had a leadership capacity to do that.

The Awami League–led government signed the historic Ganga Water Treaty without wasting time. It also paved the way for the thousands of Chakma refugees return to

India with the signing of a landmark accord that ended decades of tribal insurgency in the border region. Then, it sent a firm signal to insurgents operating all across north-eastern India, many of whom, as claimed by India, enjoyed sanctuary in Bangladesh. She took bold steps to stop insurgency problems and sincerely wanted a good relation with India. The people of Bangladesh were happy to see the progressive decision taken by the government of the grand alliance led by the daughter of the slain founding father of Bangladesh, Sheikh Mujibur Rahman, is not without its limitations and in the expansion of economy with neighbour country India by her effort to improve relation with India. The positive response of the people had been seen in 2008 election. A land slide victory in the December 2008 elections, with a two-thirds-plus majority in Parliament was a clear verdict in her favour supporting her policy of the government.

This enabled Ms Hasina's government to amend the constitution and bring about certain changes that it felt was needed to initiate a new journey that Bangladesh needs to undertake in order to get back on the right track. Having achieved independence from Pakistan in the aftermath and as a consequence of the devastating war of 1971, Bangladesh did not get adequate time to consolidate itself and put itself on a firm democratic footing. However India helped the Bengali freedom fighters to a great extent, and finally formed a joint military command to counteract Pakistani attack.

At the high-level meetings between Bangladesh and India over the important issues, concerning important bilateral aspects are in the process to be held particularly between the heads of governments to carry out the process of trade and all kinds of administration. Bangladesh is now ruled by secular democratic forces, known as the 'pro-liberation' forces. But the forces which opposed independence and which developed a fix economic foundation and constituted a base among them by the ruling the country for the past few decades, have now become quite alert and aggressive. They have been quickly joined by some other forces, who were direct beneficiaries of the 1975 massacre and who ruled the country for long thirty years have now unleashed a propaganda war.

The fundamentalists and the local Taliban do not want Bangladesh to remain friendly with India; to them India is 'the enemy state'. But again the Bangladesh Nationalist Party (BNP), which is but a mixture of soft Islamists, fundamentalists are cooperating 1975 massacre Party to come back to power by force if necessary. When the national media projected the prime minister's visit to India optimistically—as an opportunity to begin a new era and resolve certain outstanding issues—Begum Khaleda Zia, BNP chairperson and chief of the four-party rightist alliance in which the Jamaat-e-Islami plays the vital role, posed an open warning to the Hasina government. Why? A good relation with economically advanced country India would enhance the economy of Bangladesh, if so the chance of BNP government to come back to power would vanish forever, that thinking made the BNP restless. She stated publicly that any agreement with India, detrimental to nation would be strewn with thorns because India is an enemy country to Pakistan so to BNP. This is an open challenge posed before the one-year-old government. But the government was determined to see the end of the war criminals. The Supreme Court's verdict would be honoured and executed. To oppose the visit of Hasina to India is nothing but political propaganda. Any meeting with the Indian leader could somehow lead to an eventual surrender of national interests is nothing but a political gambling.

[2]

The picture of Bangladesh is changing with the change of time. Who were the Bengali freedom fighters? Originally, it was the Bengali freedom fighters and their local collaborators on the warfront who were called 'patriots' along with the vast majority of people who helped to fight the war against the Pakistan army. This concept was valid up to 1975. But after 1975, the definition of freedom fighters had changed. History was re-written; history was distorted, by a set of military and pseudo-democratic rulers. But Hasina government's attempt is now looking forward in removing the distortions of the history of independence of Bangladesh as a younger generation of Bangladeshis seeks to know what really had happened.

The BNP is fighting hard to establish its presence in Bangladesh. The Khaleda Zia-led combine, is likely to be soon under the command of her son Tareq Rahman, who is now in London and who is under training how to run either an office or an administration of a government. The nation would definitely look after him. As Ms Hasina prepared to go to New Delhi, the leader of the opposition chose to question the patriotism of Hasina and also the people who belong to the ruling party. The BNP Party chief might have forgotten that Hasina is the daughter of Bonga-Bandu, the whole family had been sacrificed and by God's grace Hasina survived and questioning her patriotism is below of her dignity. People in no way would be ready to believe her allegation against Hasina's patriotism. People know how to answer the question in right time. However, such kind of utterance would further increase the popularity of Hasina.

However, India is a friendly or enemy country to Bangladesh, only the record of history would speak the truth. India sheltered 100 million refugees, who migrated from the former East Pakistan to India when the Pakistan army began a genocidal war against unarmed civilians, and also extended significant support to Bangladesh's war that finally culminated in the creation of a new country Bangladesh. Bangladesh faced its first shock in August 1975 with the assassination of Mujibur Rahman. The military and pseudo-democratic rulers captured the power, ruled for two decades; Bangladesh found a new ethos that practically negated the secular spirit of 1971. By the time in India, tremendous transformation and development had occurred. Therefore forgetting the past the best is to do well whatever way it brings development to Bangladesh. India and Bangladesh must practically resolve the issues that have confronted them, and seek to put their relations on a solid foundation.

Since India is a big neighbour, some psychological impact on both sides of the border is inevitable. Bangladesh covers a relatively small territory. But its enormous potential and strategic significance no one can overrule. Close relations with India to resolve all major outstanding issues should be a key requirement for Bangladesh to make a new beginning. Despite having been in office only for a short period of time Sheikh Hasina government has shown considerable courage and determination to free its soil from anti-India activity. Many would, therefore, hope for suitable reciprocal gestures to strengthen the polity. An economically strong, secular and democratic Bangladesh is crucial and very essential for New Delhi and the rest of the region. The development of Bangladesh not only depended on Bangladesh, but it also depended on the cooperation and goodwill of India in particular in addition to all other country of South-east Asia. As such a democratic and secular India, and a secular Bangladesh, that has started its renewed march towards a stable democratic polity despite the muscle flexing by some extremists, or terrorists should work together for a stable South Asia.

[3]

Narendra Modi, a new prime minister, has arrived to Delhi with a massive vote and people support because a man of poor family understands the pain and sufferings of the common people. The present prime minister is now a pride of the nation of India. He sometimes expressed in public that once he was a tea-boy, but today he is the PM of India. He openly said it is the people of India who had chosen a tea-boy to the post of prime minister—it is his magnanimity and great heart. His achievement has been reflected in the administration of Gujarat. The state machinery was made as such that all the big entrepreneurs big or small, Indian or foreigners flocked together to establish industry in Gujarat, making the State economically number one state of India. The people of India had taken him to Delhi, made him the PM of India. By his short span of time, he had sharpened his administration, to stop corruption. He had made a marathon visit to the countries of East, West, and North and South. He had acquired a wonderful power to win the heart of any leader as well as the common people. Everywhere in every country people flocked together to hear him, because he is speaking something different than any other world leaders. It is astonishing to see, wherever he went people found to roaring with the cry of Modi, Modi disrupting the silence of open sky.

Bangladesh is separated from India but its geographical back ground is not separated and it is difficult to separate as God has not permitted to do that. Modi reiterated that India would do everything for the growth, peace, and prosperity of Bangladesh. Indian Prime Minister Narendra Modi has said the past, the present and the future of India and Bangladesh are interlinked. He made the remark when Foreign Minister AH Mahmood Ali called on him in New Delhi at a certain time. He further said,'Bangabandhu founded Bangladesh and his daughter, Sheikh Hasina, saved Bangladesh.' Bangabandhu was the pride of past and Sheikh Hasina is the pride of present and will remain a pride of Bangladesh for the future too.

Modi is frank and fair. He likes Bangladesh as well as the Bengali people of Bengal of this Bengal or that Bengal of Bangladesh because he is a follower of an inborn Bengali saint who is Swami Vivekananda. The Indian prime minister reiterated that India would do everything for the growth, peace, and prosperity of Bangladesh. He emphasised on regional cooperation for the collective development of this region and expressed his satisfaction over the significant progress made in power sector cooperation between the two countries. He had pointed out the potential of benefit in the increase of people-to-people contact in the sphere of cultural activity, in economy of trade and commerce and above all in the sphere of tourism between the two friendly neighbours. He is interested to talk how to improve the communication system through the sea of water, through the surface of earth building new rail lines and through the open space of air by plane. It would enhance the future opportunities for further trade and commerce through sea and river routes. The dream of Modi government a vibrant 'Look East' policy would remain incomplete if the government failed to bring Bangladesh under its environment.

He expressed his happiness on seeing Mahmood was meeting with Indian Water Resources Minister Uma Bharti to find out the ways to sort out the issue of interim agreement for sharing waters of Teesta. The Indian water resources minister reiterated that India would not implement any project that may have adverse impact on Bangladesh. Mahmood Ali met Indian Power, Coal, New, and Renewable Energy Minister Piyush Goyal and expressed satisfaction that significant progress had been made in power sector cooperation between the two countries in the last five years. The Indian power minister assured that India would extend all out support to Bangladesh to further enhance and accelerate the pace of cooperation in the power sector. The prime minister gets a pleasure of immense satisfaction on seeing the Bangladeshi foreign minister had a meeting with Arun Jaitley, Indian union minister for finance, defence, and corporate affairs, and Indian National Security Adviser Ajit Doval to lead the relation a step further to lead India-Bangladesh relation to such a level of high magnitude that India government could set it as a record of testimony for the present as well as for the future growth to other South Asian countries.

The concept of regional cooperation for the increase of trade was originated in Dhaka as 'The South Asian Association for Regional Cooperation'(SAARC) originated in Dhaka in 1985. Asian nations that included Bangladesh, Bhutan, India, Maldives, Nepal, Pakistan, and Sri Lanka agreed upon the creation of a trade bloc and to provide a platform for the people of South Asia to work together in a spirit of friendship, trust, and understanding. President Ziaur Rahman made his spectacular address, presenting his vision of thought for the future of the region. He thought it long time before in 1977 and expressed his idea during his visit to India, Nepal, and Sri Lanka behind the idea of sharing river waters among South Asian countries. However by the time its member states included Afghanistan, Bangladesh, Bhutan, India, Nepal, the Maldives, Pakistan, and Sri Lanka. SAARC compromises 3% of the world's area, 21% of the world's population, and 9.12% of the global economy, as of 2015. The purpose of the organisation is to promote development in economic front and the progress of unity through regional integration. It had launched the South Asian Free Trade since 2006.

India, the largest economy and the most populous country in the region, has initiated its efforts to revitalise the SAARC as the pre-eminent forum of regional cooperation and economic integration. In its endeavour in the opening of university, food bank, and disaster management probe might have initially provided appreciable steps, but in the long run it doesn't create any big step in accelerating the economy of the region.

The campaigns like **Make in India** and **Start-up India** forwarded by Narendra Modi government are expected to bring a lot of manufacturer to India and thereby enhancing in creating favourable environment for its own people to establish industries. They are going to increase huge markets for its operation. SAARC countries could be the biggest market if cross border trade and their full liberty is facilitated and entrusted along with the removal of tariff barriers. If the give and take policy is carried out in cordial atmosphere, among the SAARC nations the improvement of the region would not be far away.

It is the challenging task of the region to prove to the world that the densest area of the world in terms of population is a boon to the region as the bigger population gives quicker response of the product in the market. This can help India to export its great variety of products through less regulated trade channels and earn unlimited foreign exchange. There is no doubt if the clashes between India and its neighbouring countries is prevented, India will become the third largest economy in the world before 2030 and Bangladesh would be the greatest beneficiary. It was because the position of Bangladesh is as such that if the India government wishes to develop the Easter region of India, the development of Bangladesh, the road communication of Bangladesh through land and water is absolutely a necessity. A better day is waiting for the people of North-east as well as the necessary regions of Bangladesh if the good will of both the government works for better future.

The primary economic objective behind the establishment of SAARC was the promotion of closer cooperation between the participating countries. Eventually, the member nations wanted to create a free trade zone which would be a catalyst for economic activity, although the concept has been on the drawing board since 1995, but no concrete steps have been taken as far as execution is concerned. Closer economic ties and loosening of trade restrictions would greatly benefit not only India but also the other SAARC members. However political differences have made it difficult for the SAARC nations to make significant progress on this front having Pakistan's repeated refusal to grant India the MFN status being a clear example of political complications. To give some perspective of the potential of the SAARC economies, as of 2013, China-Taiwan annual bilateral trade stood at ~$197 bn while the corresponding figure for India-Pakistan was ~$2.4 bn. Having said that, the Indian economy can make significant gains if we can develop closer economic ties with other SAARC nations particularly with Sri Lankaand Bangladesh as both the countries are very much connected with water root.

The election of Prime Minister Narendra Modi and his government's proactive focus on foreign policy has ushered a new era for India-SAARC Relations. In the past several years, the SAARC countries had seen the momentous events on the ground but after the change of government in India a new initiative had found to be seen. The PM's decision to invite SAARC leaders to his oath taking ceremony or SAARC Summit, 2014 or Foreign Secretary S. Jaishankar's SAARC Yatra all are the records of prospective events. These events have raised the aspirations and hopes of the entire world that SAARC will finally come good on its potential. SAARC however remains a mixed bag of Strengths, Weaknesses, Opportunities, and Threats. <u>There might have been initial</u> set back but the ultimate goal would be reached one day by the people's cooperation because the nature of the people of both the country is the same and originally they belong to the same country India. A lot needs to be done on ground to keep it going for the growth. Let us hope for the best.

[4]

The South Asian Association for Regional Cooperation (SAARC) is a geopolitical organisation of eight countries of South Asia—Afghanistan, Bangladesh, Bhutan, India, Maldives, Nepal, Pakistan, and Sri Lanka, being establishment—1985, keeping its headquarters at Kathmandu, Nepal. There are other countries although they were not members but State Observer.

The countries are Australia, China, the European Union, Iran, Japan, Mauritius, Myanmar, South Korea, and the United States.

SAARC Preferential Trading Arrangement (SAPTA) was signed in 1993 and entered into force in 1995. It was an agreement that reflected the desire of the member states to promote and sustain mutual trade and economic cooperation within the SAARC region through the exchange of concessions.

Again the South Asian Free Trade Area (SAFTA) is an agreement reached in 2004 to create SAARC free trade area. The members of SAARC signed a framework agreement on SAFTA to reduce custom duties of all traded goods to zero by the year 2016. The SAFTA agreement came into force on 1 January 2006 and is operational following the ratification of the agreement by the seven governments. Though SAPTA, SAFTA has not been able to improve the trade relations of SAARC members significantly yet attempts are going on how to improve the relation and how these coordinated efforts of all members would be taken into account to improve the system of economic cooperation and integration. We are separate country but here is an attempt how to speak together, how to speak together for development. But behind the entire operation, the unity of growth depends upon the exchange of the unity of cultural identity. However a day might come when the development of each culture would lead to an Empire of Culture and the people would enjoy the taste of each culture.

SAARC 18th Summit 2014 comes to end at Kathmandu. The 36-point concluding Kathmandu Declaration states that members will continue their efforts to intensify regional cooperation on connectivity, connectivity through road, rail, water, or in space and renew their commitment to a South Asian Economic Union, strengthen the SAARC Development Fund, and reiterate their commitment to vanish poverty from South Asia. Apartment from development topics, SAARC has also given importance to the very sensitive subject of fighting terrorism. The recent terrorist attack on the URI Sector of India with the loss of eighteen Indian armies had brought a lot of unhappiness and misunderstanding among SAARC nations and threatened its stability by nullifying the annual SAARC meeting at Islamabad. However the people expected for the best for the future.

------------THE END------------

Printed in the United States
By Bookmasters